one spice, two spice

one spice, two spice

AMERICAN FOOD, INDIAN FLAVORS

Floyd Cardoz with Jane Daniels Lear

WM
WILLIAM MORROW
An Imprint of HarperCollins*Publishers*

FIRST EDITION

Designed by Lorie Pagnozzi

Library of Congress Cataloging-in-Publication Data

Cardoz, Floyd.
    One spice, two spice: American food, Indian flavors / Floyd Cardoz with Jane Daniels
Lear.
      p. cm.
    ISBN-13: 978-0-06-073501-2
    ISBN-10: 0-06-073501-5
    1. Cookery, Indic.   2. Cookery, American.   3. Tabla (Restaurand)   I. Lear, Jane
Daniels.   II. Title.
TX724.5.I4C28 2006
641.5954—dc22   2006041903

07 08 09 10 WBC/CW 10 9 8 7 6 5 4 3 2

To Barkha, Peter, and Justin

contents

acknowledgments

This book couldn't have been possible without the help and inspiration of many people. My heartfelt thanks to:

My sous-chefs past and present, Dan Kluger, Andrea Bergquist, Ty Kotz, Chris Jaeckle, Mohan Ismail, Ben Pollinger, Saleh Uddin, Livio Velardo, and Ross Mendoza, who believe in spices the way I do and are the chief tasters of my food. Our pastry team, who make every meal at Tabla complete and who patiently lent me their measuring cups while we were writing this book. My entire kitchen crew, past and present, who enjoy cooking this food and who do a great job of cooking the best food they can every single day. All the servers and managers at Tabla, who help communicate my spice message to our guests. General manager Tracy Wilson, who held down the fort on days when I was working on this book.

The farmers and other purveyors who produce all of the great ingredients we use at Tabla.

Gray Kunz, who harnessed the flavors of Asia, opening the door for me to do the same with India. All the great cooks I've worked alongside, who shared their knowledge with me when I was a young cook.

Amy Kalyn Sims, a very talented and accommodating photographer, and Marina Malchin, who propped the photographs with style and discernment. Rick Ellis, who elegantly styled some of the food for photographs. Allison Ehri, who tested every recipe meticulously with passion and commitment, and Penelope Hoblyn, who helped finish the testing in the ninth inning.

Beryl and Peter Cardoz, my mom and dad, who gave me the gift of taste, my talent, and a passion for food. My siblings, Dionne, Bryan, Debra, Kim, and Brett, for having such different palates—and for showing me such a variety of food. Especially my brother Bryan and his wife, Marilyn, who were instrumental in bringing me to the United States and helped me early in my career. My grandmother, Nana Esme, for teaching me the wonder of using everything and wasting nothing and for showing me where true flavor lay.

My partners, for believing in me and in my food:

Danny Meyer, for his extraordinary vision and love of excellence and good food; Michael Romano, whose love for things Indian and Indian food made this possible; Paul Bolles-Beaven, for supporting Tabla and helping me along the way; Richard Coraine, for being my scaffolding when the restaurant and this food were being introduced to the American public; and David Swinghamer, for showing me how to make things work financially.

Susan Friedland, for her stellar advice and longstanding support. Harriet Bell, an amazing editor and guide for my vision, and all the terrific people at William Morrow.

David Black, for being a great friend, adviser, confidant, and the best agent there is.

Jane Daniels Lear, a writer with tremendous knowledge, passion, and immense patience with all my "chefy" quirks and stubbornness. Sam Lear, who lent me his wife to write this book. Nichol Nelson and Eric Hastie, for helping things move along quickly.

Peter and Justin, the best two sons anyone could have, who love food the way I do and cook with me on Sundays; those dishes have landed on Tabla's menu and in this book. My wonderful wife, Barkha, who has made me follow my dreams and helped me realize my passion and love for food. For always supporting me in all that I do.

And to Tabla's guests. It's an honor and a pleasure to cook for you.

foreword

The original inspiration for Tabla came to me in 1993 during one of my frequent menu meetings with Michael Romano, chef-partner at Union Square Cafe. For a long time Michael had had an urge to see India and finally journeyed there in 1994. That very close encounter with a whole new world of flavors, cooking techniques, spices, and ingredients fundamentally changed the way he looked at food. Returning home with zealous enthusiasm, he began experimenting with the palette of Indian spices by incorporating them into dishes on the Union Square Cafe menu. Our USC guests were treated to curries, chutneys, a dash of garam masala here, a little tamarind there, all lovingly cooked with the same seasonal Greenmarket ingredients we use at Union Square Cafe. It was sort of Indian food under the radar. Sometimes Michael would cook an authentic recipe he had learned while in India, and other times he would apply authentic Indian spicing techniques to American dishes (like when he created "Oysters Raga-feller"). And it all worked!

Those cross-cultural dishes became some of our most popular. Faced with that kind of enthusiastic acceptance on one hand, but knowing we didn't want to diminish or alter that Italian inflection in USC's cooking on the other, I suggested to Michael that we consider creating a *new* restaurant to be rooted in authentic Indian tradition and spices and use Western culinary techniques and local seasonal ingredients as well. Certainly, in a city where so many people associated Indian cuisine with predictable menus of raita and dal, vindaloos, keemas, curries, and chutneys, we thought there was a great opportunity to showcase the glories and range of Indian flavors in a fresh way.

As we began to explore our possibilities and prospects, we were remarkably fortunate to meet an earnest young cook named Floyd Cardoz, a native of Bombay who was then sous-chef in Gray Kunz's inventive four-star kitchen at Lespinasse. Floyd had heard about our dreams from one of his former Lespinasse colleagues, Nick Oltarsh, now a cook at Gramercy Tavern, who knew we were cooking up an Indian-style restaurant. Floyd told us he was eager to pursue his personal dream of blending the culinary traditions of India and the West just as we were getting serious about expanding our own horizons in the same directions. After Floyd prepared an eye-opening, palate-bending tasting that blew my socks off, we spoke in depth, developed a deep sense of mutual trust and respect, and agreed to create Tabla, a restaurant we would dedicate to taking a very fresh look at Indian cooking in America.

From the beginning, building on Michael's initial inspiration, our goal has been to bring to New York the gorgeous flavors of India, both in marriage with Western ingredients, which is the focus of Tabla, and via Floyd's lovingly prepared home-style cooking, which we serve downstairs at the Bread Bar.

Over the years the most common question we've been asked is how we chose the name Tabla for the restaurant. Though many have assumed it is a French way of saying *table*, here's the real story: In the days while we were dreaming up the restaurant, I took my then four-year-old daughter, Hallie, to a children's concert at the Metropolitan Museum of Art featuring the renowned clarinetist Richard Stoltzman. He taught the kids while playing recognizable riffs from *Peter and the Wolf*, and I was particularly moved when, as a surprise, he brought out a musician who sat directly on the stage with dozens of Indian drums. The two collaborated on some familiar jazz tunes, with Stoltzman sounding very American and the drummer adding a hauntingly and decidedly Indian accent.

If you've ever heard Indian music, you will recognize the compelling, almost ringing notes of that Indian drum, which is called a *tabla*. Right then I was struck by the fascinating synchronicity of the Western and Indian music forms and how perfectly they complemented each other. That was precisely what I hoped we would do in a culinary sense at our new restaurant. And that's the origin of the name Tabla.

Making Indian cooking even more accessible to a broader swath of guests has never been about dumbing down or taming any of the vibrant spices or long-held Indian culinary traditions. Rather, what Floyd has always done so brilliantly is to take our guests by the hand and educate them by letting them know what these dishes mean to him personally. In fact, every one of his recipes is made using intelligent layers of ingredients and spices. But what makes each one sing with such sensible harmony is the layered story behind it. One by one, Floyd's deeply felt stories and the recipes that so beautifully express those stories have won over thousands of our guests, who in turn have become fluent and comfortable in their own right as tour guides to Tabla.

Floyd has also willingly taken on the role of U.S. ambassador to the state of New Indian cooking. He has embraced and cheered on an enormous number of other talented cooks who are all stretching the boundaries of what we think of and imagine when someone says "Let's eat Indian tonight!" I have loved every minute of Floyd's journey and feel blessed and privileged to take this ride with someone at the culinary helm who has so much passion, integrity, and love for sharing what he adores with so many others.

—*Danny Meyer*

preface

I was named after Floyd Patterson, the late, great African-American boxer, even though I grew up on the other side of the globe, in a large middle-class household in Bombay, on the West Coast of India. We summered with my parents' relatives farther south, in Goa, a fabled trading center since antiquity and a Portuguese colony for 450 years. My way of thinking about food—about everything, really—was influenced by different heritages, different customs, that go back centuries and stretch around the world. What's known in the West as fusion food—different cultures together on a plate—started for me in the cradle, because fusion was, quite simply, a way of life for our family.

Today I see my food as a mission of sorts, a way to bridge the gap between the food of my childhood and the American palate. If you think about food in the United States over the past decade, it's become bigger and bolder. It's taken the best of culinary traditions from all over the world, from Mexico to Asia to the Mediterranean and the Middle East, and, consequently, it's gotten hotter, smokier,

sweeter, saltier, tangier, more pungent with garlic. Seasonings like soy sauce, balsamic vinegar, chipotle chiles, cilantro, and fresh ginger are no longer considered hard-to-find "ethnic" ingredients but simply part of a well-stocked American larder. What I do in my kitchen is apply the diverse flavors I grew up with to icons of the American table—steak and potatoes, roast chicken, crab cakes, a hamburger. The food I love has a place in the melting pot.

I honestly can't remember a time when I didn't love to cook—and eat. But I do remember, very clearly, the moment when I realized that it was what I wanted to do for the rest of my life. I was puttering around in my parents' house, making a chicken curry for my father. I can see their kitchen as if it were yesterday: The principal work counter was bordered on one end by what's called a *matka*—a large clay urn of drinking water, with a spigot positioned over the sink. It was illuminated by big windows from which I could see mango trees, heavy with fruit, and a drumstick tree, which sounds like something out of Lewis Carroll but really exists: its long, beanlike pods are used in soups, curries, and pickles. Underneath the counter were staples found in every Indian kitchen—tamarind, kokum (a dried fruit related to mangosteen), vinegar, sea salt from both Bombay and Goa, a coconut scraper. On the opposite counter were large Portuguese ceramic crocks filled with mango and lime pickles; beneath were bins full of rice and flour. Within easy reach were jars filled with spices: coriander, cumin, and fenugreek seeds; three or four kinds of mustard seeds; the best black peppercorns, from Tellicherry; bay leaves; turmeric; cloves; cardamom pods. Spices are the bedrock of Indian cooking, I thought as I rummaged among them. No matter how simple or complex the food, the spices are always there.

Being in the kitchen made me relaxed and happy. I was twenty years old, and, having recently come to the realization that my degree in biochemistry didn't have to mean a stifling (to me) career in medicine, I was ready to embark on something new. Maybe it was that sense of possibility bubbling up inside that inspired me to recklessly add the unexpected to that curry: rosemary from the farmers' market and part of a bottle of Riesling. The fragrance and heat of the rosemary connected with that of the ginger in the sauce and turned it into something marvelous. The wine smoothed and rounded out the flavors in a way I hadn't imagined. And my father declared it the best thing he'd ever eaten.

Three generations of fine, instinctive cooks brought me up to love being in a kitchen. Everyone—from my mother's cook, Ermine, to a handful of ancient (and all-seeing) relations—showed me the importance of ingredients: the freshest produce, the most pristine seafood, top-quality spices toasted and ground to order. Every time I ripen a mango in a bowl of rice, the way my grandmother taught me—an idiosyncratic trick of hers that somehow brings mangoes to perfection—I think about how lucky I was to have been born and raised in a large family that was all about cooking and eating together.

That modest chicken curry marked a turning point in my life and set me to learning a new trade. Off I went to hotel and culinary school, first in Bombay and then in Switzerland. (This sort of thing wasn't really done in middle-class circles in Bombay. You can imagine what my parents thought of this move.) I persevered, and a few years later I came to America and found an entry-level job in Gray Kunz's legendary kitchen at Lespinasse, in New York City.

Gray, Swiss by birth, spent years in Singapore and Hong Kong. My first sight of him spoke volumes about the kind of person he is and the kind of kitchen he runs: the chef in command of the food world was *cleaning a sink*. Not fifteen minutes later, hands still reddened from scouring, he was putting the final touches on a signature entree—steamed black sea bass served in a bowl with a Thai-inspired kaffir lime leaf emulsion. His way of marrying French and Asian flavors and textures really spoke to me. He was creating exuberant, controversial, utterly delicious food, and I knew I was in the right place at the right time. Although I was about seven thousand miles away from India, I'd never felt more at home in my life.

During the mid-nineties, I worked my way

up from chopping thousands of kaffir lime leaves into a fine powder to chef de cuisine at Lespinasse. I wasn't in any hurry because I wanted to perfect every job I had there. I never once asked for a raise, because the education I was getting was priceless. There was always something new to see, something different to do. Those were heady days in the restaurant business, and it wasn't unusual for the kitchen to rip through five hundred kilos of truffles in a season. Extravagant items like that were just the beginning. Every ingredient, no matter how humble, was the best that could be found. I was used to that mind-set—I'd grown up with it, after all—but I came to see that first-class ingredients are a jumping-off point; they are where great cooking *begins*. Beyond that you must learn to weave together the varied strands of your imagination. The next few years were demanding but incredibly thrilling for me, as I started to develop my own style.

I still remember the first dish of mine that Gray put on the menu: lamb chops with squash, lentils, carrots, and cracked wheat. It's a Muslim dish from Hyderabad, but it didn't taste right in its new setting. The black cardamom was too strong, so I adjusted that. The dish improved, but judging by the reactions of the kitchen staff, the chiles were too extreme. Gray encouraged me to tone down the chiles and let the rest of the ingredients work in concert. "Balance," he said, time and time again. "Always balance and harmony. These are the most important things."

Thinking of heat as simply one more way to round out flavors was an epiphany. I wasn't back in India, where chiles are needed to aid digestion and circulation, cooling the body down by perspiration. Indian food is very different from traditional Western food, where just a few flavors are blended in a delicious way. Indian food requires assertive ingredients—ginger, chiles, garlic, the riches of the spice trade—that when melded together produce something subtle and sophisticated, at least in experienced hands. The Indian food I'd eaten in the United States was another matter entirely—too oily, too hot, and full of mushy, mysterious ingredients that were not remotely seasonal. No wonder Americans, who had dived joyfully into the vibrant flavors of Mexico and Southeast Asia, resisted it.

In 1997, I had the chance to realize my dream when I joined forces with New York restaurateur Danny Meyer. We named the place Tabla, after the Indian drums that lend their distinctive sound to sitar music. These drums have crossed a cultural divide—today you'll hear them in Western music from jazz to electronica—and crossing that cultural divide is exactly what we wanted the food at Tabla to accomplish. We were stunned when the restaurant created a huge splash straight away, thanks in large part to a three-star review in the *New York Times*. Critic Ruth Reichl really understood what we were trying to do, and her thumbnail description of the menu, "American food seen through a kaleidoscope of Indian spices," remains Tabla's mantra to this day.

This food is also appealing on another level: it's healthful. I use very little butter or cream to enrich dishes, relying instead on good stocks, a wide variety of fresh vegetables, spices (which contain many health-giving properties), and aromatics such as ginger, shallots, and chiles (my holy trinity) to make food satisfying and delicious.

Spices are my catalyst, of course, but I'm also a firm believer in cooking with the seasons. I look forward to the first local asparagus and tender, sweet carrots; the watermelons, tomatoes, and corn in the summer months; autumn's pumpkins and cooking greens; and winter's hearty, warming braises. And I still get excited about nontraditional ingredients. Take soft-shell crabs, for instance; they're one of my spring passions. We eat plenty of crabs in coastal India, but the soft-shells are thrown back into the sea. Now I can't imagine life without them. I panfry the crabs very simply, after first dredging them in a mixture of Cream of Wheat (the closest thing to Indian semolina) and freshly ground black pepper. And even though we have morels and asparagus in India, they are not readily available to home cooks. Here I sauté the mushrooms with asparagus, cumin seeds, shallots, ginger, and fresh green chiles. I use canola oil or extra-virgin olive oil because it's hard to find quality peanut oil here (it's often harsh tasting or rancid), and I like how the olive and canola oils interact with my food, making things lighter and cleaner tasting.

Over the years I've honed my ability to adapt Indian spices to American ingredients by building layers of well-balanced flavors. What, after all, makes people say "just one more bite"? It's the ever-alluring balance between sweet and sour, cool and spicy, crunchy and silky-smooth. Just one more bite.

I also incorporate the Western style of organizing meals around a main course, because a typical Indian meal—with its large assortment of stews and other dishes that hit the table all at once—isn't a feasible option unless you have help in the kitchen. That's still common in Indian middle-class households, but not in the United States.

There are no menus in this book (although there are plenty of serving suggestions) because I'm a big fan of component cooking. Don't turn to this book only when you have the time or inclination to make an entire meal from it. Most of the recipes can be slipped into your culinary repertoire with ease. A good example is the recipe for hanger steak on page 148. The preparation is simple: Marinate the steak (really, any cut will do) in a straightforward rub of coarsely ground coriander, cumin, and mustard seeds, plus cloves and black peppercorns. You'll find it is an extremely versatile main course because you can pair it with all sorts of accompaniments. I like to serve it with a yogurt raita brightened with horseradish and ginger (see page 249), but a dollop of horseradish mayonnaise or a tomatillo salsa would add pizzazz as well. Sometimes I add mashed potatoes with a smattering of lentils (a takeoff on the filling for the crisp, thin Indian crêpe called *dosa*; see page 218), but an all-American potato salad or baked potato makes a great accompaniment too. Try the raita with lamb burgers, crudités, or pita chips.

The recipes that follow include simple dishes that can be done quickly as well as some Tabla favorites that are more involved. There's a chapter devoted to spices and how to use them, as well as a glossary and mail-order sources. It all comes down to the spices, you see. It's as true today as it was back in my parents' kitchen all those years ago. Once you get to know Indian spices, they'll spark your imagination the way they do mine.

using spices:
the essentials

Building a pantry: spices and other seasonings

The world of spices is rich, vast, and multi-layered, but don't be intimidated. Once you start incorporating new flavors into your culinary repertoire, you'll be surprised and delighted at how easy they are to use. I like to classify them into the following five groups. *For more information, see the Glossary and Sources at the back of the book.*

SPICES YOU KNOW AND LOVE

These familiar spices are used the world over to season everything from gingerbread to Italian cured meats. You've probably got them in your pantry, but I'll show you how to use them in a different context.

> **Black peppercorns**
> **Cinnamon**
> **Cloves**
> **Bay leaves**
> **Cayenne or hot red pepper flakes**

BASIC YET VERSATILE SPICES

These spices lie at the heart of Indian cooking. Adding them to your pantry is a way to ease into Indian flavors.

> **Cumin seeds**
> **Coriander seeds**
> **Mustard seeds (brown or yellow)**
> **Turmeric**
> **Paprika**

MORE ADVENTUROUS SPICES

Once you're comfortable with more accessible spices, try these more assertive flavorings.

When used in combination with the preceding spices, they produce a more complex dish.

> **Fennel seeds**
> **Cardamom pods (black and green)**
> **Anise seeds**
> **Star anise**

COMPLEX SPICES

These are potent, so take care in using them. Although they add layers of flavor to a dish, they can easily overpower it. And once you put too much mace or Szechwan peppercorns, for instance, into a dish, you can't really fix the balance.

> **Dried ginger**
> **Allspice**
> **Mace**
> **Dried chiles**
> **Szechwan peppercorns**
> **Ajwain seeds**
> **Fenugreek seeds or leaves**
> **Nigella seeds**
> **Black cumin**

HERBS, CHILES, AND OTHER FLAVORINGS

Here are ingredients that will add freshness, depth, or acid to a dish.

> **Fresh ginger**
> **Fresh chiles (green or red)**
> **Cilantro**
> **Rosemary**
> **Thyme**
> **Curry leaves**
> **Shallots**

Onions
Aleppo pepper
Tamarind
Kokum

How to buy and store spices

I always buy whole spices (except turmeric, paprika, and cayenne) and grind only the amount I'll need for a recipe. I know that's not very convenient—especially when a recipe calls for a quarter teaspoon of this and a half teaspoon of that—but it really does make a difference. Commercially ground spices lose their potency very quickly, and you might as well be adding colored (and expensive) dust to your food.

Buy spices from a store with high turnover. Indian and Middle Eastern markets usually do a brisk business. Many grocery stores have a good selection of the basics. My favorite mail-order sources are listed at the back of this book.

Light, heat, and air are detrimental to spices, so keep them in airtight containers in a kitchen drawer or cupboard, not over the stove. The best place for anything with a high oil content—mustard seeds, for instance—is the freezer.

Grinding spices

Grinding spices releases their aromatic oils, and that's where the flavor is. A fine grind of spices evenly blends the flavors into a subtle mosaic; a coarse grind adds bursts of flavor and texture to a dish.

The only piece of equipment that I suggest you invest in is an electric coffee grinder that you keep just for spices. An inexpensive grinder costs about twenty dollars and can be found at any kitchenware shop (see Sources).

Spices: releasing their flavor and aroma

You've bought fresh whole spices and want to get the very best out of them. Grinding them is part of the story, but what really makes those aromatic oils reach their full potential is heat; it tends to mellow them out and bring harmony to a dish. Some spices, of course, such as black pepper, can be used without heating. Toasting whole spices, whether in a dry skillet or in a little oil, is very easy.

DRY-TOASTING WHOLE SPICES
Toasting whole spices in a dry skillet evaporates their moisture; they take on a warm, earthy, slightly smoky flavor that can be very different from that of the raw spices. Take black peppercorns, for instance: raw, they are sharp and pungent, but toasting brings out their fruitiness and woodsy, lemony notes. Dry-toasting also decreases the heat in dried chiles.

Because raw ground spices burn easily and become bitter, toast spices whole and then grind them. And, until toasting spices becomes second nature to you, toast only one spice at a time. If you toast a mixture of spices, with their varying sizes and shapes, some will get scorched before the others are done. Let the toasted spices cool before grinding them. The recipe for Crispy Shrimp with Toasted Spice Curry on page 97 illustrates this technique.

Heat a dry small skillet or sauté pan over moderately low heat. Add the whole spice, such as coriander seeds or cumin seeds, and cook, shaking the skillet to keep the spice moving around and control the browning. You'll want to toast the spice until fragrant and a couple of shades darker, usually just a few minutes. Immediately turn out the spice onto a small plate or tray to stop the cooking. When the spice is cool, it's ready to grind.

Experiment with dry-toasted spices by adding them to a dish toward the end of cooking. Use a combination of cumin seeds, coriander seeds, and mustard seeds to give new life to your favorite recipes for meat, fish, or vegetables.

COOKING WHOLE SPICES IN OIL

The combination of heat and oil extracts flavor and aroma from spices very quickly, allowing the spices to "bloom." I compare cooking whole spices in hot oil to sautéing a vegetable because it's fast and yields a bright flavor. Because things will move quickly, have your spices measured out and at the ready before heating the oil. An example of this technique is in the recipe for Corn and Potato Chowder (page 44).

HOW TO COOK WHOLE SPICES IN OIL

Heat canola oil in a skillet over moderate heat until it shimmers. Add the whole spices all at the same time and cook, stirring, until fragrant and little bubbles form around the spices. Then add the other ingredients as specified and proceed with the recipe.

If you're cooking a large spice, such as cardamom pods, cloves, or a cinnamon stick, remove them from the finished dish before serving so guests don't bite into them.

Stews, soups, and braises are ideal vehicles for experimenting with cooking spices in oil. Add spices to the cooking oil at the beginning of a recipe, before adding aromatic vegetables such as carrots, onion, and celery. Or pour in a tarka to finish the dish.

WHAT IS A TARKA?

A tarka is a tempering of sorts, a way of adding a little extra richness and depth by blooming whole, small edible spices and often fresh curry leaves, with their citrusy aroma, in hot oil, then immediately pouring them into a dish at the beginning or, more commonly, at the end of cooking, as in the Pumpkin Rasam on page 40. This classic Indian technique is fast (it takes about a minute) and fabulous.

Spices in India: background notes

Spices play an enormous role in Indian culture, not just in the kitchen. They are valued for their medicinal as well as culinary properties, so traditional Indian cooking is truly holistic. Turmeric is considered to be an antioxidant and antiseptic, for instance; chiles are rich in vitamin C and are thought to have antibiotic qualities—no small matter in a hot, humid climate where healing can be slow.

While I use Indian spices with ingredients that would never be found on an Indian table, when it comes to the actual complementary or contrasting spice mixture in a particular dish, I'm a real traditionalist. For thousands of years, spices have been thought to belong to various "families" and have been combined deftly to bring subtlety and complexity to food. They're also seasonal: The classic spice blend called *garam masala*, for instance, is used only in winter in northern India, where it originated. (*Garam* means "warming.") Sweet spices are considered warming spices and include cinnamon, cloves, cardamom, mace, and nutmeg; they are avoided or used in very limited quantities during the summer months. "Cooling" spices help keep the body comfortable during hot, sultry weather. Cooling spices include black peppercorns, ginger, mustard and coriander seeds, and chiles. Fenugreek and ajwain seeds are bitter or astringent spices, and tamarind, kokum (a dried fruit related to mangosteen), and amchoor (powdered dried green mango) are acidic and fruity flavorings.

In Indian cooking, by the way, you'll notice the importance of acid. Tamarind, say, gives a complexity and depth of flavor that you will never get from lemon or lime juice. Tomatoes, green mangoes, vinegars, and yogurt all add different kinds of acid to meals.

how to use this book:
 assorted tips and techniques

Salt, pepper . . . and sugar

Seasoning is all important. I prefer to use sea salt in seafood dishes and kosher salt in everything else; it just feels natural to me. You can certainly use whatever salt is available to you. When I call for freshly ground black pepper, I mean whole peppercorns that have been ground in a pepper mill, not ground pepper from a tin. Like other spices, pepper is more aromatic and flavorful when freshly ground. A pepper mill isn't expensive, and it's one kitchen tool that will change your life. Sugar is a balancing element in savory dishes; it smooths out an acidic edge.

Stocks and broths

If you're using stock for a soup or sauce in which it's going to act as a background flavor, then it's fine to use canned broth as a substitute. I recommend using reduced-sodium broths because the regular strength is generally too salty. If you are reducing stock for a glaze or concentrated sauce, then you should make your own stock because canned broth will be too salty and doesn't have enough natural gelatin to give you the body and flavor you need.

Cooking in batches . . . or not

Many of the recipes in this book are perfect for entertaining, which is why they all serve six people. But the downside is that pieces of fish or individual steaks or chops will need to be cooked in batches. If you have two 10- to 12-inch skillets, feel free to cook multiple batches simultaneously rather than keeping one batch warm in a low oven while cooking another. In some recipes, I use two heat sources. I'll start something on the stovetop and then finish it in the oven. For example, in the Rice Flake–Crisped Halibut on Watercress with Watermelon Curry on page 61, I sauté the fish first to brown the coating and create a delicious exterior. Then I roast the fish in the oven for a few minutes so that it becomes tender yet firm. In this type of recipe, I'll sauté the fish in batches on the stovetop and transfer each batch as cooked to a baking sheet with sides—that is, an old-fashioned cookie sheet, about ½ to 1 inch deep, or a shallow roasting pan.

How to make chiffonade

The French technique called *chiffonade* is a handy way to chop fresh leafy herbs or greens. Discard any tough stems and bundle the herbs or greens together, like you would roll up a cigar. Then cut them crosswise into thin strips or shreds.

How to peel and slice a mango

Use a vegetable peeler or sharp paring knife to remove the peel. Stand the mango on one end and slice off a wide "fillet" from the two flatter sides with a large, sharp knife. (Cut as close to the flat, oval pit as possible.) Then lay the pit flat and slice off the narrower sides. Cut the fillets lengthwise into pieces about 1 inch thick, then cut them crosswise about ⅛ inch thick. Cut the narrower pieces crosswise about ⅛ inch thick.

How to roast, peel, and seed chiles

If you have a gas stove, put the chile over a burner turned to moderately high heat. Roast the chile, turning it with tongs, until softened and charred on all sides. If you have an electric stove, put the chile under the broiler, turning and roasting it the same way for about 2½ minutes. While the chile is still hot, wrap it in plastic wrap or put it in an airtight container and let it sit until cool enough to handle, about 10 minutes. Unwrap the chile and rub off the charred skin under cold running water. Remove the top of the chile. Gently split the chile open and discard the seeds.

first courses
and salads

goan spiced crab cakes

The spicy tomato base here is what makes Goan-style crabs so extraordinary, but I wasn't quite sure how to deliver the flavors to Americans. And then I thought of crab cakes, and voilà—this is the one dish that has been on Tabla's menu since we opened. Crab cakes are frequently fried, but I prefer them gently sautéed. An easy fish mousse helps bind them together. They can be coated in different ways—fresh bread crumbs, for instance, or flour—but I use panko, the crisp, crunchy Japanese dried bread crumbs that are available at seafood stores and many supermarkets. They are actually Portuguese in origin; the Portuguese took their bread-making methods to Japan about a hundred years after they colonized Goa. I serve crab cakes on top of a handful of young, tender greens, alongside Avocado Salad (page 18) and a dab of Tamarind Chutney (page 238); the flavors are great together.

FOR THE TOMATO BASE

2¼ teaspoons cumin seeds
2¼ teaspoons coriander seeds
Scant ½ teaspoon ground turmeric
Scant ½ teaspoon cayenne
2 teaspoons canola oil
1½ cups diced white onion
1 tablespoon minced peeled ginger
1½ teaspoons minced garlic
½ cup diced tomato
Kosher salt

FOR THE FISH MOUSSE

3 ounces skinless white fish fillet, such as cod, bass, or pollack
1 whole egg
1 egg white
2 teaspoons grated lime zest (from about 1½ limes)
2 tablespoons finely chopped cilantro
2 tablespoons finely sliced chives

¼ cup fresh lime juice (from about 1½ limes)
Sea salt and freshly ground black pepper
1 pound lump crabmeat, gently picked over for shell pieces
2 cups panko
3 tablespoons canola oil

Finely grind the cumin and coriander seeds in an electric coffee/spice grinder, then blend with the turmeric and cayenne in a small bowl. Heat the oil in a 10-inch skillet over moderately high heat until it shimmers. Add the onion, ginger, and garlic and sauté for 5 minutes, or until the onion is softened. Stir in the tomato, spice mixture, and salt to taste. Cook the mixture over moderately low heat, stirring often, until it releases its liquid and then thickens, about 30 minutes. Cool the base, uncovered. *The base can be made a day ahead and kept, covered, in the refrigerator.*

Puree the fish, egg, and egg white in a food processor until smooth. Transfer the fish puree to a bowl big enough to later hold the tomato base and crabmeat, then stir in the lime zest, cilantro, and chives. (You should have about 1 cup fish mousse.)

Stir the tomato base and lime juice into the fish mousse and season generously with salt and pepper. Fold in the crabmeat.

Spread the panko on a tray. Form 1 small test patty of the crab mixture and roll it in the panko. Sauté it in a lightly oiled pan (about 1 minute on each side) and taste. Correct the seasoning to suit your taste. Gently form the remaining crab mixture into 12 equal balls and roll them in panko. Pat the balls into cakes (about 2½ inches by ¾ inch), taking care not to squeeze them tightly.

Preheat the oven to 225°F.

Heat 1½ tablespoons of the canola oil in a heavy 10- to 12-inch skillet over moderately high heat until it shimmers. Add half the crab cakes and sauté for about 3 minutes, or until golden on the bottom. Turn them over carefully and sauté for about 3 minutes longer, or until golden on the bottom. Transfer to paper towels or brown paper to drain, then place on a baking sheet with sides. Keep the crab cakes warm in the middle of the oven while sautéing the remaining crab cakes the same way. Serve the crab cakes warm.

green mango— marinated fluke or halibut with pickled daikon and beetroot

If you're lucky enough to be able to get impeccably fresh raw fish, you're in for a treat. Raw fluke has a delicate flavor and a beautifully firm texture. Here it is marinated in a citrusy blend that includes limes, green mango (a Granny Smith apple is an able stand-in), fresh green chile, and aromatic spices. Pickled beets and daikon—a hefty mild white radish called *mooli* in India—adds jewel-like brightness to both plate and palate. The pickled vegetables and the marinade can be made ahead.

FOR THE PICKLED DAIKON
AND BEETS

6 ounces daikon

1 small beet

2 tablespoons white wine vinegar

¾ teaspoon sugar

1 teaspoon minced peeled ginger

1 teaspoon thinly sliced mild to
    moderately hot fresh green chile

¼ teaspoon sea salt

FOR THE GREEN MANGO MARINADE

A 4-ounce piece green (unripe)
    mango or ½ Granny Smith apple

1½ teaspoons coriander seeds

½ teaspoon black peppercorns

⅛ teaspoon fenugreek seeds

1 teaspoon minced peeled ginger

Sea salt

3 limes

¼ cup extra virgin olive oil

½ teaspoon sugar

A 9-ounce piece fluke or halibut fillet,
    sliced ¼ inch thick on the diagonal

2 tablespoons thinly sliced cilantro
    leaves

Sea salt

3 cups loosely packed watercress

Freshly ground black pepper

SPECIAL EQUIPMENT: *a handheld slicer such as a mandoline or Benriner*

Cut the daikon into very thin slices with the handheld slicer. Peel the beet and cut into very thin slices with the handheld slicer. Stack 3 or 4 beet slices together at a time and cut into julienne strips with a knife.

Bring 1/3 cup water, the vinegar, sugar, ginger, chile, and salt to a boil in a 1-quart saucepan over high heat. Add the beets and let steep off the heat for 30 minutes.

Pour the beets and liquid over the daikon slices in a bowl and let marinate. The daikon will turn a beautiful pink. *The pickled daikon and beets can be made up to 8 hours ahead and refrigerated, covered.*

Peel the green mango and cut into very thin lengthwise slices with the handheld slicer. Stack 3 or 4 slices together at a time and cut into julienne strips with a knife. Cut the julienne strips into 1/8-inch dice.

Toast the coriander seeds in a dry small skillet over moderately low heat, shaking the skillet, until fragrant and a couple of shades darker, about 3 minutes. Turn the seeds out on a small tray or plate to cool. Toast the peppercorns the same way, turning them out to cool. Toast the fenugreek seeds the same way, turning them out to cool. Finely grind the seeds in an electric coffee/spice grinder. Combine the ground spices with the ginger, green mango, and salt in a medium bowl. Add the grated zest of 2 of the limes and the juice of all 3 to the green mango mixture and stir in the olive oil and sugar. *The marinade can be made up to 1 day in advance and refrigerated, covered.*

Add the fluke, cilantro, and salt to the marinade and combine well. (Your scrupulously clean hands are the best tool for the job.) Let sit for 5 minutes.

Arrange the daikon slices on a platter and scatter with a few beet strips. Top with the watercress and scatter the remaining beets on top. Surround the watercress with the fluke and season with pepper. Drizzle with the remaining marinade.

tuna tartare
with apples

Texture adds a mysterious, complex element to a dish. In this tartare, there is a unique synergy from the different textures of apple, vegetables, and tuna. Toasted spices give a smoky note to the tuna, providing another layer of flavor, and a tiny bit of mustard oil gives a little astringency. For a more substantial first course, serve this on a bed of greens, dressed with Cider Vinaigrette I (page 251). Fish served raw must be impeccably fresh: buy from a fishmonger you trust and tell him the fish will be eaten raw.

1 tablespoon coriander seeds
1½ teaspoons black peppercorns
¼ fresh red Thai chile, about 2 inches long, very finely minced
1 heaping tablespoon minced peeled ginger
⅓ cup thinly sliced quartered radishes
⅓ cup finely chopped red onion
1 cup finely diced apple such as Empire, McIntosh, or Gala

½ cup coarsely crushed salted peanuts (see Note)
2 tablespoons chopped cilantro
2 tablespoons chopped chives
18 ounces sashimi-grade tuna, sliced ¼ inch thick and then diced
Generous pinch of chaat masala
Sea salt
3 tablespoons extra virgin olive oil
½ teaspoon mustard oil (optional)
1½ tablespoons lime juice

Toast the coriander seeds in a dry small skillet over moderately low heat, shaking the skillet, until fragrant and a couple of shades darker, about 3 minutes. Transfer the seeds to a small tray or plate to cool. Toast the peppercorns the same way and transfer them to the tray to cool. Finely grind the coriander seeds and peppercorns together in an electric coffee/spice grinder.

Put the chile in a bowl and add the ginger, radishes, onion, apple, peanuts, ground spices, cilantro, and chives. Add the tuna to the chile mixture. Add the chaat masala, salt to taste, the olive oil, and the mustard oil, if using, and gently stir everything together. Stir in the lime juice just before serving, and serve in a chilled bowl.

NOTE: *Wrap the the peanuts in plastic first to keep them from scattering, then pound them a few times with a rolling pin.*

avocado salad

Cilantro, cumin, lime, chile—these ingredients are common to hot regions around the world, including India and tropical America. They have a real affinity for avocado, which is native to Mexico. (When buying avocados, look for the Hass variety, which is small with dark, rough skin. The flesh is buttery-rich, denser, and more fully flavored than that of other varieties.)

This salad falls into the "instant classic" category. It has been on the menu at Tabla ever since the restaurant opened and remains there by popular demand. Think of it as guacamole Tabla style; try it as an accompaniment for the Goan Spiced Crab Cakes (page 12), as a dip with toasted pappadums or corn chips, or as a sandwich filling. You can either serve this right away or refrigerate it for a couple of hours to allow the flavors to develop. If not serving the salad immediately, press a sheet of plastic wrap over the surface to prevent it from discoloring.

2½ teaspoons cumin seeds
6 ripe but firm Hass avocados
2 teaspoons grated lime zest (from about 2 limes)
⅓ cup lime juice (from about 2 limes)
½ cup finely chopped red onion

1 cup diced plum tomato
2 tablespoons finely sliced cilantro
¼ cup extra virgin olive oil
⅛ teaspoon cayenne
Pinch of sugar
Kosher salt and freshly ground black pepper

Toast the cumin seeds in a dry small skillet over moderately low heat, shaking the skillet, until fragrant and a couple of shades darker, about 3 minutes. Turn them out on a tray or small plate to cool. Finely grind the seeds in an electric spice/coffee grinder.

Cut each avocado in half lengthwise and remove the pit. Scoop out each half in one piece with a large spoon and lay it, cut side down, on a cutting board. Cut each into ½-inch pieces and transfer to a large bowl. Gently toss the avocado pieces with the lime zest and juice. Fold the onion, tomato, and cilantro into the avocados. Fold everything together carefully so that you don't smash the avocados or tomatoes. Fold in the oil, cumin, cayenne, sugar, and salt and pepper to taste. Serve immediately or refrigerate, surface covered with plastic wrap, for up to 2 hours.

salad of baked apple and roasted root vegetables

SERVES 6

I grew up eating incredible apples from Kashmir, and I think of them whenever I make this salad. Part of the inspiration comes from my wife, who loves to sprinkle chaat masala—a tangy spice blend that includes smoky black salt, cumin, and green mango powder—on slices of raw apple. Parsnips, which have a great affinity for apples, and celery root give the salad a suave sweetness, and the flattened onions called *cipollini* supply a mellow richness. I peel the carrots and parsnips before roasting and the celery root, turnips, and onions after roasting. The reason is simple: it's the easiest way to peel each vegetable.

FOR BAKING THE APPLE AND ROASTING THE VEGETABLES

1 large apple such as Empire, McIntosh, or Gala, peeled, cored, and lightly brushed with melted unsalted butter

3 medium carrots, peeled

Canola oil

Kosher salt and freshly ground pepper

1 pound parsnips (about 6), peeled

1 medium celery root, unpeeled

2 medium turnips, unpeeled

½ pound cipollini onions, unpeeled

FOR THE VINAIGRETTE

2 cups apple cider

2 tablespoons finely chopped shallot

1 tablespoon finely chopped peeled ginger

1 packed tablespoon grated fresh horseradish or drained bottled horseradish

1 tablespoon yellow mustard seeds

1 star anise

¼ cup cider vinegar

Kosher salt

1 tablespoon coriander seeds

1 teaspoon black peppercorns

½ teaspoon ground ginger

¼ cup canola oil

FOR FINISHING THE SALAD
1 teaspoon cumin seeds
¼ teaspoon chaat masala

Kosher salt
¼ cup sliced chives

Preheat the oven to 350°F.

Put the apple in a small baking dish. Put the carrots on a piece of foil and drizzle with a little oil. Season with salt and pepper to taste and wrap up the foil to make a package. Make separate packages in the same way with the parsnips, celery root, turnips, and onions. Put the foil packages of vegetables in the middle of the oven along with the apple and roast until the apple and vegetables are tender, about 1 hour.

Let the apple and vegetables cool. Peel the celery root and turnips and slip the skins off the onions. Cut the apple into 1½-inch-thick pieces. Cut the carrots and parsnips on the bias into 1½-inch pieces. Cut the celery root and turnips in half, then cut each half into 1½-inch pieces. Quarter the onions. Mix the apple and vegetables together in a serving bowl.

Put the apple cider, shallot, fresh ginger, horseradish, mustard seeds, star anise, and cider vinegar in a 2- to 3-quart saucepan and simmer over moderately high heat until reduced to about 1 cup, about 20 minutes. Let the vinaigrette cool and remove the star anise. Add a pinch of salt.

Toast the coriander seeds in a dry small skillet over moderately low heat, shaking the skillet, until fragrant and a couple of shades darker, about 3 minutes. Transfer the seeds to a small tray or plate to cool. Toast the peppercorns the same way and transfer them to the tray or plate to cool. Finely grind the coriander seeds and peppercorns in an electric coffee/spice grinder. Add the ground ginger to the ground coriander and pepper and stir into the vinaigrette. Whisk the oil into the vinaigrette and add salt to taste.

Toast the cumin seeds in a dry small skillet over moderately low heat until fragrant and a few shades darker, about 1 minute. Transfer to a small tray or plate to cool, then finely grind them in an electric coffee/spice grinder. Sprinkle the cumin seeds and chaat masala over the salad and gently toss with the vinaigrette. Add salt to taste, sprinkle with the chives, and serve on a platter.

roasted fennel salad with pumpkin orange vinaigrette

SERVES 6

This autumnal salad goes well with any type of bird, especially the Spice-Crusted Duck Breasts (page 134). Coarse sea salt gives the salad an extra, delicate crunch.

1 small sugar pumpkin or Delicata squash, about 1 pound, peeled, seeded, and cut into 1-inch pieces (3 cups)

fennel bulbs, about 2 pounds, halved lengthwise, cored, and reserved fronds thinly sliced and chopped

2 tablespoons extra virgin olive oil

Kosher salt and freshly ground black pepper

2 cloves

¼ cinnamon stick

¼ teaspoon black peppercorns

½ teaspoon brown mustard seeds

1 whole star anise

1 cup orange juice

1 tablespoon finely chopped peeled ginger

Juice of 1 lime or ½ lemon

⅓ cup plain whole-milk yogurt

1 teaspoon chaat masala

6 cups torn bitter greens such as arugula, watercress, and/or shredded Belgian endive

Coarse sea salt such as Maldon

Preheat the oven to 400°F.

Put the pumpkin on a parchment-lined baking sheet. Toss the fennel slices with the olive oil in a bowl and season with salt and pepper to taste. Put the fennel on another parchment-lined baking sheet. Roast the pumpkin and fennel in the middle of the oven for 25 minutes, until the fennel is tender but still firm. Remove the fennel and continue roasting the pumpkin for another 5 minutes, until tender. Remove the pumpkin and let cool to room temperature.

Finely grind the cloves, cinnamon, peppercorns, mustard seeds, and star anise in an electric coffee/spice grinder.

Put the orange juice in a small saucepan and cook over moderately high heat until reduced to ½ cup, 3 to 5 minutes.

Puree the roasted pumpkin, ginger, reduced orange juice, and lime juice in a food processor until smooth. Gradually add the yogurt while pureeing and puree to blend. Transfer the puree to a medium bowl and stir in the ground spices.

Put the roasted fennel in another medium bowl and stir in the chaat masala. Add the pumpkin orange vinaigrette and season with pepper. Serve the fennel over the greens and sprinkle with coarse sea salt.

heirloom tomato salad with spiced parmesan crisps

SERVES 6

This simple salad, made with flavorful, old-fashioned varieties of tomatoes, is one of my absolute favorites. My inspiration for the spice blend here comes from the Hyderabadi method of stir-frying vegetables and the Indian cheese called *paneer* in a *kadhai*—essentially a small deep wok. The spicy, cheesy crisps are easy to prepare and make great cocktail nibbles as well.

FOR THE SPICE BLEND

1 tablespoon fennel seeds
1 tablespoon coriander seeds
1½ teaspoons cumin seeds
¾ teaspoon black peppercorns
Pinch of Aleppo pepper or cayenne

FOR THE SPICED PARMESAN CRISPS

Heaping ¾ cup finely grated
 Parmigiano-Reggiano or grana
 padano

FOR THE HEIRLOOM TOMATO SALAD

3 pounds mixed ripe heirloom
 tomatoes, cut into even wedges
1½ teaspoons chopped peeled ginger
1½ teaspoons chopped mild to
 moderately hot fresh green chile
¼ cup chopped chives
¼ cup whole cilantro leaves
¼ cup plus 2 tablespoons Thai or
 regular basil leaves, cut into
 ¼-inch slices
Small pinch of sugar
1 teaspoon chaat masala
¼ cup extra virgin olive oil
2 tablespoons balsamic vinegar

Toast the fennel seeds in a dry small skillet over moderately low heat, shaking the skillet, until fragrant and a couple of shades darker, about 3 minutes. Transfer the seeds to a small tray or a plate to cool. Toast the coriander seeds in the same way and transfer to the tray or plate to cool. Toast the cumin seeds, and then the peppercorns, transferring each as done to the tray or plate to cool. Finely grind all the toasted spices together in an electric coffee/spice grinder. (You should have about 3 tablespoons.) Evenly divide the ground spices between one medium bowl and one large bowl. Set the large bowl aside. Add the Aleppo pepper to the medium bowl. Set aside that bowl for the Parmesan crisps.

Preheat the oven to 300°F. Line a baking sheet with a Silpat liner or parchment.

Add the grated cheese to the medium bowl of spice blend (with the Aleppo pepper) and mix well. (Your freshly washed hands are the best tool for the job.) Divide the cheese mixture into 6 mounds on the lined baking sheet. Flatten the mounds into 3½-inch rounds. Bake the cheese crisps in the middle of the oven until brown, for about 20 minutes.

Put the tomatoes into the large bowl with the spice mixture. Add the ginger, chile, chives, cilantro, Thai basil, sugar, chaat masala, oil, and vinegar and stir gently to mix well. Divide the salad, along with any juices that have accumulated in the bowl, among 6 plates and top each serving with a cheese crisp.

roasted beet salad

SERVES 6

This dish always reminds me of monsoon season in Goa. Because of the heavy rains, fishing boats can't go out for weeks at a time, so people tend to rely on salted fish such as bacalao, or salt cod—a reminder that Goa was a Portuguese colony for hundreds of years. Salt cod is generally soaked before using, but here thin slices of it are simply toasted in a dry skillet until golden and charred in places, a technique I use often. Once the fish is cool, it is easily shredded (just rub it between your hands) and blended into the salad, providing a slightly mysterious, smoky backnote of flavor that balances the earthy sweetness of beets and the acidity of red wine vinegar. Toasted, shredded salt cod is also an easy, quick way to add complexity to a simple dish of rice and *dal*, or hulled split legumes. This is a great prelude to steaks on the grill.

3 pounds beets
Sea salt and freshly ground black
  pepper
¼ cup plus 1 tablespoon extra virgin
  olive oil
3 ounces salt cod, excess salt
  brushed off
1½ cups quartered and thinly sliced
  red onion

2 tablespoons halved, seeded, and
  thinly sliced mild to moderately
  hot fresh green chile
2 teaspoons minced peeled ginger
¼ cup tightly packed thinly sliced
  cilantro
Sugar
¼ cup red wine vinegar

Preheat the oven to 350°F.

Put the beets on a piece of heavy-duty foil large enough to enclose them and season with salt and pepper. Drizzle the beets with 1 tablespoon of the oil and wrap the foil around them to form a snug packet. Put the packet on a baking sheet in the middle of the oven and roast until the beets are tender when pierced with a fork, 45 minutes to 1½ hours, depending on the size of the beets. Let the beets cool, then peel them and cut into ½-inch pieces. (You should have about 6 cups.)

While the beets are roasting, cut the salt cod on the diagonal into thin slices. Toast the salt cod in a dry small skillet over moderately high heat for 3 to 5 minutes, or until crisp, golden, and lightly charred.

Combine the beets, onion, chile, ginger, cilantro, sugar to taste, vinegar, and remaining ¼ cup oil in a bowl. Season with pepper. Shred the salt cod over the beets (your clean hands are the best tool for the task) and blend together. Taste and adjust the seasoning if necessary. Serve the salad in a large bowl. *The salad deepens in flavor if made 1 day ahead.*

sprouted bean salad with spicy yogurt dressing

SERVES 6

This fresh-tasting, protein-packed salad is all about texture, including the addictively crunchy fried chickpea noodles called *sev* (available at Indian markets or by mail order; see Sources) that are an added garnish. The tangy, spicy yogurt dressing is very refreshing on a hot day. Sprouted beans such as chickpeas, mung beans, and *urad dal* are available at farmers' markets and many grocery stores. We grow our own at Tabla, and it's easy enough to do if you know how. Soak the beans overnight in water to cover by a couple of inches. Wrap them in a kitchen towel and hang them up in a warm corner of the kitchen. Spray the towel with water occasionally to keep it moist. (You could also keep the beans in a bowl, covered with a moist towel.) The beans will sprout in two or three days.

FOR THE SALAD

3 cups (about 1 pound) sprouted chickpeas, mung beans, *urad dal*, and/or Bengal gram (*chana dal*)

1 large baking potato, peeled and cut into ½-inch dice

1 large apple such as Empire, McIntosh, or Gala

Kosher salt and freshly ground black pepper

1 teaspoon chaat masala

2 tablespoons lime juice

¼ cup plain whole-milk yogurt

½ cup Mint Coriander Chutney (page 234) or store-bought chutney

⅓ cup Tamarind Chutney (page 238) or store-bought chutney

FOR GARNISH

1½ cups sev

2 tablespoons cilantro chiffonade (see page 8)

2 tablespoons finely chopped chives

Bring a 6- to 8-quart pot of salted water to a boil and add the sprouted beans. After the water returns to a rolling boil, blanch the beans for 1 minute, then transfer them with a slotted spoon to a tray or platter to cool.

Return the water in the pot to a boil and cook the potato until tender yet still firm, about 5 minutes. Drain the potato in a strainer and set aside.

Peel and core the apple and cut into ½-inch dice. Put the apple, potato, and sprouted beans in a large bowl and season with salt and pepper. Stir in the chaat masala, lime juice, yogurt, and chutneys. Serve the salad on a platter or in individual bowls. Just before serving, garnish the salad with the sev, cilantro, and chives.

waldorf salad with duck confit

When I opened Tabla, I wasn't that familiar with American lunch salads, but I knew that guests would expect them. How to find something they would connect with? I remembered my days as a young cook at Bombay's Taj Mahal hotel and the ten different salads we made daily for the Ballroom Buffet. Among them was (naturally) a Waldorf. I took a fresh look at this period piece and gave it a lift with flavorful apples from the farmers' market and fresh, crunchy walnuts. Crisp pieces of sautéed duck confit take it over the top, but the salad is excellent by itself.

FOR THE DRESSING

1 quart orange juice

2 star anise

1 cinnamon stick, broken into pieces

3 cloves

1 cup thinly sliced peeled ginger plus
   1 tablespoon finely chopped

3 cups Chicken Stock (page 274)

1 tablespoon finely chopped shallot

1 tablespoon dry mustard

Kosher salt and freshly ground black
   pepper

½ cup canola oil

½ cup extra virgin olive oil

FOR THE SALAD

4 medium apples such as Empire,
   McIntosh, or Gala

1 tablespoon lime juice

2 cups chopped celery hearts

1 tablespoon chopped peeled pale
   green celery leaves

1 teaspoon finely chopped peeled
   ginger

1 teaspoon finely chopped mild to
   moderately hot fresh green chile

1 teaspoon chaat masala

¼ cup cilantro chiffonade
   (see page 8)

1 tablespoon chopped chives

Kosher salt

1 tablespoon extra virgin olive oil

1 cup walnuts, coarsely chopped

½ teaspoon sugar

FOR THE DUCK CONFIT

3 confit duck legs (1½ pounds) at
   room temperature

3 tablespoons canola oil

Freshly ground black pepper

Put the orange juice, star anise, cinnamon, cloves, and thinly sliced ginger in a 6-quart pot. Bring to a boil and boil until reduced to 1 cup, about 20 minutes. At the same time, put the chicken stock, finely chopped ginger, and shallot in a 3-to 4-quart pot, bring to a boil, and boil until reduced to ½ cup, about 20 minutes.

Strain the orange juice reduction through a fine strainer into a bowl, pressing on the solids with the back of a ladle. You should have about ½ cup liquid. Add the strained orange juice reduction to the chicken stock reduction. Whisk in the dry mustard and salt to taste. Whisk in the canola oil and olive oil in a stream and season with salt and pepper. Transfer the dressing to a bowl and refrigerate, covered.

Peel and core the apples. Cut them into eighths and cut crosswise into ¼-inch slices. Put them in a large bowl and toss with the lime juice. Gently stir in the rest of the salad ingredients. Stir in ¼ cup of the chilled dressing.

Preheat the oven to 350°F.

Scrape the fat off the duck legs. Remove and discard the bones, leaving the leg meat in large chunks. Heat the oil in a 10- to 12-inch ovenproof skillet over moderately high heat until shimmering and sauté the duck, skin side side down, until crisp, 4 to 5 minutes. Turn the duck skin side up and roast in the middle of the oven for 6 minutes.

Serve the duck on top of the salad, drizzled with additional dressing and seasoned with pepper.

watermelon
lime salad

The heat of freshly ground black pepper is a spicy contrast to the coolness of watermelon and lime (it's one of my wife's favorite flavor combinations). I've also included radish for added pepperiness as well as crunch. Serve this salad on its own as a first course or make a main course out of it by serving it with the Panfried Black Pepper Shrimp (page 96). It is best when made and enjoyed immediately. Pureed, this also makes a great chilled soup.

2 limes
1 teaspoon minced peeled ginger
½ teaspoon minced mild to
    moderately hot fresh green chile
¾ teaspoon chaat masala
Fine sea salt and freshly ground black
    pepper
2 tablespoons extra virgin olive oil

9 generous cups seeded diced
    watermelon (from a 7-pound piece
    of melon)
¼ cup thinly sliced radishes, halved
    crosswise if large
½ cup packed chopped mint leaves
¼ cup packed chopped cilantro

Remove the zest from 1 lime with a peeler and cut it into thin strips. Cut the lime segments from the membranes, as you would an orange or grapefruit. (You should have about 2 tablespoons lime segments.) Squeeze the juice from the membranes into a small bowl. Cut the remaining lime in half and squeeze the juice into the bowl. (You should have about ¼ cup lime juice.)

Combine the lime zest, juice, ginger, chile, chaat masala, salt and pepper to taste, and olive oil in a bowl.

Combine the watermelon, radishes, lime segments, mint, and cilantro in a serving bowl.

Just before serving, slowly pour the dressing over the watermelon mixture and combine gently.

soups

chilled tomato soup with fennel, celery, and ginger

My take on gazpacho stands on its own, but at the restaurant I often serve it over a little crabmeat or lobster. I also love it with a mixture of seafood—steamed clams, say, and calamari that's been flash-seared. (Heat oil in a pan until it's really hot but not smoking and quickly sear the squid.) All you need is some crusty French bread and you're set.

The soup develops its flavors if made a day ahead, although you should toast and add the spices right before serving. And even though this soup is served chilled, heat comes from several different sources: black peppercorns, mustard seeds, Tabasco, and radish. If you can't find ripe, flavorful tomatoes, substitute canned. At home, I make a double batch at a time.

FOR THE SOUP
¼ cup extra virgin olive oil
I medium white onion, chopped
I medium carrot, chopped
2 celery stalks, chopped
2 garlic cloves, chopped
I fennel bulb, white and green parts chopped and some fronds reserved for garnish
I large red bell pepper, chopped
2 tablespoons finely chopped peeled ginger
Kosher salt
4 large tomatoes, chopped

2 quarts Vegetable Stock (page 282) or water

FOR THE SPICE BLEND
I teaspoon cumin seeds
I teaspoon coriander seeds
I teaspoon fennel seeds
½ teaspoon black peppercorns
½ teaspoon brown mustard seeds
⅛ teaspoon fenugreek seeds

2 teaspoons sugar, or to taste
Kosher salt
Tabasco sauce
3 tablespoons lemon juice

1 tablespoon fennel seeds

2 tablespoons chopped chives

1 tablespoon thinly sliced celery

1 tablespoon chopped pale green celery leaves

1 tablespoon thinly sliced radish

Heat the oil in a 6- to 8-quart pot over moderate heat until it shimmers. Add the onion, carrot, celery, and garlic and cook, stirring frequently, until softened but not colored, about 8 minutes. Add the fennel, bell pepper, ginger, and salt to taste and cook, stirring occasionally, until aromatic, about 4 minutes. Add the tomatoes and continue cooking until they begin to break down, about 4 minutes longer. Add the stock and cook the soup at a slow boil until the liquid is reduced by one-third, about 30 minutes.

Puree the soup in a blender until smooth (be careful—it's hot) and strain through a sieve into a bowl, pressing hard on the solids with the back of a ladle. Discard the solids. Put the bowl into a larger bowl of ice water and refrigerate until cold, about 2 hours. *The soup can be made up to this point 1 day ahead and refrigerated, covered.*

Toast the cumin seeds in a dry small skillet over moderately low heat, shaking the skillet, until fragrant and a couple of shades darker, about 3 minutes. Transfer to a small tray or plate to cool. Separately toast the coriander seeds, fennel seeds, peppercorns, mustard seeds, and fenugreek seeds all in the same way, turning them out to cool as toasted. Finely grind the spices together in an electric coffee/spice grinder. Toast and coarsely grind the fennel seeds for the garnish as well and keep them separate.

Season the chilled soup with the spice blend, sugar, salt, Tabasco, and lemon juice. Serve the soup in bowls, garnished with the toasted ground fennel seeds, chives, celery, celery leaves, and radish.

chilled cucumber soup with mint and basil

SERVES *6* AS A FIRST COURSE

Chilled cucumber soup is one of the glories of summer. I use seedless cucumbers or a mixture of seedless cukes and Kirbys. I am not someone who advocates products that are labeled *low-fat,* but in the case of this soup, a good-quality low-fat yogurt works better than the full-fat kind. The soup will be rich but light and refreshing. It also has beautiful body, which comes from whisking most of the yogurt into the soup instead of pureeing it all in a blender, which causes it to become too thin. The garnishes here add bursts of flavor as well as texture and color, particularly in the case of the basil seeds (*takamaria*), which are often used in summer drinks in India and can be found at Indian markets or ordered by mail (see Sources). Soaked in water, the tiny black seeds bloom, absorbing the water and turning a beautiful blue. The soup is delicious without the seeds, of course, but with them it's a dramatic first course.

FOR THE SOUP

1½ teaspoons cumin seeds

3 seedless cucumbers or a combination of seedless and Kirby cucumbers (about 2¼ pounds total)

2½ cups plain low-fat yogurt

2 tablespoons thinly sliced peeled ginger

2 tablespoons sugar

Kosher salt

Pinch of cayenne

1½ teaspoons lemon juice

Freshly ground black pepper

FOR GARNISH

1 tablespoon basil seeds (labeled *takamaria*, optional)

1 scallion

2 radishes

About ¾ cup basil (preferably Thai basil) chiffonade (see page 8)

About ¾ cup mint chiffonade (see page 8)

2 tablespoons cilantro chiffonade (see page 8)

Toast the cumin seeds in a dry small skillet over moderately low heat, shaking the skillet, until fragrant and a couple of shades darker, about 4 minutes. Finely grind the cumin seeds in an electric coffee/spice grinder, then set aside.

Cut the cucumbers into ½-inch-thick slices. Put 1 cup of the yogurt in a blender and add about half of the cucumbers and all of the ginger and sugar, a generous pinch of salt, and the cayenne. Puree the mixture until very smooth. Pour three-quarters of the puree into a bowl and add the remaining cucumber to the blender (do not add any more yogurt). Puree the mixture until very smooth.

Whisk the remaining 1½ cups yogurt in a small bowl to lighten it, then add it to the puree, whisking to blend. Whisk in 1 teaspoon toasted cumin, the lemon juice, a generous pinch of salt, and black pepper to taste. *Chill the soup, covered, in the refrigerator for at least 2 and up to 8 hours.*

Soak the basil seeds, if using, in ½ cup water for 10 to 15 minutes.

Discard any tough parts from the scallion and cut the remaining white and green parts into thin slices on a diagonal. Cut the radishes into paper-thin slices. (If you have a handheld slicer such as a Benriner or mandoline, now is the time to use it.)

Taste the chilled soup and season with salt and pepper. Serve the soup in bowls, garnished with the scallion, radishes, the remaining ½ teaspoon toasted cumin, the herbs, and basil seeds.

chilled carrot soup

The inspiration for this pureed soup lies in the beautiful, juicy bunch (horse) carrots I find at the farmers' market in the early summer. Cashews, which give the soup body, remind me of the wild cashew trees in the hills of Goa. We used to eat the cashew fruit from the trees and then bring the nuts back to my great-grandmother's house and roast them in a little kiln.

3 green cardamom pods

1 tablespoon coriander seeds

1 teaspoon black peppercorns

2 tablespoons canola oil

1 heaping cup chopped leek, white and pale green parts only (about 1 leek), washed well

2 tablespoons thinly sliced peeled ginger

1 cup chopped celery

3 cups thinly sliced carrots

½ cup raw cashews

Kosher salt and freshly ground pepper

2½ cups carrot juice (see Note)

FOR GARNISH

2 tablespoons chopped cilantro

2 tablespoons chopped chives

Splash of lime juice

Toast the cardamom pods in a dry small skillet over moderately low heat, shaking the skillet, until fragrant and a couple of shades darker, about 3 minutes. Turn the pods out on a small tray or plate to cool. Toast the coriander seeds, then the peppercorns, the same way, turning them out to cool with the cardamom. Finely grind the toasted spices together in an electric coffee/spice grinder.

Heat the oil in a 6- to 8-quart pot over moderately high heat until it shimmers. Add the leek, ginger, and celery and cook, stirring and taking care not to let the aromatics color, for about 2 minutes, or until soft. Add the carrots and cashews and cook, stirring, for 2 minutes. Add 2 quarts water and 2 teaspoons salt. Increase the heat to high and bring the soup to a boil. Cook until the carrots are tender but still firm, 10 to 12 minutes. Stir in the carrot juice and toasted ground spices and return the soup to a boil. As soon as the soup boils, remove it from the heat.

Puree the soup in a blender (be careful—it's hot) until very smooth and add salt to taste. Transfer the soup to a bowl. Put the bowl in another, larger bowl of ice water and refrigerate until very cold, at least 4 and up to 8 hours.

Taste the chilled soup and season with salt and pepper. Serve the soup in bowls, garnished with the cilantro, chives, and lime juice.

NOTE: *If you don't have a juicer, all is not lost; carrot juice is readily available at health food stores and many grocery stores.*

pumpkin
rasam

A *rasam* (Hindi for "essence") is a thin, spicy soup. Its brothiness, however, doesn't mean that it doesn't have body. This one, with its light yet complex flavors, would make a perfect first course for Thanksgiving.

FOR THE SOUP

1 medium red onion, skin rubbed
    with canola oil
2 heaping teaspoons coriander seeds
1 teaspoon cumin seeds
1 teaspoon black peppercorns
2 cloves
1 bay leaf
½ teaspoon fenugreek seeds
1 small dried red chile (see Glossary)
3 unpeeled garlic cloves, smashed
2 tablespoons thinly sliced peeled
    ginger
1 cup loosely packed grated fresh
    coconut (see page 283) or
    unsweetened desiccated coconut
2 cups coarsely chopped carrots
1 cup coarsely chopped peeled celery
    root
¼ cup canola oil

5 cups chopped peeled sugar
    pumpkin or acorn squash (from
    about ½ pumpkin or 2 squash)
1 heaping cup diced tomato (from 1
    large beefsteak)
¾ cup *toor dal* (skinned split yellow
    lentils), picked over, washed well,
    and soaked for 20 minutes
1 tablespoon salt
¼ cup Tamarind Paste (page 284)

FOR THE TARKA

2 tablespoons canola oil
1 teaspoon brown mustard seeds
20 fresh curry leaves

FOR GARNISH

¼ cup chopped chives
¼ cup chopped cilantro
¼ cup toasted green hulled pumpkin
    seeds

Preheat the oven to 375°F. Put the onion on a small baking sheet or in a baking dish and roast in the middle of the oven until tender, 45 to 50 minutes. When the onion is cool enough to handle, peel, chop, and set aside.

Toast the coriander seeds in a dry small skillet over moderately low heat, shaking the skillet, until fragrant and a couple of shades darker, about 3 minutes. Transfer them to a small tray or plate to cool. Toast the cumin seeds in the same way, transferring them to the tray to cool. Toast the peppercorns and cloves together in the same way, about 2½ minutes. Add the bay leaf and toast for 30 seconds longer. Transfer to the tray to cool. Toast the fenugreek seeds in the same way, about 2 minutes. Add the chile, broken in half, and toast for 1 minute longer. Transfer to the tray to cool. When all the spices are cool, finely grind them all together in an electric coffee/spice grinder.

Toast the unpeeled garlic cloves in a heavy 6-quart pot over low heat, stirring occasionally, until the garlic is charred in spots, 5 to 8 minutes. Add the ginger and toast until lightly colored, about 2 minutes. Add the coconut and toast until lightly colored, about 2 minutes longer. Increase the heat to moderately high and add the carrots, celery root, and oil. Cook, stirring occasionally, for 3 minutes. Stir in the pumpkin and cook, stirring occasionally, for 2 minutes longer. Stir in the tomatoes, *toor dal,* roasted onion, salt, and 3 quarts water and simmer for 30 minutes. Stir in the ground spices and tamarind paste and simmer for 2 minutes longer.

Strain the soup through a sieve into a large bowl, pressing on the solids so that about 20 percent goes through the sieve. Discard the rest of the solids and return the strained soup to the pot. Bring the soup to a vigorous simmer.

Heat the oil in a small skillet over moderate heat until it shimmers and cook the mustard seeds until they pop and are fragrant, about 30 seconds. Add the curry leaves and cook, shaking the skillet, for 30 seconds.

Immediately pour the sizzling tarka into the soup and stir to blend. Serve the soup in bowls, garnished with the chives, cilantro, and toasted pumpkin seeds.

lentil
soup

This soup was the first one we put on Tabla's menu, and it remains a perennial favorite. I use two kinds of lentils—pink lentils, which are common all over India, and the tiny green French ones known as *lentilles du Puy*. The combination cooks quickly and manages to be hearty and sophisticated at the same time.

FOR THE LENTIL SOUP

2 teaspoons brown mustard seeds

1 teaspoon cumin seeds

2 teaspoons coriander seeds

½ teaspoon fenugreek seeds

½ teaspoon black peppercorns

½ piece mace

1 small dried red chile (see Glossary)

¾ cup *masoor dal* (pink lentils), picked over for stones

¾ cup French green lentils (*lentilles du Puy*), picked over for stones

¼ cup canola oil

2 cups diced white onion

1 cup diced carrot

1 cup diced celery

2 garlic cloves, smashed and peeled

2 tablespoons julienne strips peeled ginger

Scant 2 cups diced fresh or drained canned tomatoes

¼ teaspoon ground turmeric

1 bay leaf

2 cloves

One 5-inch rosemary sprig

Four 4-inch thyme sprigs

Kosher salt

FOR GARNISH

1 cup French green lentils (*lentilles du Puy*), picked over for stones

¼ cup plus 2 tablespoons plain whole-milk yogurt

¼ cup finely chopped chives

¼ cup cilantro chiffonade (see page 8)

Finely grind 1 teaspoon of the mustard seeds with the cumin seeds, coriander seeds, fenugreek seeds, peppercorns, mace, and chile in an electric coffee/spice grinder.

Rinse the lentils until the water runs clear. Combine them in a bowl and soak in water to cover for about 10 minutes. Drain the lentils.

Heat the canola oil in a heavy 4- to 6-quart pot over moderate heat until it shimmers and cook the remaining teaspoon mustard seeds until they pop, about 30 seconds. Reduce the heat to low and stir in the onion, carrot, celery, garlic, ginger, and ground spice mixture. Cook, stirring occasionally, until the vegetables are slightly softened, about 10 minutes. Stir in the tomatoes, turmeric, 6 cups water, lentils, bay leaf, cloves, rosemary, and thyme and bring to a boil. Reduce the heat and simmer for 20 to 30 minutes, until the lentils are tender. Remove and discard the bay leaf, cloves, and herb sprigs.

Puree the soup in batches in a blender. (Be careful—it's hot.) Season generously with salt.

Return the soup to the pot and keep hot over low heat while you make the lentil garnish.

Rinse the lentils until the water runs clear. Bring a 2½-quart pot of water to a boil and add the lentils. Bring the water back to a boil and cook for 20 minutes, or until the lentils are tender but still firm. Drain the lentils and cover with cold water.

Drain the lentils and divide among 6 bowls. Ladle the soup over the lentils. Top with a dollop of yogurt and a scattering of chives and cilantro.

corn and potato chowder

This chunky chowder, which has a gentle heat that builds, gets its depth and richness from roasted garlic and tangy yogurt. Get the freshest corn you can for this recipe, as it gives its all: after cutting off the kernels and scraping the cobs clear of their sweet milk, use the cobs to make a stock. If you develop a craving for a taste of August's bounty in midwinter, you can successfully make this soup with frozen corn; just substitute chicken stock for the corn stock. Chop the leek, celery, onion, and potato into pieces roughly the same size as the corn kernels; that way everything will cook evenly and look beautiful. Garnishing this soup with chives and tarragon gives it polish, but what really makes it sparkle is the ground toasted cumin. It was a last-minute addition to this recipe, but a welcome reminder of the wonderful affinity between corn and cumin.

6 unpeeled garlic cloves
Extra virgin olive oil
Kosher salt
5 ears corn, shucked
5 cloves
4 star anise
3 bay leaves
1 teaspoon black peppercorns
1 tablespoon coriander seeds
3 tablespoons canola oil
1 small dried red chile (see
    Glossary)
1 cup finely chopped white
    onion

1 cup packed finely chopped leek,
    white and pale green parts only
    (about 1 leek), thoroughly washed
¾ cup finely chopped celery
1 tablespoon minced peeled ginger
1 small baking potato, peeled and
    diced (about 1 heaping cup)
2 cups plain whole-milk or low-fat
    yogurt
One 7-inch rosemary sprig

FOR GARNISH
1½ teaspoons cumin seeds
1 tablespoon finely chopped chives
1 tablespoon finely chopped tarragon

Preheat the oven to 350°F. Put the garlic cloves on a piece of foil. Drizzle the garlic with the olive oil and sprinkle with salt. Wrap the garlic tightly in the foil and roast in the middle of the oven for 30 to 35 minutes, or until the garlic is soft. Slip the skin off the garlic cloves.

Cut the corn kernels from the ears into a bowl. Scrape the milky residue from the ears into another bowl. Break the cobs in half and put them in a heavy 6- to 8-quart pot. Add 6 cups water, 2 cloves, 2 star anise, and 2 bay leaves. Bring the mixture to a boil over high heat, then reduce the heat and simmer for 40 minutes. Pour the stock through a sieve into a bowl. (You should have about 1 quart stock; if you have less, add enough water to make 1 quart.)

Finely grind the peppercorns and coriander seeds in an electric coffee/spice grinder.

Wipe out the pot and heat the canola oil over moderately high heat until it shimmers. Add the remaining 3 cloves, 2 star anise, and bay leaf, along with the dried chile. Cook, stirring, for 30 seconds, and reduce the heat to moderate. Add the onion and cook until softened, about 2 minutes. Add the ground spices, leek, celery, ginger, and ¼ teaspoon salt and cook, stirring, for 2 minutes longer. Stir in the potato, corn kernels, and corn stock. Bring the mixture to a simmer and cook until the potatoes are just barely tender, about 5 minutes.

Meanwhile, puree the milky corn residue, yogurt, and roasted garlic in a blender until smooth.

Remove the cloves, star anise, bay leaf, and chile from the soup and discard. Stir the puree into the soup, add the rosemary sprig, and season the soup with about 2 teaspoons salt, or to taste. Simmer the soup for about 10 minutes longer. Remove and discard the rosemary.

Meanwhile, toast the cumin seeds in a dry small skillet over moderately low heat, shaking the skillet, until fragrant and a couple of shades darker, about 3 minutes. Finely grind them in the electric coffee/spice grinder until ground fine. Serve the soup in bowls, garnished with the chives, tarragon, and cumin.

french onion soup

Recently, my wife, Barkha, ordered onion soup in a little French restaurant in California, and it was terrible—it had no flavor or body whatsoever. I made up my mind then and there to make a good one to see us through the winter. At Tabla, I serve an Indian-inspired onion soup with a piece of rosemary naan toast topped with melted Gruyère and a cheese called Vivace Bambino, from Cato Corner Farm, which has a stall at the local farmers' market, in New York City's Union Square. You could also use just Gruyère or a combination of Gruyère and Edam. Any country-style bread works well, too—you want something that will hold together in the hot soup without dissolving.

FOR THE SOUP

¼ cup extra virgin olive oil

1½ teaspoons cumin seeds

4 cloves

2 bay leaves

3 large garlic cloves, cut into julienne strips

2 tablespoons julienne strips peeled ginger

2 medium red onions, thinly sliced

1 large white onion, thinly sliced

½ teaspoon ground turmeric

⅛ teaspoon Aleppo pepper or cayenne

One 2-inch piece dried pasilla de Oaxaca chile

½ cup dry white wine

2 tablespoons brandy

Kosher salt and freshly ground black pepper

2 quarts Chicken Stock (page 274) or reduced-sodium canned chicken broth

A bouquet garni made of one 7-inch rosemary sprig, four 5-inch thyme sprigs, and 4 cilantro stems and/or roots, tied together with kitchen string

FOR THE CHEESE TOASTS

¼ cup plus 2 tablespoons grated Gruyère

¼ cup plus 2 tablespoons grated Edam

½ teaspoon minced peeled ginger

¼ teaspoon Aleppo pepper or cayenne

¼ teaspoon cumin seeds

6 pieces naan or country-style bread cut to fit the bottom of soup bowls

Heat the oil in a 6- to 8-quart pot over moderate heat until it shimmers and cook the cumin seeds, cloves, and bay leaves for 1 minute. Add the garlic and continue to cook, stirring occasionally, until the garlic is softened and lightly colored, about 2 minutes. Stir in the ginger and onions and cook, stirring, until nicely caramelized, about 40 minutes. Add the turmeric, Aleppo pepper, chile, wine, and brandy, scraping the caramelized bits from the bottom of the pot. Add 1 teaspoon salt, the chicken stock, and the bouquet garni, then simmer briskly, stirring occasionally, for 30 minutes.

Remove the pot from the heat and add salt and pepper to taste. Remove the cloves, bay leaves, chile (if you want more heat, chop up the chile and return it to the soup), and bouquet garni. Return the soup to very low heat to keep it warm, covered.

Preheat the oven to 350°F. Stir the grated cheeses, ginger, Aleppo pepper, and cumin seeds together in a bowl. Pat the cheese mixture on top of the bread and put on a parchment-lined baking sheet. Toast in the middle of the oven until the cheese is hot and bubbling, about 5 minutes.

Put the cheese toasts in the bottom of 6 bowls and ladle the soup over to serve.

spice-infused wild mushroom broth

This spicy, brothy soup is similar to a consommé in that it's thin in consistency but full-bodied in flavor and beautifully balanced. Goan cooks always add a little sugar for that complex dance between sweet and sour. Dried shiitake mushrooms, which are full of earthy essence and found at many supermarkets these days, are the secret; they're a mainstay of my pantry. For this soup I like to use both dried and fresh shiitake as well as white button and cremini mushrooms. If you can find oyster mushrooms, toss them in as well.

1¾ ounces dried shiitake mushrooms (about 2 cups)
1 tablespoon cumin seeds
2 tablespoons coriander seeds
½ tablespoon black peppercorns
1 teaspoon brown mustard seeds
¼ cup canola oil
1 small dried red chile (see Glossary)
3 green cardamom pods
¼ teaspoon ground mace
Kosher salt
1 large white onion, chopped
3 large shallots, sliced
4 large garlic cloves, smashed and peeled
1 leek, white and pale green parts, washed well and chopped

2 celery stalks, chopped
2 tablespoons plus 1 teaspoon chopped peeled ginger
3 tablespoons Tamarind Paste (page 284)
1 quart Chicken Stock (page 274) or reduced-sodium canned chicken broth
1 cup dry white wine
4 cups mixed quartered white, cremini, and fresh shiitake mushrooms, including stems
1 teaspoon sugar
2 cups baby spinach leaves, thinly sliced crosswise
⅛ teaspoon tarragon leaves, thinly sliced crosswise

Soak the dried mushrooms in 3 cups lukewarm water for 30 minutes. Remove the mushrooms from the soaking liquid. Strain the liquid through a sieve lined with cheesecloth or a coffee filter and reserve it.

Coarsely grind the cumin seeds, coriander seeds, peppercorns, and mustard seeds in an electric coffee/spice grinder.

Heat 3 tablespoons of the oil in a 5- to 6-quart pot over moderately high heat until it shimmers and add the ground spices, chile, cardamom pods, mace, and ¼ teaspoon salt. Cook, stirring, until the spices are fragrant and a couple of shades darker, about 1 minute. Add the onion, shallots, and garlic to the spice blend and cook, stirring, for 2 minutes. Add the leek, celery, and 2 tablespoons of the ginger and cook, stirring occasionally, until tender, about 5 minutes.

Add the rehydrated mushrooms and their reserved soaking liquid, the tamarind paste, 1 quart water, the stock, and the wine and bring to a boil. Lower the heat and simmer briskly until reduced by half, about 1½ hours. Season with salt and strain through a sieve into a bowl. Remove the rehydrated mushrooms from the sieve. Discard the stems and thinly slice the caps. (They're a little chewy if you leave them whole.)

In a 10-inch skillet, heat the remaining tablespoon of canola oil over moderately high heat until it shimmers and cook the fresh mushrooms, reserved rehydrated mushrooms, and remaining teaspoon of ginger, stirring occasionally, until the liquid is evaporated, about 7 minutes.

Pour the reserved mushroom broth back into the cleaned 5- to 6-quart pot and add the cooked mushrooms. Bring the broth to a boil, add the sugar, and stir in the spinach. Cook until the spinach is wilted and the broth is heated through, 5 to 7 minutes. Serve the broth in bowls, garnished with the tarragon.

caldo verde
with peanuts

The potato-thickened soup called *caldo verde* is a staple in Portugal, where it's made with cabbage and the sausage called *chouriço*. Because Goa was a Portuguese colony for 450 years, I give this classic an Indian twist. Peanuts are ubiquitous in India (where they're called *monkey nuts*), but in fact they were brought from the New World by (you guessed it) the Portuguese. If you've never tasted raw peanuts before, you're in for a treat: their earthy, almost vegetal taste reminds you that you are eating a legume, not a true nut. Raw peanuts, both in the skin and out (with the red skin removed) are available at Indian and Asian markets and many natural foods stores. Shelling and skinning the peanuts yourself can be fiddly, time-consuming work, but you will get the best flavor that way. The skins will easily slip off if you soak them first in a bowl of water for a minute or so. This pureed soup is silky smooth and a vibrant green.

½ cup canola oil
1 tablespoon brown mustard seeds
1 clove
½ cinnamon stick
1 tablespoon cumin seeds
2 tablespoons coriander seeds
½ cup thinly sliced shallot
1 cup thinly sliced red onion
1 cup thinly sliced white onion
¼ cup thinly sliced garlic
1 bay leaf
1 heaping tablespoon sliced peeled ginger
1 cup raw peanuts

2 large Yukon Gold potatoes, diced (2 cups)
1 large baking potato, diced (2 cups)
3 quarts Chicken Stock (page 274) or reduced-sodium canned chicken broth
Kosher salt and freshly ground black pepper
½ pound fresh spinach, coarsely chopped
1 cup cilantro leaves
1 mild to moderately hot fresh green chile, roasted, peeled, and seeded (see page 9), then chopped

Heat the oil in a 6- to 8-quart pot over moderate heat until it shimmers. Add the mustard seeds, clove, cinnamon, cumin seeds, and coriander seeds and cook, stirring, until fragrant and a shade darker, for about 2 minutes. Add the shallot, onion, garlic, and bay leaf and cook, stirring, for 2 minutes longer. Stir in the ginger, peanuts, potatoes, stock, and salt and pepper to taste, and bring the soup to a simmer. Simmer for about 25 minutes, then stir in the spinach, cilantro leaves, and chopped roasted chile. Increase the heat and boil the soup, uncovered, until the potatoes are done and the spinach is tender, about 5 minutes.

Remove and discard the clove, cinnamon stick, and bay leaf. Puree the soup in a blender (be careful—it's hot) until very smooth. Add salt to taste. Serve the soup in bowls, garnished with the cilantro, chives, and peanuts.

chicken noodle soup

This is a meal in itself. To make the "noodles," I use a spaetzle maker (available at kitchen stores) or force the batter through the holes of a slotted spoon into the stock.

FOR THE BROTH

2½ quarts Chicken Stock (page 274) or reduced-sodium canned chicken broth

1 teaspoon ground turmeric

5 unpeeled garlic cloves, smashed

1 bay leaf

4 cloves

2 tablespoons thinly sliced peeled ginger

30 cilantro stems with roots

1½ teaspoons coriander seeds, coarsely crushed in a mortar or with a rolling pin

2 tablespoons black peppercorns

1½ pounds chicken pieces

FOR THE SOUP

¼ cup canola oil

1 tablespoon cumin seeds

½ large white onion, halved and thinly sliced crosswise

2 cups thinly sliced leek, white and pale green parts only (about 2 leeks), washed well

1 cup thinly sliced carrot

¼ cup julienne strips peeled ginger

2 tablespoons thinly sliced mild to moderately hot fresh green chile

Kosher salt

2 tablespoons Tamarind Paste (page 284)

FOR THE NOODLES

1 cup chickpea flour (besan)

½ cup all-purpose flour

2 tablespoons finely chopped cilantro leaves

½ teaspoon cumin seeds

1 teaspoon kosher salt

¼ teaspoon Aleppo pepper or cayenne

FOR GARNISH

¼ cup chopped chives

¼ cup chopped cilantro

Freshly ground black pepper

Put the stock, turmeric, garlic, bay leaf, cloves, ginger, cilantro stems with roots, crushed coriander seeds, and peppercorns in a 6-quart pot and bring to a boil over high heat. Add the chicken, reduce the heat, and simmer until the chicken is almost falling off the bone, about 45 minutes. Remove the chicken from the broth, reserving the broth. When the chicken is cool enough to handle, discard the skin and pull the chicken meat off the bones. Shred the meat or cut it into bite-sized pieces, then set aside.

Heat the oil in a 6- to 8-quart pot over moderately high heat until it shimmers and cook the cumin seeds, shaking the pot occasionally, until fragrant and a couple of shades darker, about 1 minute. Add the onion and leek and cook, stirring, for 1 minute. Add the carrot and ginger and cook, stirring, until the vegetables are softened and lightly colored, about 4 minutes. Then add the chile. Strain the reserved chicken broth through a sieve into the vegetable mixture and add salt to taste. Bring the soup to a gentle simmer.

Meanwhile, bring a large pot of water to a boil over high heat and salt the water. Have a bowl of cold water ready.

Put the flours, cilantro, cumin seeds, salt, and Aleppo pepper in a bowl and stir together well. Add ¾ cup water and whisk until a batter is formed. Push about half the batter through a spaetzle maker or the holes of a slotted spoon into the boiling water. When the noodles float to the top, after 2 to 3 minutes, scoop them out and put them in the cold water. Cook the rest of the batter in the same way. When the noodles are completely cold, drain them.

Stir the tamarind paste into the soup, then add the chicken and noodles. Simmer the soup 5 minutes. Serve the soup in bowls, garnished with the chives, cilantro, and black pepper to taste.

spiced shellfish nage

SERVES 6 TO 8 AS A FIRST COURSE

The French word *nage* means "swim," and here it refers to shellfish or crustaceans poached in an aromatic liquid. And if you are a shellfish fan as I am, this recipe is worth the effort. Here I use a mixture of crabs, mussels, and littleneck or manila clams. If I can find razor clams, I toss them in as well. I've also added a little calamari—for their texture. Frankly, the more seafood you put in this, the better. The garnishes also add great contrast: Scallions and lotus root or jícama add crunch; mushrooms add a delicate woodsiness; and smoky, salty bacon plays up the sweetness of the seafood.

2 tablespoons coriander seeds

2 tablespoons fennel seeds

3 cloves

¼ cup extra virgin olive oil

1 tablespoon brown mustard seeds

1 cup roughly sliced shallot

¼ cup roughly sliced garlic

½ dried pasilla de Oaxaca chile (see Note)

1 tablespoon black peppercorns

12 mussels, scrubbed and debearded

1 pound littleneck or manila clams

1 cup dry white wine

½ cup white port

5 cups White Fish Stock (page 275), Chicken Stock (page 274), or reduced-sodium canned chicken broth

2 medium tomatoes, chopped

4 live Atlantic blue crabs, roughly cut into large pieces with a knife or scissors (see Note)

One 10-inch rosemary sprig

Three 6-inch thyme sprigs

Two 3-inch cilantro stems with roots

8 razor or steamer clams (optional)

1 pound cleaned calamari, cut into rings and tentacles and roughly chopped

Sea salt

1½ cups small mushrooms such as enoki or chopped white mushrooms

½ pound lotus root or jícama, peeled and very thinly sliced (about 1½ cups)

¼ pound bacon, finely diced and fried until crisp

2 tablespoons packed chopped
cilantro

2 tablespoons packed thinly sliced
chives

2 cups thinly sliced scallions (from
about 1½ bunches)

A squeeze of lime

Coarsely grind the coriander and fennel seeds in an electric coffee/spice grinder.

Cook the cloves in the oil in a 6-quart pot over moderately low heat for 3 minutes. Add the mustard seeds and cook until they pop and are fragrant, about 1 minute. Add the shallot, garlic, and chile and cook over moderately high heat, stirring, until the shallot begins to soften, about 1 minute. Stir in the peppercorns, ground spices, mussels, and clams and cook for 1 minute longer.

Stir in the wine, port, and stock and simmer, covered, for 3 minutes, or until the mussels and clams just open wide. (Discard any mussels or clams that have not opened.) Transfer the shellfish to a bowl with a slotted spoon.

Add the tomatoes and crabs to the broth, along with the rosemary, thyme, and cilantro stems and roots.

Pull the "sleeve" off the meat of the razor clams or steamers if using and add the sleeves to the broth. Remove the razor clams from their shells and roughly chop them. Remove the remaining clams and mussels from their shells and transfer them to a small bowl, along with the chopped razor clams. Before discarding the shells, shake any liquid and aromatics remaining in them into the broth, along with any liquid and aromatics remaining in the bowl. Simmer the broth for 30 minutes.

Remove the broth from the heat and strain it into a large bowl, discarding the crab pieces and pressing hard on the remaining solids with the back of a ladle. Transfer the strained broth to the (uncleaned) pot.

Season the calamari with salt and let sit for 3 minutes. Bring the nage to a simmer, covered. Add the calamari, mushrooms, lotus root, and bacon to the nage and simmer gently for about 2 minutes, or until the calamari is just opaque. Serve the nage in bowls garnished with cilantro, chives, and scallions, with lime squeezed over it.

NOTE: *If you desire more heat in the broth, break the chile into smaller pieces. Before cutting the crabs into pieces, freeze them for 4 hours.*

fish

a note on buying fish

How can a home cook be assured of finding high-quality fish and other seafood? Shop at a busy fish market; high turnover is key. There should be a good variety of whole fish (they stay fresher longer), and everything should be lavishly iced. The fish should look unblemished and just caught; the flesh should look firm and spring back after being touched lightly. As far as fish fillets go, avoid those packed in ice or wrapped in plastic. Ask your fishmonger to fillet fish for you and give you the bones as well for stock. Soft-shell crabs, lobsters, and shellfish should be alive. (Bivalves should be closed; if open, they should shut immediately if put in cold water.) Frozen lobsters and soft-shells aren't as good as fresh, obviously, but will do in a pinch. The store itself should smell clean, the lobster tank should look clean, and what you are buying should smell fresh and of the ocean, not of ammonia or decay. While fish counters at grocery stores are getting better, their products are generally never of the best quality. When you find a fish market you like, cultivate a salesperson there. Don't be shy about asking questions: What is freshest today? Where did it come from? Is it in season? Is it farmed or wild? If it's farmed, is it farmed responsibly?

I've given you a wide range of fish recipes, and some of the fish I've called for may, in fact, be problematic at this reading because sustainability information can change relatively quickly. If a fish is unavailable or perhaps not the most mindful choice at that time, any good fish purveyor will be able to suggest alternatives. No matter where you live, try to eat what's available locally, in season. You'll get the best quality that way.

pan-roasted salmon in banana leaves with mustard greens

SERVES 6

Cooking fish in banana leaf packages reminds me of our Parsi neighbors in Bombay. The Parsis are followers of Zoroastrianism, an ancient Persian religion. Banana leaves are a common Parsi wrapping for food—they lend an herbal, earthy flavor to what's inside. Wrapping fish in a package is a technique that works especially well for salmon or more delicate fish. Substitute other tropical leaves such as taro, bamboo, or lotus leaves or use parchment paper. Banana leaves are not edible; for more information about them, see Glossary. This dish is delicious with penne or macaroni on the side to soak up the sauce.

1 bunch of mustard greens (about 13 ounces), tough coarse leaves discarded

2 tablespoons Tamarind Paste (page 284) or lime juice

1 tablespoon thinly sliced peeled ginger

3 large garlic cloves, thinly sliced

2 tablespoons minced mild to moderately hot fresh red or green chile

½ cup plus 2 tablespoons canola oil

1 tablespoon coriander seeds

1 tablespoon black peppercorns

½ teaspoon cumin seeds

1 tablespoon yellow mustard seeds

Sea salt and freshly ground black pepper

3 banana leaves (from a 1-pound package, see headnote), thawed if frozen, or parchment paper

Six 6-ounce pieces skinless salmon fillet

Bring a pot of water to a boil and blanch the mustard greens for 30 seconds. Drain them and put immediately in a bowl of ice water to set the color. Squeeze the excess water from the greens with your hands and chop roughly. (You should have about 1¾ cups, lightly packed.)

Puree the mustard greens with the tamarind paste, ginger, garlic, chile, ¼ cup water, and 2 tablespoons of the canola oil in a blender until smooth. (You should have about 2 cups puree. Resist the urge to add more water to make blending easier; the puree will be too thin.) *The puree can be made 1 day ahead and chilled, its surface covered with plastic wrap to prevent discoloration.*

Toast the coriander seeds, peppercorns, and cumin seeds in a dry small heavy skillet over moderately low heat, shaking the skillet, until fragrant and a couple of shades darker, about 3 minutes, and transfer to a small tray or plate to cool. Finely grind the toasted spices along with the untoasted mustard seeds and stir into the puree. Season the puree with salt.

Unfold the banana leaves and cut them into six 12-inch squares. To make them pliable, fold them in half and, holding them with tongs, toast them on both sides over a gas or electric burner on moderately high heat for 10 to 15 seconds. (They will become very shiny.)

Preheat the oven to 400°F and pat the salmon dry. Season the salmon with salt and pepper.

Put about 2½ tablespoons (more or less, depending on whether you have more or less than 2 cups total) mustard green puree on a banana leaf, put a salmon piece on top, then put another 2½ tablespoons puree on top of the fish. Fold 2 sides of the leaf over the fish (as you would fold a letter), then fold in the opposite sides to form a package. Wrap the remaining salmon pieces in the remaining banana leaves.

Heat ¼ cup of the remaining oil in a 12-inch skillet over moderately high heat until it shimmers. Put half of the fish packages in the skillet, flap sides down, and cook for 2 minutes. Transfer the packages to a baking sheet with sides. Heat the remaining ¼ cup oil in the skillet and cook the remaining fish packages in the same way, transferring them when cooked to the baking sheet. Turn the packages over and finish cooking in the middle of the oven, 6 to 8 minutes. To serve, transfer the packages, flap side up, to a platter.

rice flake–crisped halibut on watercress with watermelon curry

My son Peter was perched on the kitchen counter at home watching me cut watermelon for his midmorning snack and asked me if people ate spices with everything in India. "Just about," I replied. "Even watermelon?" he said. I told him that my father ate watermelon with salt and black pepper. Peter then wondered if I could make a curry out of watermelon. "Why not?" I thought, and then I made this. You can substitute any mild white-fleshed fish—black bass, for instance—for the halibut. The dollop of lime relish is more than a garnish; the acidity counteracts the sweetness of the watermelon. Rice flakes, one of my favorite coatings for seafood because it crisps up beautifully, are made of crushed parboiled rice that is then dried.

FOR THE CURRY

4 pounds seedless watermelon
½ teaspoon coriander seeds
¼ teaspoon Aleppo pepper or cayenne
2½ tablespoons extra virgin
    olive oil
I teaspoon cumin seeds
I large garlic clove, finely chopped
1½ teaspoons finely minced peeled
    ginger
⅛ teaspoon ground turmeric
Sea salt
3 to 4 tablespoons fresh lime juice

FOR THE LIME RELISH

2 limes
2 teaspoons extra virgin olive oil
2 tablespoons coarsely chopped
    cilantro
2 tablespoons finely sliced chives

FOR THE FISH

I large egg
2 tablespoons all-purpose flour
Sea salt and freshly ground black
    pepper

1 cup (4 ounces) rice flakes or
    crushed unsweetened puffed rice
    cereal
Six 6-ounce pieces skinless halibut
    fillet, ¾ to 1 inch thick

½ cup canola oil
1 tablespoon lime juice
3 cups loosely packed watercress,
    tough stems discarded (about
    6 ounces)

Cut enough watermelon flesh into ½-inch cubes to yield 3 cups of fruit and set aside. Put the trimmings (but not the rind) in a blender along with the rest of the melon, coarsely chopped, and any juice from the cutting board. Blend until smooth to make watermelon juice. (You should have about 3 cups.)

Grind the coriander seeds with the Aleppo pepper in an electric coffee/spice grinder.

Heat 2 tablespoons of the olive oil in a heavy 1-quart pot over moderate heat until it shimmers and cook the cumin seeds, stirring constantly, until fragrant and a couple of shades darker, about 30 seconds. Reduce the heat to moderately low and add the garlic, ginger, and ground spices. Cook until the garlic is softened and fragrant about 2 minutes, stirring constantly so that the garlic doesn't color. Add the turmeric and cook for a few seconds longer, stirring. Add the watermelon juice and boil over moderately high heat, stirring occasionally, until reduced to about 1½ cups, about 15 minutes. *The curry can be made up to this point 1 day ahead and chilled, covered.* Season the curry with salt and lime juice.

Remove the zest from the limes with a zester (be careful not to include any white pith) and put in a small bowl. Immediately add the olive oil, then stir in the cilantro and chives.

Cut the sections out of the limes as you would from a grapefruit, then cut the sections into thirds. Squeeze out any remaining juice from the membranes into the zest mixture and stir in the lime sections.

Preheat the oven to 400°F. Beat the egg, flour, ⅛ teaspoon salt, and ⅛ teaspoon pepper together with a fork in a small bowl to make an egg wash. Pour the rice flakes into a medium bowl.

Generously brush the skinned side of 1 halibut piece with egg wash to coat and gently dredge the coated side in rice flakes. Repeat with the remaining pieces. *The fish can be coated 2 hours ahead and chilled, covered with plastic wrap.*

Season the halibut with the salt and pepper. Heat ¼ cup of the canola oil in an ovenproof 10- to 12-inch skillet over moderately high heat until it shimmers and add half of the halibut, coated sides down. Cook the fish, without turning it, until the coating is golden brown, about 1½ minutes. Turn the halibut coating side up and transfer to a baking sheet with sides. Cook the remaining fish in the same way and transfer to the baking sheet, coating side up. Roast the fish on the baking sheet in the middle of the oven for 2 to 4 minutes, depending on the thickness of the fish, or until firm and just cooked through.

Meanwhile, reheat the watermelon curry over low heat and keep it warm.

Heat the remaining ½ tablespoon olive oil in a 3- to 4-quart pan over moderately high heat and sauté the reserved watermelon cubes, stirring, until warm, about 2 minutes. Add the curry and continue to sauté until warmed through, stirring carefully so that the watermelon cubes don't fall apart, 1 to 2 minutes longer. Season the curry with ½ teaspoon salt, pepper to taste, and the lime juice.

Arrange the watercress on a platter and spoon the curry over it. Top with the halibut and lime relish.

poached halibut in coriander broth

Halibut is mild in flavor but holds its own in this light, gently spiced broth. It's virtually impossible to overcook if you poach it slowly. Because the texture is so delicate, I cut the pieces of fillet in half crosswise; that little trick makes the fish much easier to transfer from pan to plate. An optional garnish here is *dhana dal*, roasted split coriander seeds. They add a clean, citrusy note to the finished dish. I serve this in wide, shallow bowls or soup plates.

FOR THE POACHING BROTH

I tablespoon coriander seeds

I tablespoon mustard oil plus
  I tablespoon canola oil, or all
  canola oil

I tablespoon brown mustard seeds

6 large garlic cloves, thinly sliced

½ cup thinly sliced shallot

I tablespoon chopped peeled ginger

⅛ teaspoon ground turmeric

¼ cup thinly sliced mild to
  moderately hot fresh green chile

5 cups White Fish Stock (page 275),
  Chicken Stock (page 274), or
  reduced-sodium canned chicken
  broth

Six 3- to 4-inch cilantro stems with
  roots

8 pieces kokum (labeled "wet
  kokum"), thinly sliced

I scant tablespoon balsamic vinegar

½ teaspoon sugar

Sea salt

FOR THE FISH

Six 6-ounce pieces skinless halibut
  fillet, about 1¼ inches thick, cut
  in half crosswise

Sea salt and freshly ground black
  pepper

I heaping tablespoon chopped
  cilantro

FOR GARNISH

I tablespoon thinly sliced chives

I tablespoon *dhana dal* (optional)

Coarsely crush the coriander seeds with a mortar and pestle or a rolling pin.

If you're using the mustard oil, heat it in a wide, relatively shallow 6- to 8-quart pan over moderately high heat until it smokes, then remove from the heat. (Mustard oil is very pungent, so don't breathe it in when it's smoking.) Add the canola oil, return the pan to moderately high heat, and heat the oil until it shimmers. (If you're not using mustard oil, simply heat 2 tablespoons canola oil in the pan until it shimmers.) Add the mustard seeds and, when they pop and are fragrant, after about 30 seconds, add the crushed coriander seeds and the garlic, stirring constantly. Reduce the heat to moderate and stir in the shallot, ginger, turmeric, and chile. Gently simmer the mixture for 20 minutes, then stir in the stock, cilantro stems with roots, kokum, vinegar, sugar, and salt to taste.

Season the fish with salt and pepper and let sit for 5 minutes. Remove the cilantro stems with roots from the poaching broth and add the chopped cilantro. Add the fish to the poaching broth and cover the pan. (Don't worry if the fish isn't covered with broth; simply spoon the broth over it several times during cooking.) Poach the fish at a gentle simmer 8 to 10 minutes, or until just cooked through. (Do not turn the fish over.)

Divide the broth among 6 wide soup bowls, put a piece of fish on top, and garnish with chives and *dhana dal* if desired.

taro-crusted red snapper with white beans and mustard greens

SERVES 6

This dish is about flavor, of course, but it's also about texture with a capital *T*. Here, velvety white beans and tender mustard greens—given a lift with an intriguing little acid burst from green mango powder—make a bed for mild, sweet-fleshed red snapper. The fish is topped by a thatch of taro, a South American starchy tuber that's increasingly available at grocery stores. In a technique I learned at Lespinasse, I pat a thin layer of a simple fish mousse over the pieces of fish fillet and then coat the mousse with a layer of taro matchsticks. That insulation, so to speak, keeps the fish moist and succulent during cooking. Any kind of dried white beans—navy or Great Northern, for instance—will do. I use rice beans, so called because they're just a little bit bigger than grains of basmati. Asian in origin, they were once grown extensively in northeast India.

FOR THE BEANS AND GREENS

1 cup dried white beans such as navy, Great Northern, or rice beans, picked over for stones
Sea salt
5 unpeeled garlic cloves
Extra virgin olive oil
1 pound mustard greens, tough center ribs cut out and leaves roughly chopped (about 5 cups)
2 tablespoons brown mustard seeds
3 tablespoons canola oil
3 cloves
1 tablespoon cumin seeds

2 tablespoons finely chopped shallot
3 tablespoons finely chopped peeled ginger
1 tablespoon unsalted butter
1 mild to moderately hot fresh green chile, halved lengthwise and finely sliced crosswise (about 2 tablespoons)
1 teaspoon Aleppo pepper or cayenne
1½ cups Chicken Stock (page 274) or reduced-sodium canned chicken broth
Four 4-inch thyme sprigs
One 6-inch rosemary sprig

1 tablespoon green mango powder
2 tablespoons chopped cilantro
Freshly ground black pepper

FOR THE FISH MOUSSE
½ pound fish from red snapper,
    halibut, or striped bass
2 garlic cloves, peeled
1 mild to moderately hot fresh green
    chile, roughly chopped (about 3
    tablespoons)
1 tablespoon roughly chopped peeled
    ginger

1 egg
¼ cup roughly chopped cilantro
2 tablespoons heavy cream
Sea salt and freshly ground black
    pepper

FOR THE FISH
One 9-ounce piece taro, peeled
Six 6-ounce pieces red snapper fillet
    with skin
Sea salt and freshly ground black
    pepper
1 cup canola oil

Put the beans and 5 cups water in a 3-quart pot and bring to a boil. Boil the beans for 2 minutes, turn off the heat, and let the beans soak, uncovered, for 1 hour.

Drain the beans and return to the pot with enough water to cover them by 2 inches. Simmer the beans, partially covered, until just tender, about 45 minutes. Generously salt the beans and let sit for 5 minutes.

While the beans are cooking, preheat the oven to 350°F and put a large pot of water on to boil. Put the unpeeled garlic cloves on a piece of foil. Drizzle the garlic with some olive oil and sprinkle with salt. Wrap the garlic tightly in the foil and roast in the middle of the oven for 30 to 35 minutes, or until the garlic is soft. Slip the skins off the garlic cloves. Add some salt to the boiling water and blanch the mustard greens for 1 minute. Immediately transfer the greens to a bowl of cold water. When cold, squeeze them dry by the handful and chop roughly. (You should have about 1 cup chopped blanched greens.)

Finely grind 1 tablespoon of the mustard seeds in an electric coffee/spice grinder.

Heat the canola oil in a 4- to 6-quart pan over moderately high heat until it shimmers. Cook the remaining tablespoon of mustard seeds, the cloves, and the cumin seeds, shaking the pan, for 30 seconds. Add the shallot, ginger, butter, chile, and roasted garlic, smashing the garlic with a spatula, and cook for about 1 minute. Stir in the Aleppo pepper.

Set aside 1 cup of the beans and add the rest to the roasted garlic mixture. Stir in 1 cup of the stock and simmer for 10 minutes. Add the thyme and rosemary. Sprinkle the ground mustard seeds over the mixture and continue to simmer.

Puree the reserved beans with ½ cup water in a blender. Stir the puree into the simmering bean mixture and simmer for 10 minutes longer. Discard the herb sprigs. *The beans can be cooked and the greens chopped and blanched 1 day ahead and refrigerated, covered separately.*

Prepare the fish mousse: Pulse the ½ pound of fish, garlic, chile, ginger, and egg in a food processor until very smooth and transfer to a bowl. Gently fold in the cilantro, cream, a pinch of salt, and a generous amount of pepper. Put the mousse in the refrigerator until ready to use.

Cut the piece of taro in half lengthwise and cut each half into ⅛-inch-thick slices with a mandoline or large sharp knife. Then cut the thin slices into matchsticks and spread them out on a cookie sheet or tray.

Lightly score the skin side of the fish to prevent curling. Pat one-sixth (about ¼ cup) of the fish mousse all over the skin side of each piece of fish. Put each piece of fish, mousse side down, onto the taro, gently pressing to help the matchsticks adhere. *The fish can be made up to this point 4 to 6 hours ahead and kept, taro side down, on a tray, covered and refrigerated.*

Finish preparing the beans and greens: Add the chopped blanched mustard greens to the bean mixture and add the remaining ½ cup stock if the mixture seems too thick (it should be the consistency of loose oatmeal). Reheat over moderately low heat. Stir in the mango powder, cilantro, and a generous amount of black pepper.

Preheat the oven to 225°F.

Season the flesh sides of the fish with salt and pepper. Turn the pieces of fish over so that the taro "thatch" is on top and press as many stray matchsticks onto the fish as you can. Season the thatch with salt and pepper.

Heat ½ cup of the oil in a 12-inch skillet over high heat until it shimmers and sauté 3 pieces of fish, taro sides down, until golden brown, about 3 minutes. Turn the fish over (2 spatulas are helpful) and cook for 3 minutes longer. Transfer the fish to a baking sheet lined with paper towels and keep warm in the middle of the oven.

Cook the remaining pieces of fish in the remaining ½ cup oil in the same way. Serve the fish over the beans and greens.

pan-roasted red snapper
with roasted chile sauce

In the southern and western cuisines of India, chiles are a star ingredient. Here you have a traditional chile sauce—rich and deep in flavor—that goes with sweet, mild snapper. I found my inspiration on a recent trip back home. I pulled off the road at a *dhabba*, a rest-stop restaurant, and saw the cooks roasting fresh green chiles over live coals for the night's fish curry. This dish is based on that curry I ate with rice. Depending on the length of the pieces of fish you get, you might be able to cook them all in one batch. This is delicious with rice or pasta.

FOR THE ROASTED CHILE SAUCE

3 unpeeled garlic cloves
Extra virgin olive oil
Sea salt
1½ tablespoons coriander seeds
1½ teaspoons cumin seeds
1½ cups packed grated fresh coconut
(see page 283) or unsweetened
desiccated coconut
2 mild to moderately hot fresh green
chiles, roasted, peeled, and seeded
(see page 9)
2 tablespoons canola oil
1 tablespoon chopped shallot

1 tablespoon chopped peeled ginger
1 cup Roasted Fish Stock (page 277),
Chicken Stock (page 274), or
reduced-sodium canned chicken
broth
1 tablespoon Tamarind Paste (page
284)
Generous pinch of sugar

FOR THE FISH

Six 6-ounce pieces red snapper fillet
with skin
Sea salt
½ cup canola oil

Preheat the oven to 350°F.

Put the unpeeled garlic cloves on a piece of foil. Drizzle the garlic with the olive oil and sprinkle with salt. Wrap the garlic tightly in the foil and roast in the middle of the oven for 30 to 35 minutes, or until the garlic is soft. Slip the skins off the garlic cloves.

Toast the coriander seeds in a dry 10-inch skillet over moderately low heat, shaking the skillet, until fragrant and a couple of shades darker, about 3 minutes. Transfer to a small tray or plate to cool. Toast the cumin seeds in the same way and add them to the coriander seeds. Finely grind the toasted spices in an electric coffee/spice grinder.

In the same skillet, toast the coconut over low heat, stirring and shaking the skillet frequently, until golden brown, 10 to 12 minutes. Spread the toasted coconut out on a tray or large plate to cool.

Puree the roasted garlic, roasted chiles, toasted coconut, and ½ cup water in a blender until smooth, adding ¼ cup water if necessary to make a smooth puree.

Heat the canola oil in a 3- to 4-quart pan over moderately high heat until it shimmers and cook the shallot and ginger, stirring, for 1 minute. Add the puree (do not clean the blender) and ground spices. Put the stock in the blender, swish it around (why waste any residual flavor?), and add to the mixture in the pan. Add the tamarind paste, sugar, and salt to taste. Simmer the sauce, stirring occasionally, until thickened slightly, about 12 minutes.

Preheat the oven to 225°F.

Lightly score the skin side of the pieces of fish to prevent curling. Season both sides of the fish with salt.

Heat ¼ cup of the oil in a 12-inch skillet over high heat until it shimmers and sauté 3 pieces of fish, skin sides down, until golden brown, about 4 minutes. Turn the fish over and cook for 2 minutes longer. Transfer the fish to a baking sheet lined with paper towels and keep warm in the middle of the oven. Cook the remaining pieces of fish in the remaining ¼ cup oil in the same way. Serve the fish on top of the sauce.

pan-roasted cod and clams with basmati kanji

SERVES 6

Kanji is a home-style dish that is similar to a soupy risotto or Chinese *jook*. This one has its roots in my childhood summers in Goa. Every morning at eleven, my grandmother would summon my brothers and me indoors. We obediently sat around the dining table to a bowl of steaming-hot kanji, accompanied by pickled mango and roasted salted dried fish, and it was the last thing on earth we wanted as a midmorning snack. Our father was deeply sentimental about the ritual, but we hated both the formality and the kanji itself. As much as I loved my grandmother, her kanji left something to be desired, so I decided to refine it. This rendition is a favorite, full of both fresh and salt cod as well as clams. Green peas add color, and tangy kokum cuts the richness of coconut milk, as does Mango Water Pickle (page 241). My children love it, quite possibly because I don't make them eat it every day of summer vacation.

1½ cups white basmati rice
1½ ounces salt cod (about ⅓ cup)
2 tablespoons canola oil
2 cloves
I bay leaf
1½ tablespoons chopped peeled ginger
¼ cup plus 2 tablespoons minced shallot or white onion
2 large garlic cloves, thinly sliced crosswise
One 6-inch rosemary sprig
2½ to 3 cups Chicken Stock (page 274) or reduced-sodium canned chicken broth

One 13- to 14-ounce can coconut milk (1¾ cups), stirred well
½ cup dry white wine
½ cup cooked mung beans (optional; see page 73)
Six 5-ounce pieces fresh cod, preferably with skin
Sea salt and freshly ground black pepper
24 littleneck or manila clams, washed thoroughly
2 tablespoons thinly sliced kokum (labeled "wet kokum")
1½ cups frozen peas

Wash the rice well (see page 258) and soak it in water to cover for 20 minutes. Drain the rice. Thinly slice the salt cod on the diagonal against the grain. Break the salt cod into roughly 1½-inch pieces and toast in a dry small heavy skillet over high heat until golden and charred in spots, about 3 minutes. Let cool and shred into small pieces.

Heat 1 tablespoon of the oil in a heavy 3- to 4-quart pan over moderately high heat until it shimmers and cook the cloves and bay leaf, stirring, until fragrant, about 1 minute. Add the ginger, shallot, garlic, and rosemary and cook, stirring, for about 5 minutes, or until the shallot and garlic are translucent. Add the drained rice and cook, stirring, until the grains are coated with oil, about 2 minutes. Add 1 cup of the stock, 1 cup of the coconut milk, the wine, and the mung beans if using. Simmer, covered, until the rice is tender and the liquid is beginning to be completely absorbed, 15 to 20 minutes. Discard the cloves, bay leaf, and rosemary and spread the rice on a tray to cool. *The rice can be made up to this point 1 day ahead.*

Preheat the oven to 350°F and season the fresh cod with salt and pepper.

Put the clams in the same (cleaned) 3- to 4-quart pan and add 1½ cups of the remaining stock. Bring to a boil. Cover the pan and cook over moderate heat until the clams open, about 2 minutes. (Discard any unopened clams.) Transfer the clams and stock to a 6-quart pan and stir in the cooled rice, salt cod, remaining coconut milk, kokum, and peas. (The mixture should be very soupy.) Reduce the heat to moderately low.

Heat the remaining tablespoon of oil in a heavy ovenproof 12-inch skillet over moderately high heat until it shimmers. Sear the fresh cod in the oil, skin side down, for 2 minutes. Turn the cod over and transfer the skillet to the middle of the oven. Cook for 4 to 8 minutes (depending on the thickness of the fish), or until the cod is just cooked through.

Stir the remaining ½ cup chicken stock into the rice if necessary to keep the rice soupy and season with salt.

Serve the cod on a bed of rice and clams.

how to cook mung beans

Dried whole mung beans, small and olive-green in color (when hulled and split, they are yellow and are referred to as moong dal *or* mung dal*), give earthy flavor and creamy texture to kanji.*

Put ¼ cup dried whole mung beans, washed well, in a small pot and add 2 cups water. Bring the beans to a simmer and simmer over moderately high heat for 15 to 20 minutes, or until tender. Drain the beans in a colander or in a slotted spoon before adding to the kanji.

seared wild striped bass with warm tomato salad and balsamic sauce

SERVES 6

Make this when your garden or farmers' market is overflowing with ripe, flavorful tomatoes. I use the beefiest beefsteaks I can find. Even though delicately flavored wild striped bass is the main event here, what makes this dish special is something called *kachumber*, a chopped salad commonly found at roadside diners in India. Tomatoes are a standard ingredient, but the salad can also include onions, cucumbers, cilantro, radishes—whatever is available and inexpensive. This dish is enormously satisfying on hot, sunny days.

FOR THE BALSAMIC SAUCE

4 large beefsteak tomatoes, chopped (about 4 cups)

1 quart White Fish Stock (page 275), Chicken Stock (page 274), or reduced-sodium canned chicken broth

½ cup balsamic vinegar

1 tablespoon coriander seeds

1 teaspoon black peppercorns

¼ teaspoon fenugreek seeds

2 tablespoons canola oil

1 tablespoon chopped shallot

1 teaspoon chopped garlic

1 teaspoon chopped peeled ginger

1½ teaspoons red wine vinegar

Scant ¼ teaspoon cayenne

1 teaspoon sugar

Sea salt

FOR THE TOMATO SALAD

6 large beefsteak tomatoes, diced (about 6 cups)

1 heaping cup quartered and very thinly sliced red onion

1 heaping tablespoon chopped peeled ginger

1 tablespoon thinly sliced chives

2 heaping tablespoons thinly sliced mild to moderately hot fresh green chile

¼ cup chopped cilantro or Thai basil

¼ cup extra virgin olive oil

1 teaspoon sugar
1 teaspoon sea salt
Freshly ground black pepper

FOR THE FISH

Six 6-ounce pieces wild striped bass
fillet with skin, 1½ to 2 inches
thick
Sea salt and freshly ground black
pepper
½ cup canola oil

Bring the tomatoes and stock to a boil in a 3- to 4-quart pan and simmer vigorously for 10 to 12 minutes, or until the tomatoes start to break down. Strain the mixture through a fine sieve into a bowl, pressing on the solids with the back of a ladle. Discard the solids. Put the strained tomato liquid in the (uncleaned) pan and add the balsamic vinegar. Simmer the mixture until reduced to the consistency of chocolate sauce, about 30 minutes, and set aside. (You should have about 1 cup.)

Toast the coriander seeds, peppercorns, and fenugreek seeds together in a dry small skillet over moderately low heat, shaking the skillet, until fragrant and a couple of shades darker, about 3 minutes. Transfer them to a small tray or plate to cool. Finely grind in an electric coffee/spice grinder.

Heat the canola oil in a 4- to 6-quart pan over moderately high heat until it shimmers and cook the shallot, garlic, and ginger, stirring constantly, until softened and translucent but not colored. Stir in the balsamic reduction, red wine vinegar, ground spices, cayenne, sugar, and salt to taste. Remove the sauce from the heat and reserve.

Put the diced tomatoes in a large ovenproof bowl or dish and gently stir in the onion, ginger, chives, chile, cilantro, olive oil, sugar, and half of the sauce. Season with the salt and pepper.

Preheat the oven to 225°F and season the fish with salt and pepper.

Heat ¼ cup of the oil in a heavy 12-inch skillet over moderately high heat until it shimmers and add 3 pieces of the fish, skin side down. Sear the fish until pale golden, about 3 minutes. Transfer the fish, skin side up, and the oil to a baking sheet with sides. Cook the remaining pieces of fish in the remaining oil in the same way, transferring to the baking sheet when done. Put the fish in the middle of the oven and roast for 8 minutes, or until just done. During the last 2 minutes of cooking, put the tomato salad in the oven to warm through (don't let it get hot). Divide the tomato salad among 6 plates. Top with the fish and drizzle with the reserved sauce.

seared striped bass with lime jaggery gastrique

A gastrique (gas-TREEK) is a classic French sauce made by reducing a seasoned mixture of sugar and vinegar until the sugar is caramelized and the liquid thickens into a lovely glaze. I'm playing around with the concept here, giving it a fresh twist by using lime juice and the Indian unrefined sugar called *jaggery*. The end result is vibrant and aromatic, with a deep underlying sweetness and a smoky spark from a pasilla de Oaxaca chile. I serve this with roasted mushrooms or grilled summer vegetables.

FOR THE SAUCE

1½ teaspoons coriander seeds
1½ teaspoons black peppercorns
¼ cup jaggery (see Glossary) or dark
   brown sugar
½ cup strained lime juice
¼ pasilla de Oaxaca or other smoked
   chile, including seeds
3 cups Roasted Fish Stock (page 277)
   reduced to ½ cup or veal
   demiglace (see Sources)
Pinch of sea salt

FOR THE FISH

Six 6-ounce pieces striped bass
   fillet with skin
Sea salt and freshly ground black
   pepper
2½ or 5 tablespoons canola oil
1 or 2 tablespoons unsalted butter

Toast the coriander seeds in a dry small skillet over moderately low heat, shaking the skillet, until fragrant and a couple of shades darker, about 3 minutes. Turn out on a small tray or plate to cool. Toast the peppercorns the same way, turning them out to cool with the coriander. Finely grind the spices together in an electric coffee/spice grinder.

Combine the jaggery with ½ cup water in a 1-quart pot and heat over moderately high heat until the jaggery starts to melt, 2 to 3 minutes. Continue to cook, stirring occasionally, until the jaggery melts and turns into a golden caramel, about 10 minutes. Add the lime juice and chile and simmer for 5 minutes, or until reduced to roughly a quarter of its volume. Add the stock and bring to a boil. Remove the chile and add the ground spices and salt. Simmer the sauce until reduced to a thick but still runny glaze (it should be the consistency of molasses), about 30 minutes. Remove the sauce from the heat and let cool to room temperature.

Lightly score the skin side of the fish to prevent curling. Season the fish generously with salt and pepper.

Heat the oil in a 12-inch skillet over moderately high heat until it shimmers, using 5 tablespoons if all the fish will fit in the pan at once, 2½ tablespoons to cook it in 2 batches. Add the fish, skin side down, and cook until golden brown on the bottom, 2 to 2½ minutes. Turn the fish over and add the butter (again all or half, for 1 or 2 batches). Cook the fish for 2 to 2½ minutes longer, basting with the melted butter in the skillet for the last minute. Serve the fish with the gastrique spooned over it.

poached wild striped bass with ginger broth

SERVES 6

One of the easiest and most angst-free ways to cook fish is by slowly poaching thick pieces of fillet in a flavorful, aromatic broth. This is a very summery dish because the broth is so light. I use ground dried ginger here because I like its peppery heat as opposed to the spicier heat of fresh ginger. At Tabla, I serve this wild striped bass in shallow wide bowls or soup plates on top of steamed bok choy with the broth spooned around it.

6 cups White Fish Stock (page 275), Chicken Stock (page 274), or reduced-sodium canned chicken broth
6 plum tomatoes, quartered
2 tablespoons canola oil
2 cloves
¼ teaspoon nigella seeds
¼ teaspoon cumin seeds
3 garlic cloves, sliced
1 cup quartered and thinly sliced white onion

1 tablespoon seeded and thinly sliced mild to moderately hot fresh green chile
¼ teaspoon ground turmeric
Six 6-ounce pieces wild striped bass fillet with skin, 1½ to 2 inches thick
Sea salt
¾ teaspoon ground dried ginger
Six 3-inch cilantro stems with roots, tied in a cheesecloth bundle
Freshly ground black pepper
Coarse sea salt such as Maldon
1 tablespoon cilantro chiffonade (see page 8)

Bring the stock and tomatoes to a boil in an ovenproof 3- to 4-quart pot. Simmer over moderately high heat until reduced by about half, about 10 minutes. Strain the mixture through a fine-mesh sieve into a bowl and discard the solids.

Preheat the oven to 275°F.

Heat the oil in pot over moderately high heat until it shimmers and add the cloves, nigella seeds, and cumin seeds. Cook for 1 minute, stirring, then add the garlic and cook for 1 minute longer, stirring. Add the onion and cook, stirring, until transparent, about 2 minutes. Add the chile and turmeric and cook, stirring, for 1 minute, then add the reduced stock mixture. Simmer the broth for 5 minutes and season with salt.

Meanwhile, generously season the fish with salt and let stand for 5 minutes.

Stir the ginger, cilantro stems with roots, and pepper to taste into the broth and add the fish. Cover the pot and put in the middle of oven until the fish is just cooked through, about 15 minutes. Serve the fish and the broth in soup plates or bowls, garnished with coarse sea salt and cilantro.

sautéed black sea bass with mustard curry

SERVES 6

Mild in flavor and firm in texture, black sea bass is one of my favorite fish to cook. The sauce is aromatic and intensely flavorful; it's not a smooth sauce, but somehow it has a velvety quality. I like to serve this in wide, shallow bowls or soup plates.

FOR THE SAUCE

2 cups chopped white onion

2 cups quartered fresh or drained canned plum tomatoes

2½ cups Chicken Stock (page 274) or reduced-sodium canned chicken broth

2 tablespoons canola oil

3 cloves

1 teaspoon brown mustard seeds

1 teaspoon cumin seeds

1 small dried red chile (see Glossary), broken in half

1 teaspoon chopped garlic

2 teaspoons chopped peeled ginger

1 tablespoon thinly sliced mild to moderately hot fresh green chile

Heaping ¼ teaspoon ground turmeric

⅛ teaspoon cayenne

12 fresh curry leaves

Sea salt and freshly ground black pepper

1 teaspoon dry mustard

FOR THE FISH

Six 6-ounce pieces black sea bass with skin, about 1 inch thick

¼ teaspoon ground turmeric

¼ teaspoon cayenne

Sea salt and freshly ground black pepper

1 cup canola oil

Puree the onion, tomatoes, and stock together in a blender until smooth (you may have to do this in batches). Transfer the puree to a 2-quart pan and bring to a boil over high heat. Reduce the heat and simmer 40 minutes, or until all of the raw onion flavor is gone. Strain the puree through a fine sieve into a bowl, pressing on the solids with the back of a ladle until the solids look dry and cakey. (You should have about 1⅔ cups liquid.) Reserve ¼ cup of the solids and discard the rest.

Heat the oil and cloves in 2-quart pan over moderately high heat until the oil is shimmering, then add the mustard seeds and cook until the seeds pop and are fragrant, about 30 seconds. Add the cumin seeds, dried chile, garlic, and ginger. Reduce the heat to moderately low and cook the mixture, stirring, until the garlic and ginger are softened, about 3 minutes. Add the fresh chile, turmeric, cayenne, curry leaves, strained stock, reserved tomato solids, and salt and pepper to taste. Bring the mixture to a simmer.

Put the dry mustard in a small bowl and whisk in a teaspoon of the simmering liquid to dissolve the mustard. Whisk in a little more liquid, enough to make the mixture pourable, and pour into the simmering liquid. Keep the sauce hot.

Preheat the oven to 225°F.

Lightly score the skin side of the fish to prevent curling. Turn the fish over and rub the turmeric and cayenne into the flesh side. Generously season both sides of the fish with salt and pepper.

Heat ½ cup oil in a 12-inch skillet over moderately high heat until it shimmers, and sauté 3 pieces of fish, skin side down, until golden brown, about 4 minutes. Turn the fish over and cook for 2 minutes longer. Transfer the fish to a baking sheet lined with paper towels and keep warm in the middle of the oven. Cook the remaining pieces of fish in the remaining ½ cup oil in the same way. Serve the fish over the sauce.

steamed black sea bass
with kokum broth

The inspiration for this dish comes from *kokum saar*, a refreshing Indian drink that can be served hot or cold. Kokum (pronounced "KOH-com") is the dried deep-purple fruit of the gamboge tree; in Indian cooking, it's used as an acid, giving a complex sweet-sour backnote of flavor that balances the richness of other ingredients—like the coconut milk used here. The kokum broth is enlivened with a traditional tarka—spices sizzled in hot oil to intensify their flavors and aromas. It's important to add the spices in the order they're called for, so that the things that burn easily, like the fresh chile and ginger, are added at the end.

FOR THE KOKUM BROTH

2 cups Roasted Fish Stock (page 277),
　　Chicken Stock (page 274),
　　or reduced-sodium canned
　　chicken broth
10 pieces kokum (labeled
　　"wet kokum")
1 tablespoon thinly sliced peeled
　　ginger
2 cloves
¼ mild to moderately hot fresh
　　green chile, split lengthwise
1 cup coconut milk, shaken well

FOR THE TARKA

2 tablespoons canola oil
1½ tablespoons thinly sliced garlic
1 teaspoon brown mustard seeds

½ teaspoon cumin seeds
About 21 fresh curry leaves (from
　　1 sprig)
¼ cup thinly sliced shallot
1 heaping tablespoon thinly sliced
　　mild to moderately hot fresh
　　green chile
1 scant tablespoon thinly sliced
　　peeled ginger
Sea salt
Pinch of sugar
Freshly ground black pepper

FOR THE FISH

Six 6-ounce pieces black sea bass
　　fillet with skin
Sea salt and freshly ground black
　　pepper

1 tablespoon unsalted butter,
softened
¼ teaspoon chopped peeled
ginger

¼ teaspoon chopped mild to
moderately hot fresh green
chile
½ teaspoon chopped cilantro

Put the stock, kokum, ginger, cloves, split chile, and coconut milk in a 3- to 4-quart pan and bring to a simmer over low heat. Simmer the mixture, pressing occasionally on the kokum and other solids to extract their essence, until the mixture is reduced to about 2 cups, about 20 minutes. Strain the broth through a sieve into a bowl, pressing hard on the solids with the back of a ladle.

Heat the oil in another 3- to 4-quart pan over moderately high heat until it shimmers. Add the garlic and cook until it just begins to color, about 1 minute. Add the mustard seeds, cumin seeds, curry leaves, shallot, chile, and ginger, stirring and shaking the pan. Add a pinch of salt, the sugar, and the kokum broth and bring to a boil. Reduce the heat and simmer the sauce for 5 minutes. Stir in a generous amount of black pepper and keep the sauce warm.

Preheat the oven to 350°F. Bring a 2-quart pot of water to a boil.

Lightly score the skin side of each piece of fish to prevent curling. Sprinkle all over with salt and pepper and rub the skin side of each piece with about ½ teaspoon butter. Sprinkle the buttered sides with the ginger, chile, and cilantro.

Pour just enough boiling water into the bottom of a 13 × 9-inch roasting pan with a rack to reach about halfway to the rack. Put the pieces of fish on the rack and cover with a tent of foil. (That way, the condensed steam will roll down the sides, not directly onto the fish.) Steam the fish in the middle of the oven until it is just done, about 12 minutes. Serve the fish over a pool of sauce.

skate with "tartar" sauce

Here, fish cooked very simply is livened up by an eggless tartar sauce. The sauce gets its richness and body from a vinaigrette made from chicken stock reduced to its flavorful essence and is made piquant by Garlic Pickle (page 242) and capers. I love it with skate, but feel free to experiment with other mild white-fleshed fish. The flour I dredge the skate in before cooking is a little unusual, but the combination of very finely ground cornmeal (sometimes marketed as corn flour), chickpea flour (*besan* in Hindi), and instant flour (a low-gluten, quickly dissolving flour used for thickening gravies), results in an ethereally light but satisfyingly crunchy coating.

FOR THE GARLIC PICKLE
VINAIGRETTE

3 cups Chicken Stock (page 274; see
  Note)
12 cloves Garlic Pickle (page 242),
  skins slipped off
¼ chile and ⅓ cup liquid from
  Garlic Pickle mixture
⅓ cup canola oil
½ teaspoon sugar
Sea salt and freshly ground black
  pepper

FOR THE TARTAR SAUCE

3 tablespoons diced sour gherkins or
  dill pickles
2 tablespoons drained capers, rinsed
  (soaked overnight if very salty) and
  minced

1 tablespoon thinly sliced chives
1 tablespoon minced cilantro
Sea salt and freshly ground black
  pepper

FOR THE FISH

Six 6-ounce pieces skinless skate
  fillet
Sea salt
1 tablespoon black peppercorns
1 tablespoon coriander seeds
⅓ cup chickpea flour (*besan*)
⅓ cup instant flour such as Wondra
⅓ cup very fine cornmeal
  (sometimes called corn flour)
1 cup canola oil
Lemon wedges

Vigorously simmer the stock in a 2-quart pan until reduced to ¾ cup, about 15 minutes. (If you reduce it too much, add water to make ¾ cup.) Remove the pan from the heat and let the reduced stock cool slightly.

Puree the reduced stock, garlic pickle cloves, chile, and garlic pickle liquid in a blender. When the puree is smooth, slowly add the oil to make a thick, mayonnaiselike vinaigrette. Add the sugar and season with salt and pepper to taste. Transfer the vinaigrette to a bowl and refrigerate, covered, for at least 2 hours and up to 6, to give the vinaigrette time to thicken to the proper consistency.

Combine the chilled vinaigrette, gherkins, capers, chives, and cilantro in a bowl and season with salt and pepper. Refrigerate, covered, until ready to serve.

Season the skate with salt and let sit for 5 minutes.

Finely grind the peppercorns and coriander seeds together in an electric coffee/spice grinder.

Preheat the oven to 225°F. Stir the chickpea flour, instant flour, cornmeal, and ground spices together in a medium bowl. Dredge the fish in the seasoned flour.

Heat a third of the oil in a 12-inch skillet over moderately high heat until it shimmers and add 2 pieces of the skate. If the fish curls up, gently flatten it with a spatula. Sauté until the underside is light golden, about 2 minutes. Turn the fish over and sauté for 1 to 2 minutes longer. Drain on paper towels and keep warm on a baking sheet with sides in the middle of the oven. Cook the remaining pieces of fish in 2 more batches in the same way, adding about a third of the oil to the skillet for each batch and transferring each batch when done to the baking sheet in the oven. Serve the fish with the tartar sauce and lemon wedges.

NOTE: *Do not substitute canned chicken broth for homemade stock in this case. It doesn't have enough body to thicken the vinaigrette.*

steamed fluke with cilantro and spices

Steamed fish is virtuous and simple, but it can be, well, boring. Not this preparation. Try this with the Fricassee of Summer Beans (page 198).

I teaspoon mustard dal
I teaspoon black peppercorns
½ teaspoon ajwain seeds
⅛ teaspoon Szechwan peppercorns
Unsalted butter, softened, or extra virgin olive oil
Six (6-ounce) pieces skinless fluke or other small, thin fillets such as black sea bass or red snapper

2 tablespoons thinly sliced shallot
I heaping tablespoon julienne strips unpeeled ginger
I teaspoon minced cilantro roots or stems
2 tablespoons chopped cilantro leaves
2 tablespoons chopped chives
I tablespoon thinly sliced mild to moderately hot fresh green chile

Finely grind the mustard dal, black peppercorns, ajwain seeds, and Szechwan peppercorns in an electric coffee/spice grinder. Brush a tray with butter or olive oil and sprinkle some of the ground spices on the tray. Put the fish on the tray and sprinkle with the rest of the spice mixture. Brush the fish with a little more softened butter or olive oil and sprinkle with the shallot, ginger, cilantro roots and leaves, chives, and chile. *Refrigerate the fish, covered loosely with foil, for 2 to 4 hours.*

Preheat the oven to 350°F. Bring a 2-quart pot of water to a boil.

Pour just enough boiling water into the bottom of a 13 × 9-inch roasting pan fitted with a 10 × 8-inch rack so that it reaches about halfway to the rack. Put the pieces of fish on the rack and cover with a tent of foil. (That way, the condensed steam will roll down the sides, not directly onto the fish.) Steam the fish in the middle of the oven until it is just done, 8 to 10 minutes, and serve immediately.

mahimahi stuffed with coconut coriander chutney

SERVES 6

Parsis are members of the Persian religion called Zoroastrianism. One of their culinary techniques is to coat fish with chutney before cooking it. Rather than putting the chutney on the outside, I tuck it inside. The mahimahi's savory juices mingle with the chutney and create a light, fragrant sauce.

1 tablespoon coriander seeds
1 tablespoon fennel seeds
1 teaspoon black peppercorns
½ cup Coconut Coriander Chutney (page 232)

Six 5-ounce pieces mahimahi fillet
Sea salt and freshly ground pepper
¼ cup canola oil

Preheat the oven to 350°F.

Finely grind the coriander seeds, fennel seeds, and peppercorns together in an electric coffee/spice grinder. Stir the ground spices and chutney together in a small bowl.

Starting at a narrow end of each piece of mahimahi, cut a slit in each piece with a small paring knife, cutting almost all the way down to the other narrow end. (Don't go all the way through.) Stuff each piece of fish with a generous tablespoon of stuffing. Season the fish all over with salt and pepper and let sit for 5 minutes.

Heat the oil in a 12-inch ovenproof skillet over moderately high heat until it shimmers and sauté the fish until golden on the bottom, 2 to 3 minutes. Turn the fish over with a spatula and transfer the skillet to the middle of the oven. Roast the fish until just done, 5 to 6 minutes. Serve the fish in wide shallow bowls or soup plates with the sauce.

fish curry with eggplant and okra

In coastal Bengal, far to the northeast of Goa, seafood is abundant and yellow-flowering mustard fields are everywhere. With plenty of mustard seeds and vegetables in addition to fish, this is a classic *machor jhol*, or Bengali curry. The heat, very clear and pungent in this dish, is reminiscent of a Southeast Asian curry—which makes sense when you realize that Burma is not far away. Serve the curry over rice.

3½ pounds fish heads and/or fish bones and trimmings, washed

1½ tablespoons coriander seeds

1 teaspoon cumin seeds

2 teaspoons brown mustard seeds

1 teaspoon ground turmeric

¼ teaspoon cayenne

3 tablespoons canola oil

3 cloves

2 bay leaves

3 cups quartered and thinly sliced white onion

1 tablespoon minced peeled ginger

1 tablespoon minced garlic

2 large vine-ripe beefsteak tomatoes, seeded and chopped (about 2 cups)

Sea salt and freshly ground black pepper

1 mild to moderately hot fresh green chile, slit down 1 side

½ cup dry white wine

1 large Japanese eggplant (about 6 ounces), cut into large bite-sized pieces (about 2 cups)

2 large Yukon Gold potatoes, cut into large bite-sized pieces (about 2 cups)

½ pound okra, trimmed

Six 1½-inch cilantro stems with roots

Six 6-ounce pieces wild striped bass or cod fillet

Make a quick fish stock by putting the fish heads and/or bones and trimmings and 6 cups water in a 5- to 6-quart pan. Bring the mixture to a boil and simmer, skimming the froth occasionally, for 30 minutes. Strain the stock through a sieve into a bowl, pressing hard on the solids with the back of a ladle.

Finely grind the coriander seeds, cumin seeds, and 1 teaspoon of the mustard seeds in an electric coffee/spice grinder. Transfer the ground spices to a small bowl and add the turmeric and cayenne. Stir in 2 tablespoons water to make a paste.

Heat the oil in the (cleaned) pan over moderately high heat until it shimmers and add the cloves, bay leaves, and remaining teaspoon of mustard seeds. Cook, stirring, until the mustard seeds pop and the spices are fragrant, about 30 seconds. Stir in the onion, ginger, and garlic and cook until the onion is translucent, about 5 minutes. Add the spice paste, tomatoes, and 2½ teaspoons salt and cook, stirring, until the tomatoes are softened, about 2 minutes. Add the green chile, white wine, and fish stock and bring the sauce to a boil. *The curry can be made up to this point 1 day ahead, cooled completely, uncovered, and refrigerated, covered.*

Bring the sauce to a boil and add the eggplant, potatoes, okra, and cilantro stems with roots. Simmer the sauce until the eggplant and potato are tender, about 20 minutes.

Season the fish with salt and pepper and let sit for 5 minutes. Completely submerge the fish in the sauce and bring to a boil. Simmer the curry for 5 minutes, then turn off the heat and tightly cover the pan. Let sit for 5 minutes longer.

esme's bacalao stew

My grandmother Esme made this for me at her house in Goa. Bacalao (salt cod) was always considered a special ingredient in our family because of the Portuguese connection. In Goa, salt cod and other dried fish and shrimp are staples during the summer's rainy season. That's monsoon time, when torrential downpours and rough seas prevent the small fishing boats from going out for weeks at a time, so Goan cooks rely instead on salt fish. In this stew, the salt cod isn't the least bit overpowering. It flakes and falls apart beautifully during cooking and gives the dish a deep richness. I serve this in large shallow bowls with roast chicken on top. It's even delicious with nothing more than some crusty French bread.

FOR THE STEW

¼ pound salt cod, rinsed well and cut into small pieces

¼ cup plus 2 tablespoons extra virgin olive oil

2 cloves

½ cinnamon stick

1 teaspoon brown mustard seeds

½ teaspoon cumin seeds

1 small dried red chile (see Glossary), crumbled

1 bay leaf

One 6-inch rosemary sprig

5 garlic cloves, sliced

2 cups halved and thinly sliced white onion

½ teaspoon ground turmeric

½ cup dry white wine

1 quart Chicken Stock (page 274) or reduced-sodium canned chicken broth

Freshly ground black pepper

3 plum tomatoes, cut into thin rounds

3 pounds Yukon Gold potatoes (about 6 medium), cut into ¼-inch rounds

2 tablespoons dry mustard

1 tablespoon balsamic vinegar

¼ pound baby mustard greens or watercress, coarse stems discarded

2 tablespoons cilantro chiffonade (see page 8)

2 tablespoons finely chopped chives

Soak the cod in cold water to cover, refrigerated, changing the water 3 times a day for 1 to 3 days (see Note). Drain.

Heat ¼ cup of the oil in a 6-quart pot over moderately high heat until it shimmers. Add the cloves and cinnamon and cook, stirring, just until fragrant, about 45 seconds. Add the mustard seeds, cumin seeds, chile, bay leaf, and rosemary and cook until the spices are fragrant and a couple of shades darker, about 15 seconds. Stir in the garlic and cook until softened, about 1 minute. Add the onion and cook, stirring, until softened, about 5 minutes. Add the turmeric and salt cod, and cook, stirring, until the salt cod is softened, about 2 minutes. Stir in the wine and increase the heat to high. Deglaze the pan, scraping up any caramelized bits of garlic and onion in the bottom of the pot. Stir in the stock and bring to a boil. Season the stew with black pepper (the cod supplies plenty of salt).

Layer first the tomato rounds, then the potato rounds, on top of the stew, overlapping them, and simmer briskly, uncovered, 20 minutes, or until the potatoes are softened and fully cooked. Gently stir in the dry mustard (you don't want to break up the potatoes).

Whisk together the balsamic vinegar and the remaining 2 tablespoons oil in a small bowl and gently stir into the stew.

Put a handful of greens into the bottom of 6 large shallow bowls and generously ladle the stew over it, including plenty of potatoes and tomatoes. Garnish with the cilantro and chives.

NOTE: *How salty salt cod is depends on the brand. A less salty piece of fish might need only 1 day of soaking, while another could require longer. To test it, taste a small piece after 1 day. It's supposed to be pleasantly briny, not overwhelmingly salty.*

shellfish and
other seafood

goan shrimp curry

Goa is on the coast of the Arabian Sea, which teems with many varieties of fish and shellfish. This curry, rich with shrimp (called *prawns* in India), coconut, and chiles, is one of the glories of Goan cuisine. It was my favorite curry as a child. The following day, any leftover sauce was thickened and served with fried eggs for breakfast, a tradition that lives on in my household today. If you can find heads-on shrimp, buy them; that's a sign that they are impeccably fresh, and the heads are full of flavor. Remove them before serving if desired. This curry has a gentle heat that builds. If you want a spicier curry, add more dried red chile. Serve this with Plain Basmati Rice (page 258) or other cooked white rice.

1½ cups roughly chopped white onion

5 garlic cloves, peeled

1½ cups grated fresh coconut (see page 283) or frozen coconut

1 tablespoon coriander seeds

1½ teaspoons cumin seeds

3 small dried red chiles (see Glossary)

1 tablespoon paprika

½ teaspoon ground turmeric

1 tablespoon canola oil

6 cups Quick Shrimp Stock (see Note) or water

1 mild to moderately hot fresh green chile, or more to taste, slit down 1 side

30 extra-large shrimp (16 to 20 count), peeled and deveined, heads left on if desired

Sea salt

2 tablespoons Tamarind Paste (page 284)

½ pound okra, trimmed

One 13- to 14-ounce can coconut milk (1¾ cups), stirred well

Put the onion, garlic, coconut, and ½ cup water in a blender and puree until smooth, starting at low speed and increasing to high. If necessary to keep the blades moving, add a little more water.

Finely grind the coriander seeds, cumin seeds, and dried red chiles together in an electric coffee/spice grinder. Transfer to a small bowl or plate and combine with the paprika and turmeric.

Heat the oil in a 4- to 6-quart pan over moderately high heat until it shimmers and add the spice blend and coconut puree. Put 3 cups of the stock into the (uncleaned) blender and pulse to blend any residual puree. Add that mixture to the puree in the pan along with the green chile. Bring the sauce to a boil, stirring occasionally.

Cook the sauce over moderately high heat, stirring occasionally, until it is the consistency of thick paste, about 15 to 20 minutes. (Do not let it scorch.) While the sauce is reducing, season the shrimp with salt and let sit for about 20 minutes.

Stir the remaining stock, tamarind paste, and okra into the sauce and bring to a simmer. Simmer mixture until the okra is barely tender, about 3 minutes. Stir in the coconut milk and bring the sauce to a boil. Add the shrimp and simmer until the shrimp are just cooked through, about 3 minutes. Season with salt before serving.

NOTE: *To make Quick Shrimp Stock, cover the shrimp shells with 6½ cups cold water, bring to a boil, and simmer, uncovered, for 30 minutes. Strain the liquid through a sieve into a bowl, pressing hard on the shells with the back of a ladle, and use the liquid as a stock.*

panfried black pepper shrimp

While I was growing up, my family lived near fishing villages in both Bombay and Goa, so we were able to get the freshest shrimp imaginable. As a child, I looked forward to Fridays because we always had shrimp for lunch. (We Cardoz children didn't eat lunch at school like many other children but went home for the midday meal.) The sweetness of the shrimp, the heat of freshly ground black peppercorns, and the citrusy flavor of the coriander seeds make a great combination. I serve this with Watermelon Lime Salad (page 31) or cucumber and onion salad. For a first course, simply halve the recipe. The shrimp can be grilled, too, but first brush the rack with oil so they don't stick. I call for extra-large shrimp, but use whatever size is local or freshest and adjust the cooking time accordingly.

2 tablespoons black peppercorns
2 tablespoons coriander seeds
2 tablespoons extra virgin olive oil
30 extra-large shrimp (16 to 20
    count), peeled and deveined

½ teaspoon sea salt
1 cup canola oil
Juice of 1 lime (2 to 3
    tablespoons)

Grind the peppercorns and coriander seeds separately in an electric coffee/spice grinder until medium-fine. Combine the ground spices with the olive oil in a bowl and mix well. Add the shrimp, tossing to coat well. *Marinate the shrimp, covered and chilled, for at least 1 and up to 24 hours.*

Season the shrimp with the salt. Heat ½ cup of the canola oil in a heavy 12-inch skillet over moderately high heat until the oil just begins to shimmer. Carefully put half the shrimp in the skillet and panfry them until crisp, about 2 minutes on each side. Drain the shrimp on paper towels or brown paper and drizzle with the lime juice.

Cook the remaining shrimp in the remaining oil and drizzle with lime juice in the same way.

crispy shrimp with toasted spice curry

Cooking shrimp with a coating of *rawa,* Indian semolina, is very typical in coastal western India. It results in a crisp, pale golden crust that is light and neutral in flavor, bringing out the best in the seafood. I substitute Cream of Wheat for the semolina. I butterfly the shrimp, which allows more surface area to be coated; it also ensures that the shrimp cook evenly. This isn't a brothy curry but one that is more saucelike.

3 cups Shrimp Stock (page 280)
I tablespoon minced peeled ginger
I tablespoon coriander seeds
I teaspoon cumin seeds
I small dried red chile (see Glossary), broken in half
I clove
¼ teaspoon Aleppo pepper or cayenne
¼ teaspoon ground turmeric

6 pieces kokum (labeled "wet kokum"), cut into julienne strips (I tablespoon)
30 extra-large shrimp (16 to 20 count), peeled, tails left intact, and deveined
Sea salt
I cup Cream of Wheat
½ cup canola oil
2 tablespoons unsalted butter

Simmer the stock in a heavy 3- to 4-quart pan until reduced to 1½ cups, about 6 minutes. Add the ginger and reduce by about ½ cup more, or until it measures 1 scant cup, about 6 minutes longer. (It should be thick enough to coat the back of a spoon.)

Toast the coriander seeds in a dry small skillet over moderately low heat, stirring and shaking the pan occasionally, until fragrant and a couple of shades darker, about 3 minutes. Transfer the coriander seeds to a small tray or plate. Toast the cumin seeds the same way and turn them out on the tray. Toast the chile and clove together for 1 minute and turn out to cool. Coarsely grind all the toasted spices and chile together in an electric coffee/spice grinder.

Stir the ground spice mixture, Aleppo pepper, turmeric, and kokum into the reduced stock and simmer for 2 minutes. Keep the sauce warm on the stove.

Butterfly the shrimp by turning your knife parallel to the deveined side of each shrimp and cutting inward, from the top side to the bottom side of the shrimp and parallel to the work surface. Don't cut through the shrimp entirely; stop just before you reach the other side and then flatten the shrimp out gently. After butterflying the shrimp, sprinkle both sides with salt and let sit 3 to 5 minutes.

Preheat the oven to 225°F. Put the Cream of Wheat in a bowl and dredge the shrimp in it, brushing off the excess.

Heat 2 tablespoons of the oil in a 12-inch skillet over moderately high heat until it shimmers and add about a quarter of the shrimp, butterflied side down. Cook the shrimp for 1 minute, or until light golden on the bottom, and flip them over. Swirl 1½ teaspoons butter into the skillet and cook the shrimp for 1 minute longer. Drain the shrimp on paper towels (or brown paper) and keep them warm on a baking sheet with sides in the middle of the oven.

Cook the remaining shrimp in 3 more batches in the same way, wiping out the skillet with a paper towel between batches and adding 2 tablespoons oil to the skillet for each batch. Transfer each batch when done to the baking sheet in the oven.

Heat the sauce until hot and serve the shrimp with the sauce spooned around it.

panfried shrimp with roasted coconut curry

SERVES 6

Here I panfry shrimp quickly and embellish them with a Maharashtran-style curry, the sort that I grew up eating in Bombay. I like to use heads-on shrimp if I can find them: the heads are full of flavor, and you can easily remove them before serving if you like. (The sauce is also delicious made with eggplant and a handful of toasted dried baby shrimp.) Serve over Plain Basmati Rice (page 258) or other cooked white rice.

FOR THE ROASTED COCONUT CURRY

I cup grated fresh coconut (see page 283), thawed frozen coconut, or unsweetened desiccated coconut

1½ teaspoons cumin seeds

1½ teaspoons coriander seeds

⅛ teaspoon Szechwan peppercorns

4 mild to moderately hot fresh green chiles, roasted, peeled, and seeded (see page 9)

2 tablespoons canola oil

I tablespoon finely chopped shallot

1½ teaspoons finely chopped garlic

I tablespoon finely chopped peeled ginger

2 tablespoons Tamarind Paste (page 284)

2 cups Shrimp Stock (page 280) or Lobster Stock (page 279)

I teaspoon sugar

Sea salt

FOR THE PANFRIED SHRIMP

30 extra-large shrimp (16 to 20 count), peeled, and deveined, heads left on if desired

Sea salt and freshly ground black pepper

I cup canola oil

Toast the coconut in a dry 10-inch skillet over low heat, stirring and shaking the skillet frequently, until golden brown, 10 to 12 minutes. Spread the toasted coconut out on a tray or large plate to cool.

Toast the cumin seeds in the dry skillet over moderately low heat, shaking the skillet, until fragrant and a couple of shades darker, about 3 minutes. Transfer the seeds to a small bowl or plate to cool. Toast the coriander seeds the same way and add them to the cumin seeds. Finely grind the cooled seeds together with the (untoasted) Szechwan peppercorns in an electric coffee/spice grinder.

Put the peeled chiles, toasted coconut, and 1 cup water in a blender and puree until smooth.

Heat the oil in a 3- to 4-quart pan over moderate heat until it shimmers and add the shallot, garlic, and ginger. Cook, stirring, until light golden, 3 to 4 minutes. Add the coconut-chile puree and ground spices and simmer until thickened, 3 to 4 minutes. Add the tamarind paste, stock, sugar, and salt to taste and cook, stirring occasionally, until thickened a bit more, about 5 minutes.

Preheat the oven to 225°F. Season the shrimp with salt and pepper and let sit for 5 minutes.

Heat ⅓ cup of the oil in a heavy 12-inch skillet over moderately high heat until the oil just begins to shimmer. Carefully put a third of the shrimp in the skillet and panfry them until crisp, about 2 minutes on each side. Drain the shrimp on paper towels or brown paper and keep them warm on a baking sheet with sides in the middle of the oven. Panfry the remaining shrimp in 2 more batches in ⅓ cup oil each time and drain them. Transfer each batch when done to the baking sheet in the oven. Serve the shrimp with the curry spooned over them.

shrimp gumbo

This isn't a gumbo in the strict sense of the word—in other words, if you're looking for okra and the Cajun holy trinity of onion, green bell pepper, and celery, you'll be disappointed. My gumbo is more of a sauce, one that's enriched by a roux, the classic French flour paste used to thicken most Louisiana gumbos. I make mine with chickpea flour instead of white flour. This roux imparts an earthy, roasty-toasty essence to the dish. And you'll also taste the Indian holy trinity of shallots, garlic, and ginger. Mushrooms are included for additional body. If you'd prefer this gumbo with crab, see the Note at the end of the recipe. And remember to freeze the shrimp shells to make Shrimp Stock (page 280) for other recipes. Serve this over Plain Basmati Rice (page 258) or other cooked rice.

FOR THE ROUX
8 tablespoons (1 stick) unsalted butter
1 cup chickpea flour (*besan*)

FOR THE GUMBO
¼ teaspoon fenugreek seeds
½ teaspoon black peppercorns
1 tablespoon coriander seeds
½ teaspoon cumin seeds
1 tablespoon mustard oil
¼ cup plus 3 tablespoons canola oil
1 teaspoon brown mustard seeds
½ cup sliced shallot
¼ cup sliced garlic
¼ cup sliced peeled ginger
1 pound white mushrooms, roughly
    chopped

½ cup dry white wine
1 quart Chicken Stock (page 274) or
    reduced-sodium canned chicken
    broth
½ teaspoon cayenne
Two 5-inch rosemary sprigs
Two 5-inch thyme sprigs
Two 5-inch tarragon sprigs
5 teaspoons Tamarind Paste
    (page 284)
Pinch of sugar
Sea salt and freshly ground black
    pepper
30 extra-large shrimp (16 to 20
    count), peeled, tail and last shell
    segment left intact, and deveined

SHELLFISH AND OTHER SEAFOOD 101

Melt the butter in a heavy 2-quart pan over moderately low heat and add the flour. Cook the roux, stirring constantly and shaking the pan, for 12 to 14 minutes, or until it turns smooth and a glossy chestnut brown. (The roux will first tighten up and look too dry, but then become loose again. It will also be very hot, so be careful.) Transfer the roux to a bowl and let cool.

Coarsely grind the fenugreek seeds in an electric coffee/spice grinder. Leaving the fenugreek in the grinder, add the peppercorns and grind coarse. Repeat with the coriander seeds and then the cumin seeds.

Heat the mustard oil in a wide, relatively shallow 6- to 8-quart pan over moderately high heat until smoking, about 1 minute, then remove the pan from the heat. (Mustard oil is very pungent, so don't breathe it in when it's smoking.) Add 1 tablespoon of the canola oil, return the pan to moderately high heat, and heat the oil until it shimmers. Add the mustard seeds, and as soon as they pop and are fragrant, after about 30 seconds, reduce the heat to moderate and add the shallot, garlic, ginger, and the ground spices. Cook, stirring, for 3 minutes, then stir in the mushrooms, white wine, roux, and stock. Whisk in the cayenne and add the rosemary, thyme, and tarragon. Simmer the mixture for 5 minutes and stir in the tamarind paste. Reduce the mixture until it measures about 1 quart, about 20 minutes, and season with the sugar, and salt and pepper to taste.

Strain the sauce through a sieve set over a bowl, pressing on the solids with the back of a ladle. Discard the solids and keep the sauce warm on the stove.

Preheat the oven to 225°F and sprinkle the shrimp with salt and pepper.

Heat 2 tablespoons of the remaining oil in a 12-inch skillet over high heat until it shimmers and add about a third of the shrimp. Sear the shrimp, turning after 30 seconds and shaking the skillet occasionally until the shrimp are lightly browned (the caramelization adds wonderful flavor), about 1 minute. Transfer the shrimp to a baking sheet with sides. Wipe out the skillet with a paper towel. Cook the remaining shrimp in 2 more batches in the same way, wiping out the skillet with a paper towel between batches and adding 2 tablespoons oil to the skillet. Transfer each batch of shrimp as cooked to the baking sheet. Roast all the shrimp in the middle of the oven for 2 minutes.

Put the shrimp on a large platter and spoon the sauce over it to serve.

bay scallops
rasam

Scallops aren't available in India, so it wasn't until I traveled in Europe that I discovered how wonderful they are. In this dish I use small, sweet bay scallops. If you see scallops from Nantucket Bay, splurge on them—they are especially delicate. Here, the scallops, gentle briny sweetness plays off the acidity and earthy elegance of the rasam, or spicy broth. Two unusual ingredients you'll see below are *toor dal* (hulled split yellow lentils) and *chana dal* (hulled split yellow Indian chickpeas). They're roasted here for flavor, as they are all over southern India. And one technique that you might not be familiar with is the tarka, which is simply popping spices in hot oil to intensify their flavors before swirling them into a dish.

FOR THE RASAM

1¼ cups dried shiitake mushrooms (1¾ ounces)

½ cup plus 1 tablespoon *toor dal* (hulled split yellow lentils), picked over and washed

5 unpeeled garlic cloves, cut in half crosswise

2 tablespoons canola oil

1 cup chopped red onion

1 cup chopped carrot

1 cup chopped celery

7 or 8 fresh shiitake mushrooms (2½ ounces), stems removed and reserved

Sea salt

1 tablespoon *chana dal* (hulled split yellow Indian chickpeas), picked over and washed

1 tablespoon coriander seeds

½ teaspoon cumin seeds

1 small dried red chile (see Glossary)

1½ teaspoons black peppercorns

16 fresh curry leaves

¼ teaspoon ground turmeric

¼ cup julienne strips peeled ginger

2 tablespoons Tamarind Paste (page 284)

Sugar

FOR THE TARKA

2 tablespoons canola oil

1 teaspoon brown mustard seeds

Pinch of asafetida

12 fresh curry leaves

Sea salt

FOR THE SCALLOPS
2 pounds bay scallops
Sea salt and freshly ground black
    pepper

½ cup canola oil
2 tablespoons unsalted butter
1½ teaspoons chopped cilantro
A squeeze of lemon

Put the dried shiitake mushrooms in a small bowl and soak them in enough lukewarm water to cover by a couple of inches for 15 minutes. Put ½ cup of the *toor dal* in a small bowl and soak in enough water to cover by a couple of inches for 15 minutes.

Toast the unpeeled garlic in a 4-quart saucepan over low heat, stirring, until the garlic begins to color, about 10 minutes. Add the oil, onion, carrot, celery, and fresh shiitake mushrooms and their stems. Add 2 quarts water, the soaked mushrooms and their soaking water, and a pinch of salt. Drain the *toor dal* and add the *dal* to the mixture. Bring to a boil over moderately high heat, then reduce the heat and simmer for 20 minutes.

Toast the *chana dal* and the remaining tablespoon *toor dal* in a dry small skillet over low heat, stirring constantly and shaking the skillet so that the *dals* don't burn, until lightly colored, about 8 minutes. Transfer the *dals* to a plate to cool and discard any that are over-toasted.

Toast the coriander seeds in the skillet over moderately low heat, shaking the skillet, until fragrant and a couple of shades darker, about 3 minutes. Transfer the seeds to the plate of *dals* to cool. Then toast the cumin seeds with the chile in the same way and transfer to the plate to cool. Toast the peppercorns in the same way and add them to the cooled spices. Toast the curry leaves for 1½ minutes and add the turmeric to the skillet, stirring to blend it with the curry leaves and toasting it for 30 seconds. (Don't worry—it will smoke a little.) Transfer the curry leaves and turmeric to the plate of spices. When all the spices are cool, finely grind them all together in an electric coffee/spice grinder. Transfer them to a small bowl.

Strain the mushroom mixture through a sieve into a large bowl. (You should have about 6 cups liquid.) Pick through the solids in the sieve and pull out the mushroom caps of both the fresh and dried mushrooms. Discard the rest of the solids and, when the mushroom caps are cool, cut them into thin slices.

Return the strained liquid to the 4-quart pan and add the ginger and the ground spices. Bring the rasam to a boil and add the tamarind paste, generous pinches of salt and sugar, and the sliced mushrooms. *The rasam can be made 1 day ahead and cooled, uncovered, before being refrigerated, covered.*

Heat the oil in a small skillet over moderate heat until it shimmers and add the mustard seeds. Cook the mustard seeds, shaking the skillet, until they start to pop, about

30 seconds. Add the asafetida and curry leaves and cook for about 30 seconds more, shaking the skillet. Immediately swirl the tarka into the rasam and return to a boil. Season with salt.

Season the scallops with salt and pepper to taste and let sit for 5 minutes.

Heat ¼ cup of the oil and 1 tablespoon of the butter in a 12-inch skillet over high heat until the butter starts turning brown and the oil is almost beginning to smoke. Add half of the scallops and cook, stirring and turning the scallops, for 3 minutes. Transfer the scallops to a platter. Wipe out the skillet with a paper towel. Cook the remaining scallops in the remaining oil and butter in the same way. Transfer to the platter when done.

Scatter the scallops with cilantro, spoon the rasam over them, and anoint with a squeeze of lemon.

seared sea scallops with lime jaggery glaze

Most Indians eat their seafood with a squirt of lime juice. Here the sweetness of meaty sea scallops is tempered by a satiny glaze made acidic by lime and mellowed by the Indian unrefined sugar called *jaggery*. Any unrefined sugar or even dark brown sugar can be substituted. The caramel-like quality of the sugar plays off the caramelization that occurs when the scallops are seared. This dish is delicious with braising greens—kale or mustard greens, for example—and cauliflower tossed with a little oil and roasted. And one last thing: I blanch the garlic three times to give it the mellowness it needs here.

FOR THE GLAZE
¼ cup thinly sliced garlic cloves
¾ cup fresh lime juice (from about 4 limes)
⅓ cup jaggery or dark brown sugar
Zest of 2 limes (about 2 teaspoons)
1 tablespoon finely chopped peeled ginger
1½ teaspoons coriander seeds
1½ teaspoons black peppercorns

8 Szechwan peppercorns
¼ teaspoon ajwain seeds

FOR THE SCALLOPS
2½ pounds sea scallops (about 30)
Sea salt and freshly ground black pepper
½ cup canola oil
3 tablespoons unsalted butter
Four 3-inch thyme sprigs

Half-fill your 3 smallest pots with water and bring to a boil all at the same time. Blanch the garlic in one pot of water for 15 seconds and strain in a sieve. Put the garlic in the second pot of water and blanch for another 15 seconds. Repeat the blanching process for the third time in the last pot of water. Rinse the garlic under cold running water and set aside. (I like to blanch sliced garlic like this; if you use just one pot and 3 changes of water, the garlic will turn mushy between blanchings.)

Put the lime juice in a 3- to 4-quart saucepan and add the jaggery and ½ cup water. Heat the mixture over low heat, breaking up the jaggery with a wooden spoon or spatula. When the jaggery is completely melted, add the lime zest, ginger, and blanched garlic, then reduce the liquid to a thick, syrupy glaze, about 8 minutes.

Toast the coriander seeds in a dry small skillet over moderately low heat, shaking the skillet, until fragrant and a couple of shades darker, about 3 minutes. Transfer them to a small tray or plate to cool. Toast the black peppercorns in the same way and transfer them to the tray with the coriander seeds to cool.

Toast the Szechwan peppercorns in the same way for about 1½ minutes. Add the ajwain seeds and toast for about 1½ minutes longer, stirring and shaking the skillet. Transfer the Szechwan peppercorns and ajwain seeds to the tray of toasted spices and let them cool. Finely grind all the spices together in an electric coffee/spice grinder and stir into the reduced glaze. Remove the glaze from the heat.

Preheat the oven to 350°F. Remove the little ligament from the side of each scallop if it hasn't already been removed. Season the scallops with salt and pepper and let sit for 5 minutes.

Heat ¼ cup of the oil in a 12-inch skillet over high heat until it shimmers. Sear half the scallops for 2 minutes. Turn the scallops over and add 1½ tablespoons of the butter and 2 of the thyme sprigs. When the butter melts, tilt the skillet and use a spoon to baste the scallops with the fat in the pan. Transfer the scallops to a baking sheet with sides. Sear the remaining scallops in the same way, using the remaining oil, butter, and thyme. Transfer them to the baking sheet and roast all the scallops in the middle of the oven for 3 minutes. (Be careful not to overcook them; they'll lose their delicate taste.) Serve the scallops topped with the glaze.

scallops with silk squash, eggplant, and dried shrimp

I love the textures at play in this dish. The scallops are meaty and tender, toasted dried baby shrimp add a roasty crunch, and then there are the vegetables—unctuous eggplant and ultra smooth silk squash. The squash, by the way, is thought to have originated in India but is grown and enjoyed all over Asia; it's often sold under the name *Chinese okra* or *angled loofah* in Chinese markets. It's mild in flavor, like a summer squash, but the key to its appeal is its texture—when slices are cooked, the insides turn satiny while the edges stay slightly crisp. It's addictive. You can substitute zucchini for the silk squash; the texture will be different but still delicious.

½ cup dried baby shrimp

1½ tablespoons coriander seeds

2 small dried red chiles (see Glossary), broken in half

¾ cup canola oil

2 tablespoons finely chopped shallot

1½ teaspoons finely chopped garlic

½ teaspoon Aleppo pepper or cayenne

2½ cups Shrimp Stock (page 280), Chicken Stock (page 274), or reduced-sodium canned chicken broth

1½ tablespoons Tamarind Paste (page 284)

Sea salt

½ pound silk squash, peeled, cut in half lengthwise, and then cut into 1½-inch pieces

3 small Japanese or young Italian eggplants, cut in half lengthwise, and sliced crosswise into 1¼-inch pieces (about 4 cups)

1½ cups coconut milk, stirred well

2 tablespoons coconut vinegar or malt vinegar

Freshly ground black pepper

2½ pounds sea scallops (about 30)

3 tablespoons unsalted butter

Toast the dried shrimp in a dry small skillet over moderately high heat until fragrant with a white, almost ashy-looking coating, about 3 minutes. Transfer them to a plate to cool.

Finely grind the coriander seeds and chiles together in an electric coffee/spice grinder.

Heat ¼ cup of the oil in a 4- to 6-quart saucepan over moderately high heat until it shimmers and add the shallot, garlic, ground spices, toasted shrimp, and Aleppo pepper and cook, stirring, for 30 seconds. Stir in the stock, tamarind paste, and a pinch of salt. Bring the mixture to a boil and simmer for 5 minutes. Stir in the silk squash, eggplant, coconut milk, and vinegar and simmer until the vegetables are tender, 8 to 10 minutes. Season with salt and pepper.

Preheat the oven to 350°F. Remove the tough little ligament from the side of each scallop if it hasn't already been removed. Season the scallops with salt and pepper to taste and let sit for 5 minutes.

Heat ¼ cup of the remaining oil in a 12-inch skillet over moderately high heat until it shimmers. Sear half the scallops for 2 minutes. Turn the scallops over and add 1½ tablespoons of the butter. When the butter melts, tilt the skillet and use a spoon to baste the scallops with the fat in the pan. Transfer them to a baking sheet with sides. Sear the remaining scallops in the same way, using the remaining oil and butter. Transfer them to the baking sheet and roast all the scallops in the middle of the oven for 3 minutes. Serve the scallops on a bed of the vegetables and their sauce.

sautéed soft-shell crabs

Soft-shell crabs were new to me when I came to America. They've since become one of my favorite things about spring. Before sautéing them, I coat them with *rawa*, or Cream of Wheat (in India, I would use Indian semolina), seasoned with freshly ground black pepper. It gives a little crunch but is neutral enough to let the delicate taste of the crab shine through. Put the soft-shells between slices of brioche or any good country bread, drizzle with the sauce, and you have the makings for a killer sandwich. I once sold them that way from a street cart outside the restaurant and found I couldn't keep up with demand.

FOR THE SAUCE

1 cup grated fresh coconut (see page 283), thawed frozen coconut, or unsweetened desiccated coconut

2 small dried red chiles (see Glossary), broken in half

1-inch piece cinnamon stick

2 cloves

2 tablespoons coriander seeds

1 tablespoon cumin seeds

4 garlic cloves

2 teaspoons roughly chopped peeled ginger

3 tablespoons Tamarind Paste (page 284)

1 cup Roasted Fish Stock (page 277)

Heaping ½ teaspoon salt

FOR THE CRABS

2 teaspoons black peppercorns

1 cup quick-cooking Cream of Wheat

1 large egg

2 tablespoons all-purpose flour

⅛ teaspoon sea salt

⅛ teaspoon freshly ground black pepper

12 live soft-shell crabs, cleaned (see page 112)

¾ cup canola oil

3 tablespoons unsalted butter

Toast the coconut in a dry 10-inch skillet over low heat, stirring and shaking the skillet frequently, until golden brown, 10 to 12 minutes. Spread the toasted coconut out on a tray or large plate to cool.

Toast the chiles, including the seeds, cinnamon, and cloves in another dry small skillet over moderately low heat until the chiles are lightly colored, about 3 minutes. Transfer to a small tray or plate to cool. Toast the coriander seeds in the same skillet over moderately low heat until fragrant and a couple of shades darker, about 3 minutes. Turn out on the tray to cool. Toast the cumin seeds the same way and turn out to cool. Finely grind all the spices in an electric coffee/spice grinder.

Puree the coconut, garlic, ginger, tamarind paste, and ½ cup water in a blender until smooth (add more water if necessary to keep the blades moving). Transfer the puree to a 1-quart saucepan and cook over low heat, stirring, until very thick and dry, about 20 minutes. Stir in the ground spices and stock and simmer for 6 minutes to develop the flavors. Season with the salt and keep warm.

Grind the peppercorns until medium-fine in an electric coffee/spice grinder and stir them together with the Cream of Wheat in a bowl to make a seasoned *rawa*.

Beat together the egg, flour, salt, and pepper with a fork in a small bowl to make an egg wash.

Brush the top shell of the crabs with the egg wash and drop them, coated side down, into the *rawa*.

Heat ¼ cup of the oil in a 12-inch skillet over moderately high heat until it shimmers and sauté 4 crabs, coated sides down, for 2 minutes. Add 1 tablespoon of the butter and turn the crabs over. Sauté the crabs for 2 minutes longer, or until golden, and drain them on paper towels or brown paper. Transfer the crabs to a platter and keep them warm, loosely covered with foil. Sauté the remaining crabs in 2 more batches in the same way, using the remaining oil and butter, and transferring each batch to the platter when done. Serve the crabs with the sauce.

to clean soft-shell crabs

This is a really unpleasant job, but if you are going to cook soft-shell crabs, you have to start with live ones. Their quality deteriorates rapidly once they are dead. You can ask your fishmonger to clean them for you, but cook them as soon as you get home.

Quickly cut off the eyes and mouth with kitchen shears. (When you do this, you are also cutting off the crab's primitive central nervous system.)

Pressing out the sand sac (stomach) and pale-green mustard (hepatopancreas) is optional. The sand sac is occasionally gritty, and the mustard can be bitter, although many people love it.

Lift up the points on each side of the crab and cut away the spongy gills.

Turn the crab over. Lift up the apron (abdomen) and cut it off.

Goan Spiced Crab Cakes (page 12) with Avocado Salad (page 18)

Roasted Beet Salad (page 25)

*Sprouted Bean Salad with
Spicy Yogurt Dressing (page 27)*

Chilled Cucumber Soup with Mint and Basil (page 36)

Pan-Roasted Salmon in Banana Leaves
with Mustard Greens (page 59)

Spiced Shellfish Nage (page 54)

*Taro-Crusted Red Snapper
with White Beans and
Mustard Greens (page 66)*

*Steamed Black Sea Bass with
Kokum Broth (page 82)*

Poached Wild Striped Bass with Ginger Broth (page 78)

Panfried Black Pepper Shrimp (page 96)

Seared Sea Scallops with Lime Jaggery Glaze (page 106)

Sautéed Soft-Shell Crabs (page 110) with Braised Silk Squash and Long Squash (page 225)

Ingredients for Lobster Coconut Curry with Eggplant and Cabbage (page 115)

Crab-Stuffed Calamari with Spicy Sauce (page 121)

Panfried Quail with Lentil Salad
(page 142)

Poached Chicken with Salsa Verde
(page 130)

Coriander-and-Mustard-Crusted Strip Loin (page 149)

Roast Lamb with Mint—Black Pepper Sauce (page 161)

Barbecued Brisket (page 155) with Kashmiri Greens (page 213)

Braised Veal Roulade (page 177)

Sweetbread Chile Fry (page 184)

Stuffed Pork Chops with Mustard Shrimp Sauce (page 174)

Fricassee of Summer Beans
(page 198)

Sautéed Asparagus
and Morels (page 196)

Ramps with Spinach and Bacon (page 220), Turmeric Mashed Potatoes (page 218)

Braised Romaine (page 223)

Clockwise from top: Dried-Fruit Chutney (page 233), Warm Tomato Chutney (page 240), Mint Coriander Chutney (page 234), Mango Chutney (page 237), Tamarind Chutney (page 238), Cucumber Raita with Tiny Chickpea Puffs (page 247)

Clockwise from top: Tapioca Pilaf (page 263), Basmati Pilaf, (page 259), Cracked Wheat Pilaf (page 265)

panfried soft-shell crabs with cucumber salad and green mango vinaigrette

SERVES 6

Crab curry was a staple in our house when I was a child. Green (immature) mangoes are sour, crisp, and on the starchy side; they're treated as a vegetable, not a fruit. I roast the fruit until it is soft and has a deep tang that plays off the sweetness of the crab. I'm having fun with texture, too: I puree the roasted mango into a creamy vinaigrette (maple syrup gives it a rich, sweet undertone) that contrasts with crunchy, succulent cucumber salad and crunchy, succulent soft-shell crabs. (It all makes a great filling for hamburger buns.) I use instant flour to coat the crabs; this low-protein flour, most often used for thickening gravies and sauces, provides a neutral coating that lets the flavor of seafood shine through. It can be found at any grocery store.

FOR THE VINAIGRETTE

1 green mango (about 1 pound)
¼ cup canola oil plus oil for the mango
½ teaspoon brown mustard seeds
1 tablespoon chopped peeled ginger
1 tablespoon sliced mild to moderately hot fresh green chile
Sea salt and freshly ground black pepper
¼ teaspoon chaat masala
2 tablespoons pure maple syrup

FOR THE CUCUMBER SALAD

1 seedless cucumber, quartered lengthwise and thinly sliced (about 3 cups)
1 cup halved and thinly sliced red onion
1 cup (about 14 small) quartered radishes
1 tablespoon chopped peeled ginger
1 tablespoon chopped mild to moderately hot fresh green chile
2 tablespoons chopped cilantro
Sea salt and freshly ground black pepper
¼ teaspoon chaat masala

FOR THE CRABS

2 tablespoons all-purpose flour

2 large eggs

¼ teaspoon salt

¼ teaspoon freshly ground black
 pepper

1½ cups instant flour, such as
 Wondra

½ cup canola oil

12 live soft-shell crabs, cleaned (see
 page 112)

Preheat the oven to 450°F.

Rub the green mango with a little canola oil and roast in the middle of the oven for about 40 minutes, or until soft. When the mango is cool enough to handle, cut it in half lengthwise and scoop the flesh out into the bowl of a food processor. Discard the pit. Lightly crush the mustard seeds in a mortar or with a rolling pin. Add the mustard seeds to the mango flesh, along with the ginger and chile. Puree the mixture until very smooth. Add salt and pepper to taste, the chaat masala, maple syrup, and remaining ¼ cup oil and puree until blended well.

Put the cucumber, onion, and radishes in a large bowl. Add the ginger, chile, cilantro, salt and pepper to taste, and chaat masala. Stir together well.

Stir ½ cup of the vinaigrette into the salad.

Reduce the oven temperature to 225°F. Mix together the all-purpose flour, eggs, salt, and pepper in a wide shallow bowl or pie plate. Put the instant flour in another wide shallow bowl or pie plate. Brush the crabs all over with the egg mixture and dredge in the instant flour.

Heat ¼ cup of the oil in a 12-inch skillet over moderately high heat until it shimmers. Cook 6 of the coated crabs on both sides until golden brown, about 4 minutes total. Transfer the crabs to paper towels or brown paper to drain. Put them on a baking sheet with sides and keep them warm in the middle of the oven. Wipe out the skillet and cook the remaining crabs in the remaining oil in the same way. Serve the crabs with the salad and the remaining vinaigrette spooned around the crabs.

lobster coconut curry with eggplant and cabbage

SERVES 6

I grew up eating brothy curries like this; the aroma of coconut being toasted for them perfumed my childhood. Lobsters do double duty in this recipe: after removing the tail and claw meat, I use the carcasses for stock; then I gently poach the tail and claw meat in this curry. I cook the eggplant in the curry but blanch the cabbage first; the cabbage has a high water content and I don't want it to dilute the sauce. The eggplant, on the other hand, just absorbs all of the flavors.

FOR THE CURRY

1 cup grated fresh coconut (see page 283) or unsweetened desiccated coconut

1½ tablespoons coriander seeds

½ teaspoon ground turmeric

¼ teaspoon Aleppo pepper or cayenne

3 mild to moderately hot fresh green chiles, roasted, peeled, and seeded (see page 9)

¼ cup Tamarind Paste (page 284)

6 cups Lobster Stock (page 279)

3 tablespoons canola oil

⅓ cup thinly sliced shallot

⅓ cup thinly sliced garlic cloves

Scant ¼ cup thinly sliced peeled ginger

¼ teaspoon Szechwan peppercorns, tied in a cheesecloth bundle

FOR FINISHING THE DISH

Blanched tails and claws from six 1-pound lobsters (see page 117)

One 13- to 14-ounce can coconut milk (1¾ cups), stirred well

Sea salt

One 6-ounce Japanese eggplant

1 pound cabbage (preferably Savoy), tough center ribs discarded and leaves cut into 1-inch squares (about 6 cups)

Four 2-inch cilantro stems with roots

2 tablespoons cilantro chiffonade (see page 8), for garnish

Toast the coconut in a dry 10-inch skillet over moderately low heat, stirring and shaking the skillet frequently, for about 8 minutes, or until golden brown. (Or toast it in a pan in the middle of a preheated 350°F oven for 15 to 20 minutes.) Spread the toasted coconut out on a tray or plate to cool.

Finely grind the coriander seeds in an electric coffee/spice grinder. Add the turmeric and Aleppo pepper to the ground coriander. Stir 2 tablespoons water into the ground spices to form a paste.

Puree the coconut, chiles, tamarind paste, and 1 cup of the stock in a blender until smooth.

Heat the oil in a 6- to 8-quart pot over moderate heat until it shimmers. Add the shallot, garlic, and ginger and cook, stirring occasionally, for 3 minutes, or until very lightly colored. Stir in the ground spice paste. Reduce the heat to low and stir in the coconut puree. Cook, stirring, for 5 minutes.

Toss the Szechwan peppercorn bundle into the pot and add the remaining lobster stock. Bring the curry to a simmer and simmer for 10 minutes.

Working with 1 lobster tail at a time, put a kitchen towel over it and press down firmly on the back of the tail to crack the shell. Snip open the underside of the tail with kitchen shears. Remove the shell, leaving the last (fringy) tail segment attached to the meat. Snip a U shape into that last segment with the shears and pull out the intestine. Discard the intestine. Wrap each claw in the kitchen towel and crack with the flat side of a chef's knife. Pull out the claw meat so that it remains intact. (Needlenose pliers will help you break the shells away from the meat.)

Stir the coconut milk into the curry and simmer for about 15 minutes. While the curry is simmering, season the lobster meat with salt and let sit 3 to 5 minutes.

Cut the eggplant into ¼-inch slices and add to the curry.

Blanch the cabbage in a large pot of salted boiling water for about 2 minutes, or until barely tender. Drain the cabbage and transfer to a bowl of ice water to stop the cooking. Squeeze the excess water out of the cabbage and add to the curry along with the cilantro stems with roots. Season the curry with salt to taste and add the lobster. Reduce the heat to low and gently poach the lobster meat in the curry until the meat is just cooked through, about 5 minutes. Discard the Szechwan peppercorn bundle. Serve the curry in soup plates or shallow bowls, garnished with the cilantro.

how to blanch lobsters

This method is for 1-pound lobsters. (You can blanch two at a time.) Use the tail and claw meat for the Lobster Coconut Curry with Eggplant and Cabbage or cook the lobsters a little longer and use the meat for your favorite lobster salad or lobster rolls. The carcasses make a wonderful stock (page 279) that you can use in the curry or for seafood sauces and soups.

Bring a large kettle of water to a boil. Have a large bowl of ice water ready. Put 2 live lobsters headfirst into the boiling water and blanch for 1 minute. Transfer the lobsters with tongs to the ice water.

Return the water to a boil and blanch any remaining lobsters, 2 at a time, transferring them to the ice water as blanched. (Make sure you return the water to a boil for subsequent batches if necessary.) Leave the lobsters in the ice water until cold.

Return the water in the kettle to a boil. Remove the claws from the lobsters and boil the large claws for 1 minute. Add the smaller claws to the water and boil all of the claws for 1 minute longer. Transfer the claws to the ice water and, when cold, set them aside.

Remove the tails and set them aside with the claws. Lobster tail and claw meat may be blanched 1 day ahead and kept in resealable plastic bags in the refrigerator.

lobster pan roast
with coconut sauce

Lobster is just as prized in India as it is elsewhere in the world. The common variety there is the spiny lobster, which, unlike American and European lobsters, has no claws. (Spiny lobster is found in the United States, too, along the southern Atlantic coast and in California, but is usually sold in local fish markets or as frozen lobster tails.) Coconut has a way of enriching and rounding out the briny tang of lobster, and here I use it lavishly. It's an everyday ingredient in southern India—my grandmother had a large shed behind her house that was filled top to bottom with a year's supply of coconuts, both fresh for eating and dried shells for fuel. The technique I use for making the stock can be adapted for shrimp or crab; it makes a great base for a seafood soup.

FOR THE LOBSTER STOCK

Six 1-pound live lobsters, blanched
  (see page 117) and carcasses
  reserved
2 tablespoons canola oil
3 celery stalks, roughly chopped
1 large carrot, roughly chopped
½ large white onion, roughly
  chopped
6 unpeeled garlic cloves, smashed
¼ cup dry white wine
¼ cup brandy
1 teaspoon black peppercorns
1 bay leaf
2 cloves
3 cups Chicken Stock (page 274) or
  reduced-sodium canned chicken
  broth

FOR THE COCONUT SAUCE

1½ cups roughly chopped white
  onion
5 garlic cloves, peeled
1 cup shredded fresh coconut
  (see page 283) or frozen
  coconut
1 tablespoon coriander seeds
1½ teaspoons cumin seeds
1 dried New Mexico chile,
  broken into pieces and seeds
  discarded
1½ teaspoons paprika
¼ teaspoon ground turmeric
1 tablespoon canola oil
1 tablespoon Tamarind Paste
  (page 284)

6 tablespoons unsalted butter, cut into pieces and softened Sea salt and freshly ground black pepper to taste	3 heaping tablespoons finely chopped cilantro

SPECIAL EQUIPMENT: *12 wooden skewers*

Remove the carapaces from the lobster carcasses and discard the grain sac (often called the *stomach*, it is filled with grit). I also like to keep the green liverlike tomalley or any roe. Cut the bodies into small pieces with kitchen shears.

Heat the oil in a 6- to 8-quart pot over moderately high heat until it shimmers and cook the celery, carrot, onion, and garlic, stirring, until the vegetables are softened, 4 to 5 minutes. Add the cut-up lobster bodies and cook for 5 minutes longer. Add the wine, brandy, peppercorns, bay leaf, cloves, stock, and 2 cups water and simmer for 45 minutes. *The stock can be made 1 day ahead. Cool, uncovered, and refrigerate, covered. Put the lobster tails and claws in resealable plastic bags and refrigerate separately.*

Puree the onion, garlic, coconut, and 1 cup water in a blender until smooth.

Finely grind the coriander seeds, cumin seeds, and chile in an electric coffee/spice grinder and add to the coconut puree in the blender. Pulse the blender to incorporate the spices. Add the paprika and turmeric, pulsing to incorporate.

Heat the oil in a heavy 2-quart pan over moderately high heat until it shimmers and add the coconut-spice puree. Cook the puree until it is the consistency of thick paste and dry around the edges but not scorched, about 20 minutes.

Strain the lobster stock, pressing hard on the solids, and discard the solids. Reserve 2½ cups stock for the sauce and freeze the remaining stock for another use. Add the 2½ cups stock to the paste and simmer briskly, stirring occasionally, until reduced to about 3 cups, about 15 minutes. Stir in the tamarind paste.

Working with 1 lobster tail at a time, put a kitchen towel over it and press down firmly on the back of the tail to crack the shell. Snip open the underside of the tail with kitchen shears. Remove the shell, leaving the last (fringy) tail segment attached to the meat. Snip a U shape into that last segment with the shears and pull out the intestine. Discard the intestine and push 2 wooden skewers lengthwise through each lobster tail (about ½ inch apart) so they do not curl while roasting. Wrap each claw in the kitchen towel and crack with the flat side of a chef's knife. Pull out the claw meat so it remains intact. (Needlenose pliers will help you break the shells away from the meat.)

Rub the butter inside a 13 × 9-inch heatproof glass or enameled cast-iron baking dish and on the lobster tails and claw meat, then arrange the lobster in the baking dish. *The lobster can be made up to this point a few hours ahead and refrigerated, covered. Bring it to room temperature before cooking.*

Preheat the oven to 250°F and reheat the sauce. Season the lobster with salt and pepper and sprinkle with the cilantro. Cover the lobster with a piece of buttered parchment paper and cover the baking dish tightly to prevent moisture from escaping. Roast in the middle of the oven for 15 minutes, or until the lobster is just done. Remove the skewers. Serve the lobster with the sauce spooned around it.

crab-stuffed calamari
with spicy sauce

SERVES 6

When I was growing up, one of my favorite seafood curries, similar to this dish, was often made with cuttlefish. In the United States, squid—most often known by its Italian name, *calamari*—is more common than cuttlefish, its close relative. Calamari needs to be cooked either quickly or for a very long time—anything in between results in a tough texture. Here I stuff it with a chile-crab mixture and sear it before finishing it in the oven. The spicy sauce that I serve with the stuffed calamari is called *ambot tik*—*ambot* means "sour," and *tik* means "spicy" in Konkani, a language spoken primarily in Goa.

FOR THE SAUCE

1½ cups chopped white onion
4 dried New Mexico chiles, stems
    and seeds removed
¼ dried pasilla de Oaxaca chile
1 teaspoon sliced peeled ginger
1½ teaspoons cumin seeds
1 tablespoon canola oil
1 teaspoon brown mustard seeds
8 fresh curry leaves
2 tablespoons Tamarind Paste (page
    284)
¼ teaspoon sugar
Sea salt and freshly ground black
    pepper
5 pieces kokum (labeled "wet
    kokum")

FOR THE CALAMARI

12 cleaned squid with tentacles
¼ cup plus 3 tablespoons canola oil
1 teaspoon cumin seeds
3 cups quartered and thinly sliced
    red onion
2 tablespoons chopped peeled ginger
3 tablespoons thinly sliced kokum
    (labeled "wet kokum")
2 tablespoons thinly sliced mild to
    moderately hot fresh green chile
2 small dried red chiles (see
    Glossary), crumbled
Sea salt and freshly ground black
    pepper
3 tablespoons chopped chives
3 tablespoons chopped cilantro
½ pound lump crabmeat, picked
    over for shell pieces

Put the onion, chiles, ginger, and 1 quart water into a blender and puree, starting on low speed and increasing to high after about 3 minutes, until very smooth, about 5 minutes total.

Finely grind the cumin seeds in an electric coffee/spice grinder and stir into the puree.

Heat the oil in a 3- to 4-quart pan over moderately high heat until it shimmers and cook the mustard seeds, stirring, until they pop and are fragrant, about 30 seconds. Add the curry leaves, chile puree, 2 cups water, and the tamarind paste and boil vigorously over high heat for 5 minutes. Add the sugar and season with salt and pepper to taste. Briskly simmer the sauce for 45 minutes and stir in the kokum. Simmer for 15 minutes longer, stirring occasionally, and remove the sauce from the heat.

Chop the squid tentacles and set aside.

Heat 3 tablespoons of the oil in a 5- to 6-quart pan over moderately high heat until it shimmers. Add the cumin seeds and cook, stirring, until fragrant, about 1 minute. Add the onion, ginger, kokum, chiles, and salt to taste and cook, stirring, until the onion just begins to soften, about 3 minutes. Add the chopped squid tentacles and cook, stirring, for 2 minutes longer. Spread the mixture out on a tray or plate to cool and season with pepper.

Transfer the mixture to a medium bowl and stir in the chives and cilantro. Gently fold in the crabmeat and season with salt.

Stuff each squid body with about ¼ cup of the crab mixture, making sure to push the stuffing all the way down but not pack it too tightly. (The thin handle of a wooden spatula comes in handy.) Leave enough room at the top so that you can pin the squid closed with a toothpick or small wooden skewer.

Preheat the oven to 350°F. Pat the calamari dry.

Heat 2 tablespoons of the remaining oil in a 12-inch skillet over moderately high heat until it shimmers. Sear half of the calamari on one side for 1 minute and turn it over. Transfer the calamari to a baking sheet with sides. Cook the remaining calamari in the remaining oil in the same way, transferring it to the baking sheet. Roast all the calamari in the middle of the oven for 5 minutes. Arrange the stuffed calamari on a platter, remove the skewers, and spoon the sauce around it to serve.

clams with anise and pepper

I could eat clams almost every day. My sons could, too, and this simple preparation is for them. The sweet, slightly mysterious warmth of the spices plays up the seafood and the mild, peppery crunch of the fennel beautifully. These clams are delicious as is, in bowls with the broth. If you want to get fancy, serve them with the Fennel Gnocchi (page 270).

2 teaspoons anise seeds
½ teaspoon black peppercorns
¼ cup extra virgin olive oil
4 garlic cloves, sliced
½ cup chopped shallot
I small fennel bulb, quartered, cored, and very thinly sliced lengthwise (about 1½ cups), fronds chopped and reserved
I tablespoon julienne strips peeled ginger
I tablespoon thinly sliced fresh red chile

3 cups Chicken Stock (page 274) or reduced-sodium canned chicken broth
Sea salt
Three 3-inch cilantro stems with roots
I large tomato
2½ pounds littleneck or manila clams, scrubbed
8 pieces kokum (labeled "wet kokum"), cut into julienne strips
3 scallions, chopped

Coarsely grind the anise seeds and peppercorns together in an electric coffee/spice grinder.

Heat the olive oil in a 4-quart pot over moderately high heat until it shimmers. Reduce the heat to moderately low and add the garlic. Cook, stirring occasionally, until the garlic is softened and pale golden, about 2 minutes. Add the shallot, fennel bulb, and ginger and cook, stirring, for 2 minutes. Add the chile and ground spices and cook, stirring, for 2 minutes longer. Add the stock, salt to taste, and cilantro stems with roots. Simmer for 5 minutes to infuse the broth with the flavors. *The broth may be made up to this point 1 day ahead. Cool the broth, uncovered, and then refrigerate, covered.*

Bring a small pot of water to a boil. Score an X in the bottom of the tomato and blanch for 15 seconds, counting from the moment the tomato is slipped into the boiling water. Transfer the tomato to a bowl of ice water. Peel and dice the tomato when it is cold (you should have about 1½ cups).

Bring the anise-pepper broth to a simmer. Stir in the clams, tomato, and kokum and simmer, covered, for 3 to 5 minutes, or until the clams are opened. (Discard any unopened clams.)

Put the scallions and fennel fronds in a tureen or large bowl and arrange the clams in their shells on top. Ladle the broth over all and serve.

chicken and other birds

roast chicken
with fenugreek

Fenugreek is a commonly used spice in the kitchens of India, the Middle East, and western Asian countries like the Republic of Georgia. The seeds taste a little like celery seeds and are mildly astringent; when toasted, they develop a wonderful nutlike flavor and aroma. Take one whiff of the dried leaves and you'll understand why their Latin name, *Trigonella foenum-graecum*, translates as "Greek hay." This roast chicken is herbaceous without relying on the more usual suspects like rosemary and thyme. I make a wet paste that includes pureed fenugreek, dried pomegranate seeds (which come from the same part of the world), and fresh chiles; simply smear it under the skin. Try this and your Sunday night roast chicken may never be the same again.

1 teaspoon fenugreek seeds

1½ teaspoons black peppercorns

2 tablespoons dried pomegranate seeds

2 tablespoons dried fenugreek leaves

2 tablespoons thinly sliced peeled fresh ginger

2 tablespoons chopped garlic

1 mild to moderately hot fresh green chile

¼ cup fresh lime juice

3 tablespoons canola oil, plus oil for rubbing chickens

Kosher salt

Two 3-pound chickens, rinsed, drained, and patted dry

Toast the fenugreek seeds in a dry small heavy skillet over moderately low heat, shaking the skillet, until fragrant and a couple of shades darker, about 3 minutes. Transfer the seeds to a tray or small plate to cool. Toast the peppercorns the same way and add them to the fenugreek seeds. Finely grind the toasted spices, dried pomegranate seeds, and fenugreek leaves together in an electric coffee/spice grinder.

Puree the ginger, garlic, chile, lime juice, and 3 tablespoons oil in a mini food processor or blender until smooth. Add the ground spices and salt to taste and puree again briefly to blend.

Work your fingers underneath the skin of the chickens and loosen the skin from the meat of the chickens on both the body and the legs. (Be gentle; you don't want to tear the skin.) Generously smear half of the spice paste between the skin and meat of each bird. If you have any spice paste left over, smear it inside the cavities of the birds. Truss the chickens with kitchen string. (That way, if the skin breaks, the spice will stay on the birds.) *Marinate the chickens, covered, in the refrigerator for at least 1 and up to 12 hours. Let them sit at room temperature for about 20 minutes before roasting.*

Preheat the oven to 400°F. Rub the chickens with a little canola oil and put them on a rack inside a roasting pan.

Roast the chickens in the middle of the oven for 12 minutes. Reduce the heat to 375°F and roast for 1 hour longer, or until the juices run clear when the birds are pierced with a fork. Let the chickens stand for 10 minutes before cutting into serving pieces.

chicken
cafreal

In this Goan dish, chickens are rubbed with a garlicky cilantro paste and left to marinate for at least six hours. I add a little water to the pan before roasting the birds so that the paste makes its own sauce. (The marinated chickens are also wonderful on the grill; the only downside is that you won't have the sauce.) The end result is incredibly succulent and aromatic, delicious with the Fricassee of Summer Beans on page 198 and some rice or crusty bread to soak up the sauce. It makes a great filling for a wrap and gives chicken salad a fresh twist. Try this with Cornish hens as well.

Two 2½- to 3-pound chickens or 5 to 6 pounds chicken pieces, rinsed, drained, and patted dry

½ cup fresh lime juice

½ pound cilantro (including stems with roots), coarsely chopped

10 whole garlic cloves, peeled

¼ cup thinly sliced peeled ginger

1 mild to moderately hot fresh green chile, cut crosswise into pieces

1 tablespoon cumin seeds

1½ teaspoons black peppercorns

4 cloves

½ cinnamon stick

1 tablespoon kosher salt

Cut the backbones out of the chickens with a large heavy knife. (Freeze the backbones for making stock.) Crack the keel bone, in the center of each breast, so that the chickens lie flat. Lightly pierce the chickens all over with a kitchen fork.

Put the lime juice, cilantro, garlic, ginger, and chile in a blender or food processor and puree until smooth.

Finely grind the cumin seeds, peppercorns, cloves, and cinnamon in an electric coffee/ spice grinder.

Put the cilantro puree in a large bowl and stir in the ground spices and salt. Put each chicken in the bowl and rub all over with the marinade. Refrigerate any left-over marinade.

Put each chicken in a large resealable plastic bag and refrigerate. *Marinate the chickens in the refrigerator for at least 6 and up to 24 hours.*

Preheat the oven to 400°F. Put a tiny amount of water (about ⅛ inch) in a 13 × 9-inch roasting pan and fit the chickens into the pan. Lightly pat any remaining marinade on top of the birds.

Roast the chickens in the middle of the oven until done, about 1 hour and 15 minutes. Cut the chickens into serving pieces and serve the sauce from the pan juices on the side.

poached chicken
with salsa verde

I think chicken is a great opportunity to get creative. Take this dish, for instance. I came up with it several years ago during a long, hot summer in the city. I bought a chicken from Four Story Hill Farm at my local farmers' market and poached it, allowing it to be infused with great flavors. I use a few of my favorite ingredients here: ginger, chiles, cilantro, and lemony, peppery, pungent Thai basil. (You can substitute regular basil, of course.) The accompanying salsa verde is bright with fresh herbs, chiles, and lime. A small amount of mashed potato carries those flavors, stabilizes the olive oil, and gives the sauce body.

FOR THE POACHING BROTH
1 tablespoon black peppercorns
2 tablespoons coriander seeds
2 tablespoons fennel seeds
3 quarts Chicken Stock (page 274) or reduced-sodium canned chicken broth
3 cups roughly chopped white onion
1 cup roughly chopped celery (about 2 stalks)
1½ cups roughly chopped peeled carrots (about 2)
1 leek, white and light green parts only, cut in half lengthwise and washed thoroughly
5 unpeeled garlic cloves, smashed with the flat side of a large knife
One 4-inch-long piece ginger, peeled
1 mild to moderately hot fresh red or green chile, sliced in half lengthwise
1 teaspoon ground turmeric
2 bay leaves

FOR THE CHICKEN
Two 3-pound chickens, rinsed and drained
2 tablespoons kosher salt

FOR THE SALSA VERDE
4 garlic cloves, peeled
1½ teaspoons kosher salt
2 tablespoons cilantro chiffonade (see page 8)
1½ teaspoons chopped tarragon
1½ tablespoons Thai or regular basil chiffonade (see page 8)

2 tablespoons flat-leaf parsley
chiffonade (see page 8)
1 tablespoon finely chopped mild to
moderately hot fresh green chile
with seeds
3 tablespoons finely chopped peeled
ginger

Juice of 3 limes (about ½ cup)
Freshly ground black pepper
1 medium potato such as baking or
Yukon Gold, peeled, cut into
chunks, boiled, and mashed
(about ½ cup)
½ cup extra virgin olive oil

Coarsely grind the peppercorns, coriander seeds, and fennel seeds separately (so they grind evenly) in an electric coffee/spice grinder. Combine the stock, ground spices, onion, celery, carrots, leek, garlic, ginger, chile, turmeric, and bay leaves in a heavy 10- to 12-quart pot. Bring the liquid to a boil and simmer for 15 minutes.

Pat the chickens dry and rub with salt inside and out. Add the chickens, breast side down, to the poaching liquid, and return the liquid to a slow boil. Cook the chickens, covered, for 20 minutes. Remove the pot from the heat and let the chickens stand in the broth, covered, for 30 minutes. Remove the chickens from the broth and let it rest, covered with foil, for 10 minutes.

Blanch the garlic in a small saucepan of boiling water for 30 seconds. Drain the garlic and blanch it 2 more times, changing the water each time. (This sounds fussy, but it will remove bitterness from the garlic.) Coarsely puree the garlic with the salt in a blender or small food processor. Or roughly chop it, sprinkle it with salt, and work it into a coarse puree with the flat side of a large knife. Stir together the garlic puree, herbs, chile, ginger, lime juice, pepper to taste, mashed potato, and olive oil in a bowl.

Remove the legs (including thighs) from the chicken. Remove the skin from the breasts and slice against the grain. Arrange the chicken on a platter and spoon the salsa verde over it.

NOTE: *If desired, you can crisp the chicken legs before serving. Heat 1½ tablespoons canola oil in an ovenproof 12-inch skillet over high heat. Put the legs, skin side up, in the skillet and roast them in the middle of a preheated 400°F oven about 15 minutes, or until crisp and browned.*

To make a flavorful soup, add the chicken carcasses back to the poaching liquid, simmer for about 1 hour, and strain.

black spice–rubbed poussins with kokum jus

SERVES 6

The baby chickens called *poussins* are great for entertaining because they each serve one person. They're a bit harder to find than Cornish hens (your butcher can order them) but are worth tracking down. You could also substitute chicken pieces. The birds are rubbed with deep-flavored spices and popped into the oven; they are great on the grill as well. Kokum gives the sauce a little fruitiness. Serve this dish with a green salad and good bread; in cold weather, the Pan-Roasted Brussels Sprouts and Chanterelles on page 199 are a good accompaniment.

4 cloves
1 cinnamon stick, broken into pieces
1 tablespoon black peppercorns
½ teaspoon Szechwan peppercorns
2 star anise
1 teaspoon black cumin seeds
4 black cardamom pods
1½ teaspoons brown mustard seeds
6 allspice berries
Six 12- to 14-ounce poussins or
    Cornish hens
2 tablespoons unsalted butter

1 tablespoon finely chopped shallot
1 tablespoon finely chopped peeled
    ginger
2 tablespoons thinly sliced kokum
    (labeled "wet kokum")
3 cups Chicken Stock (page 274) or
    reduced-sodium canned chicken
    broth
2 tablespoons pure maple syrup
Two 5-inch rosemary sprigs
Kosher salt
1 cup canola oil

Finely grind the cloves, cinnamon, black peppercorns, Szechwan peppercorns, star anise, black cumin seeds, black cardamom pods, mustard seeds, and allspice berries together in an electric coffee/spice grinder. Set aside three-quarters of the spice mixture (about 3½ tablespoons) in a large bowl for the poussins. Set aside the remaining spice mixture (about 1½ tablespoons) in a small bowl for the kokum jus. Dredge the poussins, one at a time, in the large bowl of ground spices. *Marinate the poussins in large resealable plastic bags for at least 6 and up to 24 hours.*

Melt the butter in a 4-quart pan over moderate heat until light brown and fragrant, about 2 minutes. Add the shallot, ginger, remaining spice mixture, kokum, and stock, stirring, and bring the mixture to a boil. Reduce the heat and simmer the mixture for about 10 minutes. Stir in the maple syrup and simmer the mixture for about 10 minutes longer, until reduced to about one-quarter of its volume.

Transfer the mixture to a blender and puree until smooth. (Be careful—it's hot.) Return the mixture to the (uncleaned) pot and add the rosemary and salt to taste. Keep the sauce at a very gentle simmer on a back burner until the birds are ready.

Preheat the oven to 400°F. Season the poussins with salt and bring to room temperature.

Heat ½ cup of the oil in a 12-inch skillet over high heat until it shimmers. Put 3 poussins, back side down, in the skillet and sear until golden and crisp, turning once, about 4 minutes on each side. Transfer the birds to a shallow roasting pan large enough to hold all 6 birds. Heat the remaining ½ cup of oil in the skillet and sear the 3 remaining birds in the same way, transferring them to the roasting pan.

Roast the seared birds in the middle of the oven for about 10 minutes, or until they are cooked through. Discard the rosemary and serve the poussins on top of the sauce.

spice-crusted
duck breasts

Generally speaking, duck is popular with those known as "East Indians"—the term doesn't refer to a geographical region of the country but to the Catholics from around Bombay who worked for the British East India Company. The secret to this preparation is a fatty farm-raised duck, not a wild one. (I get my duck breasts from a local producer, Hudson Valley; see the sources at the back of the book.) The duck breast is cooked entirely on its fat side—I never turn it over. That way the fat gets beautifully crisp, and the meat gets even more succulent by being basted toward the end of cooking. I like my duck breast medium-rare; if you prefer well-done meat, cook it a little longer. Strictly speaking, you don't need to add the butter at the end, but it gives a wonderful roundness to the basting sauce. I like to accompany this duck with chutney. There is a whole range of options that begin on page 229, but store-bought will also do. Add a simple endive salad and serve the duck hot or at room temperature.

1 teaspoon black peppercorns

2 star anise

1 teaspoon allspice berries

Kosher salt

Three 14-ounce fresh White Pekin (sometimes called Long Island Pekin) duck breasts

1 tablespoon unsalted butter (optional)

1 unpeeled garlic clove, smashed

Two 7-inch rosemary sprigs

1½ tablespoons roughly chopped peeled ginger

Grind the peppercorns, star anise, and allspice in an electric coffee/spice grinder until medium-fine. Put the ground spices in a bowl and stir in 1 tablespoon salt.

Leaving the skin side of the duck breasts alone, trim excess fat from the sides. Then score the skin side in a crosshatch pattern through the fat almost to the flesh so that the fat renders more easily. Generously rub the spice mixture on the flesh side of the breasts, pressing firmly so that it adheres, and marinate the duck, covered and chilled, for at least 1 and up to 6 hours.

Put the duck breasts, skin side down, in a well-seasoned cast-iron or other heavy 12-inch skillet over low heat and season the duck with salt. Cook the duck very slowly for about 25 minutes, until most of the fat is rendered and the skin side is crisp. (Halfway through the cooking, pour off the rendered fat and set it aside.)

Return ¼ cup of the poured-off fat to the skillet and add the butter, garlic, rosemary, and ginger. Increase the heat to moderately high and start to baste the duck, pulling it off the heat briefly and tilting the skillet so that the fat is easy to spoon up and over the meat. Baste frequently for 5 to 7 minutes. Let the duck rest for 10 minutes before slicing it across the grain to serve.

duck with black pepper—tamarind jus

SERVES 6

The simplest way to prepare duck at home is to cook the legs and breast meat separately. (It's easy to overcook the breast while you're waiting for the legs to get tender.) Here I combine duck legs braised in a flavorful "yellow curry" (so called because of the turmeric) with sautéed duck breasts. The duck legs are even more delicious made a day ahead; all you have to do then is simply sauté the breasts before sitting down to dinner. This dish could also make two dinners—enjoy the sautéed breast one night and on another serve the rich meat from the legs with pasta.

FOR THE BRAISED DUCK LEGS
Kosher salt
6 whole fresh White Pekin (sometimes called Long Island Pekin) duck legs (about 2¾ pounds), skin discarded
¼ cup canola oil
1 cinnamon stick
4 cloves
2 pieces mace
1 tablespoon black peppercorns
5 large garlic cloves, peeled and quartered
1 cup chopped leek, white and light green parts only (about 1 leek), washed well
1 cup chopped celery
1 cup chopped carrot
1 cup chopped white onion

½ teaspoon ground turmeric
½ cup white port
1 quart Chicken Stock (page 274) or reduced-sodium canned chicken broth
One 6-inch rosemary sprig

FOR FINISHING THE SAUCE
1 teaspoon cumin seeds
1 teaspoon black peppercorns
1 small piece mace or ¼ teaspoon ground
1 clove
1 tablespoon unsalted butter
2 tablespoons finely shopped shallot
1 tablespoon finely chopped peeled ginger
1½ tablespoons Tamarind Paste (page 284)

136 one spice, two spice

Three 12- to 14-ounce fresh White
Pekin (sometimes called Long
Island Pekin) duck breasts

Kosher salt and freshly ground black
pepper
1 tablespoon unsalted butter
(optional)

Generously salt the duck legs and let sit for 30 minutes. Preheat the oven to 325°F.

Heat the oil in an ovenproof 6- to 8-quart pot over moderately high heat and sear the duck legs until browned all over, 8 to 10 minutes. Transfer them to a platter. Add the cinnamon, cloves, mace, peppercorns, garlic, leek, celery, carrot, and onion to the pot and cook, stirring, over moderate heat until the vegetables are softened and lightly colored, about 3 minutes. Add the turmeric and cook for 30 seconds, stirring. Return the duck legs to the pot and add the white port, stock, 1½ teaspoons salt, and the rosemary. Bring the duck mixture to a boil and remove it from the heat.

Tightly cover the pot and transfer it to the middle of the oven. Braise the duck legs until fork-tender, about 1½ hours. Transfer the duck legs to a platter. Strain the braising liquid through a sieve into a large bowl and skim off the fat. *The duck legs and sauce can be made to this point 1 day ahead. Let both the duck and sauce cool to room temperature, then refrigerate, covered.*

Remove the meat from the bones in large pieces and discard the bones. (Or serve the meat on the bone.)

Transfer the sauce to a pan and simmer, skimming the froth, until reduced to about 2 cups, about 15 minutes.

Finely grind the cumin seeds, peppercorns, mace, and clove in an electric coffee/spice grinder.

Melt the butter in a 3½-quart pan over moderately high heat. Add the shallot and ginger and cook, stirring constantly, until lightly colored, about 4 minutes. Stir in the ground spices and 2 tablespoons of the reduced sauce. Add the remaining sauce, tamarind paste, and meat from the duck legs. Remove the pan from the heat while you sauté the duck breasts.

Leaving the skin side of the duck breasts alone, trim the excess fat from the sides. Then score the skin side in a crosshatch pattern through the fat almost to the flesh so that the fat renders more easily. Generously salt and pepper the flesh side of the breasts. Let the duck breasts sit for 30 minutes.

Put the duck breasts, skin side down, in a well-seasoned cast-iron or other heavy 12-inch skillet over low heat. Cook the duck very slowly for about 25 minutes, until most of the fat is rendered and the skin side is crisp. (Halfway through the cooking, pour off the rendered fat and set it aside.)

Return ¼ cup of the poured-off fat to the skillet and add the butter. Increase the heat to moderately high and start to baste the duck, pulling it off the heat briefly and tilting the skillet so that the fat is easy to spoon up and over the meat. Baste frequently for 5 to 7 minutes.

Let the meat rest for 10 minutes before slicing it across the grain. Meanwhile, reheat the duck leg meat in the sauce. Serve the duck napped with the sauce.

duck orange curry

I suppose you could say this is my take on Duck a l'Orange. Roasting duck at home can be intimidating—there's a lot of fat that needs to be dealt with, and it's hard to cook the legs properly without overcooking the breast meat. Here's the secret: separate the legs from the rest of the duck and cook them (along with the wings and backs for flavor) slowly in an aromatic braising liquid. The dish can be made up to that point one day ahead; in fact, it's better that way. Then I sear the duck carcasses until they are golden brown and pop them in the oven. This is delicious with braised endive.

Two 5- to 6-pound fresh White Pekin (sometimes called Long Island Pekin) ducks

¼ cup plus I tablespoon canola oil, plus oil if needed to cook onion and shallot

4 cups halved and thinly sliced white onion

I cup thinly sliced shallot

One 5-inch dried New Mexico chile

½ small dried red chile (see Glossary)

½ dried pasilla de Oaxaca chile

I tablespoon coriander seeds

I½ teaspoons cumin seeds

I teaspoon black peppercorns

3 green cardamom pods

2 star anise

¼ teaspoon ground mace

¼ teaspoon Aleppo pepper or cayenne

¼ teaspoon ground turmeric

I½ tablespoons packed chopped peeled ginger

8 cloves Garlic Pickle (page 242), skins slipped off

2 cups orange juice

One II-inch rosemary sprig

Kosher salt and freshly ground black pepper

5 cups Chicken Stock (page 274), reduced-sodium canned chicken broth, or water

¼ cup jaggery or dark brown sugar

¼ cup red wine vinegar

Cut the wings and legs off the ducks, leaving as much of the skin on the breasts as possible. Cut out the backs up to the rib cage, but leave the rest of the carcasses whole. Trim large flaps of skin and fat and set them aside. Discard the livers but set aside the gizzards, hearts, and necks.

Put ¼ cup of the oil and the duck legs, skin side down, in a heavy ovenproof 6- to 8-quart pot over moderately high heat and sear the legs until golden brown, about 8 minutes. Turn the legs over and sear the other side until just golden, about 4 minutes. Transfer to a platter. Sear the wings, backs, flaps of skin and fat, gizzards, hearts, and necks in 2 more batches until golden brown, about 10 minutes total per batch, and transfer to the platter. Discard the flaps of skin and fat. You should have ¾ to 1 cup of fat in the pot when you're done. If you have more, pour off the excess; if you have less, add oil to make up the difference.

Add the onion and shallot to the fat in the pot and cook over moderate heat, stirring occasionally, until dark brown and charred in places, about 30 minutes. Meanwhile, preheat the oven to 350°F.

Finely grind the dried chiles, coriander seeds, cumin seeds, peppercorns, cardamom pods, and star anise in an electric coffee/spice grinder. Combine the ground spices with the mace, Aleppo pepper, and turmeric in a small bowl. Stir the spice blend, ginger, garlic pickle, and orange juice into the onion mixture. Increase the heat to high and cook the mixture, stirring, until the orange juice is reduced, about 10 minutes. (Do not let it scorch.)

Return the duck legs to the pot, then add the other duck parts (not the carcasses) and any accumulated juices from the platter. Add the rosemary, salt to taste, stock, jaggery, and vinegar and bring to a boil. Tightly cover the pot with a lid or foil and braise the mixture in the middle of the oven for 1½ hours. Remove the lid or foil and braise the duck for 1½ hours longer. Let the duck parts cool in the braising liquid.

Set the duck legs aside in a bowl and discard the other duck parts, shredding the wing meat, if desired, into the bowl with the duck legs. Skim the fat from the braising liquid and strain the liquid through a sieve into a bowl, pressing hard on the solids with the back of a ladle. (About one-third of the onions will be pushed through the sieve.) Discard the solids. Pour the sauce over the duck legs. *The dish can be made to this point 1 day ahead and refrigerated, covered. Skim the congealed fat and bring the duck legs to room temperature before finishing the dish.*

Preheat the oven to 350°F and season the duck carcasses inside and out with salt and pepper.

Put the remaining tablespoon oil and the ducks, breast sides down, in a heavy ovenproof 12-inch skillet and sear over moderate heat until nicely browned, about 10 minutes, pouring out the fat as it accumulates. Sear the ducks on the other side until nicely browned, about 10 minutes longer.

Roast the ducks, breast sides up, in the middle of the oven for 15 minutes for medium-rare meat (30 minutes for well done). Transfer them to a cutting board and let rest for 10 minutes.

Meanwhile, put the duck legs and sauce into a 4-quart pan and bring to a vigorous boil over high heat to reduce the sauce to about 3 cups, about 20 minutes.

Carve the roasted ducks down the midline and remove the breasts. Cut the breasts on the bias, holding your knife at a 45-degree angle, across the grain into ½-inch slices. Pour any accumulated juices into the sauce. Pick the leg meat off the bone. Put the leg meat and sauce on a platter and top with the breast meat to serve.

panfried quail
with lentil salad

Here lentil salad rich with lardons—salty nuggets of bacon—and grilled scallions is a wonderful foil for fast-cooking, succulent quail. A tarka (spices "bloomed" in very hot oil) flavors the oil for the vinaigrette. Halved, this recipe makes an impressive first course. For the best flavor, let the birds sit in their coriander-pepper seasoning overnight.

1½ teaspoons coriander seeds
1½ teaspoons black peppercorns
Twelve 4- to 5-ounce semiboneless
    quail, rinsed and patted dry

FOR THE VINAIGRETTE
2 cups Chicken Stock (page 274) or
    duck stock
¼ teaspoon dry mustard
2 tablespoons sherry vinegar or
    balsamic vinegar
½ teaspoon minced peeled ginger
½ teaspoon chaat masala
¼ teaspoon sugar
Kosher salt and freshly ground black
    pepper
¼ cup canola oil
1 teaspoon brown mustard seeds

FOR THE LENTIL SALAD
2 cups French green lentils (*lentilles du
    Puy*), picked over for stones and
    rinsed
Kosher salt and freshly ground black
    pepper
1½ cups diced thick-cut bacon
    (½ pound)
1 teaspoon extra virgin olive oil
1 bunch scallions, trimmed
1 heaping cup radishes halved and
    thinly sliced (about 16)
½ cup diced daikon or jícama
2 tablespoons chopped cilantro
2 tablespoons chopped chives
2 teaspoons chopped peeled ginger
2 teaspoons chopped mild to
    moderately hot fresh green chile

9 tablespoons canola oil
3 tablespoons unsalted butter

Finely grind the coriander seeds and peppercorns together in an electric coffee/spice grinder. Pat the spice blend over the quail and let them sit, loosely covered and refrigerated, for at least 2 hours and up to 1 day.

Vigorously simmer the stock in a 2-quart pan until reduced to ½ cup, about 15 minutes. (If you reduce it too much, add enough water to make ½ cup.) Whisk the dry mustard and vinegar together in a bowl. Whisk in the ginger, reduced stock, chaat masala, and sugar and season with salt and pepper.

Make a *tarka* by heating the oil in a 6-inch skillet over moderately high heat until it shimmers and add the mustard seeds. Cook the mustard seeds, stirring, until they pop and are fragrant, about 30 seconds. Immediately whisk the tarka into the vinaigrette and chill.

Put the lentils in a 2-quart pan and cover with water. Bring to a boil and blanch the lentils for 30 seconds. Drain the lentils through a sieve and return to the pan. Add 1 quart water and bring to a boil. Simmer the lentils until tender but still slightly al dente, about 15 minutes. Season with 1½ teaspoons salt and transfer the lentils and whatever water is left in the pan to a wide bowl or tray to cool and absorb the salt and liquid.

While the lentils are cooking, cook the diced bacon in a skillet over moderately high heat until golden brown. Drain on paper towels.

Put the olive oil, ⅛ teaspoon salt, and a generous amount of pepper into a small bowl. Cut the pale green and white bottom of the scallions from the green tops and put both tops and bottoms in the bowl, coating them with the seasoned oil. Cook the scallions, in batches if necessary, on a hot, well-seasoned ridged grill pan over moderately high heat, until softened and charred, about 2 to 3 minutes. Let the scallions cool and chop coarsely.

Drain the lentils 30 minutes before serving (before you cook the quail). Combine them with the bacon, grilled scallions, radishes, daikon, cilantro, chives, ginger, and chile in a large bowl.

Preheat the oven to 225°F. Season the quail with salt. Heat 3 tablespoons of the canola oil in a heavy ovenproof 12- to 14-inch skillet until it shimmers and cook 4 of the quail, breast side down, setting them an inch or so apart so that they brown evenly, for 2 minutes, or until the breasts have browned. Turn them over with tongs, add 1 tablespoon of the butter to the fat in the skillet, and cook the quail for 4 minutes longer, tilting the skillet and basting the birds with fat until the breasts are nicely browned. Transfer the birds to a roasting pan and keep warm in the middle of the oven. Cook the remaining quail in 2 more batches in the same way, wiping out the skillet with a paper towel between batches and adding 3 tablespoons oil and 1 tablespoon butter to the skillet for each batch. Transfer each batch when done to the roasting pan in the oven. Let the birds rest for 10 minutes before cutting the breast meat into slices. The breast meat should be firm and light beige, with a pinkish cast.

Spread the lentil salad on a platter. Arrange the quail legs and breast meat over the salad and drizzle the vinaigrette over all.

braised guinea hen
with yogurt sauce

Guinea hen is leaner than chicken, with darker, more flavorful meat. Here I use an Indian method of braising meat called *dum,* which makes any game bird moist and succulent. First spices are cooked in a generous amount of fat. Then the meat and other ingredients are added and the pot is sealed tightly to prevent the vapor from escaping. The *dum* cooks slowly and gently in the fragrant steam. Using pureed stewed onions as a thickener for a spice-rich yogurt sauce is a classic Indian technique. Like any braise, this is even more delicious if made a day ahead, giving the flavors a chance to meld. Semolina Pilaf (page 266) or Plain Basmati Rice (page 258) would make a good accompaniment.

FOR THE STEWED ONIONS

1½ pounds white onions, quartered
    lengthwise
1 bay leaf
2 tablespoons canola oil
4 large garlic cloves, thinly sliced
    crosswise
2 tablespoons thinly sliced peeled
    ginger

FOR THE GUINEA HEN

6 whole guinea hen legs
Kosher salt

FOR THE YOGURT SAUCE

¼ cup canola oil
½ cinnamon stick
4 green cardamom pods, cracked
½ teaspoon fenugreek seeds
1 teaspoon brown mustard seeds
1 teaspoon cumin seeds
½ teaspoon nigella seeds
1 teaspoon fennel seeds
1 mild to moderately hot fresh green
    chile
3 cups plain whole-milk yogurt
1 tablespoon coriander seeds

Put the onions, 3 cups water, the bay leaf, and the oil in a 4-quart pan and bring to a simmer. Reduce the heat to low and cook the onions, uncovered, for about 1 hour, or until very soft and tender. Discard the bay leaf and let the onions cool to room temperature. *The onions can be stewed 1 day ahead, cooled, and refrigerated, covered.*

Put the garlic and ginger in a blender and add the stewed onions and liquid. Puree the mixture until smooth.

Generously season the guinea hen legs with salt and let sit for 30 minutes. Preheat the oven to 375°F.

Heat the oil in a 10-inch skillet over moderately low heat until it shimmers. Add the cinnamon, cardamom pods, fenugreek seeds, mustard seeds, cumin seeds, nigella seeds, and fennel seeds. Poke a few holes in the chile (so that it doesn't burst) and add the chile to the spice mixture. Cook the spices and chile, swirling the skillet and basting the chile with the oil and spices, for 2 minutes.

Put the pureed onions in a heavy ovenproof 6- to 8-quart pot and add the spiced oil and chile. Whisk the yogurt into the onion mixture.

Finely grind the coriander seeds in an electric coffee/spice grinder. Add the ground coriander to the onion-yogurt mixture and season with salt to taste. Add the guinea hen legs to the pot and cover the pot with a tight-fitting lid or heavy-duty aluminum foil. Bring the mixture to a simmer on top of the stove.

Transfer the pot to the middle of the oven and cook, carefully uncovering the pot occasionally to turn the guinea hen legs, until the meat is fork-tender, about 1½ hours.

Let the meat cool, uncovered, in the pot. *The dish can be made to this point up to 1 day ahead, cooled to room temperature, and the legs refrigerated in the sauce, covered.*

Pull the meat off the bones (the legs of game birds have lots of tendons, so I like to serve the meat off the bone) and gently reheat the meat in the sauce. Serve the meat with some of the sauce ladled over it.

meat

marinated
hanger steak

People tend to be surprised when I tell them that I grew up eating beef. Our family wasn't Hindu, though, but Roman Catholic. Beef was a staple in our household, primarily because of the Portuguese influence. You can substitute flank steak for the hanger steak here. I serve this with Turmeric Mashed Potatoes (page 218) and Horseradish Ginger Raita (page 249), but it's also great with your favorite potato salad.

1½ tablespoons coriander seeds
1 tablespoon black peppercorns
1 tablespoon brown mustard seeds
1 teaspoon cumin seeds
2 cloves

1 tablespoon kosher salt
¾ cup canola oil
Six 6-ounce pieces hanger steak,
   1½ to 2 inches thick

Coarsely grind the coriander seeds, peppercorns, mustard seeds, cumin seeds, and cloves in an electric coffee/spice grinder. Sift the ground spices through a coarse sieve into a bowl. Stir in the salt and ¼ cup of the oil. Generously pat the spice rub all over the steak. *Marinate the steaks, covered and refrigerated, for at least 4 and up to 36 hours.*

Bring the steak to room temperature and preheat the oven to 375°F.

Heat ¼ cup of the remaining oil in a 12-inch skillet over moderately high heat until it shimmers and sear 3 pieces of steak on all sides, about 3 to 6 minutes. (Don't rush this step; careful browning will add great flavor.) Transfer the steak to a baking sheet with sides. Sear the remaining steak in the remaining oil in the same way and transfer to the baking sheet. Put the baking sheet in the middle of the oven and cook the steaks, without turning them, for 4 to 6 minutes for medium-rare meat.

Transfer the steaks to a cutting board and let them rest at room temperature for 5 to 10 minutes. Cut them against the grain at a 45-degree angle into ¼- to ½-inch slices. Arrange the meat on a warm platter. Pour any pan juices over it and serve at once.

coriander-and-mustard-crusted strip loin

SERVES 6

Strip loin is also known as *New York strip, Kansas City strip,* or *club steak,* depending on where you live. Here a spicy, sparky crust adds contrast to the tender, flavorful meat. My inspiration was twofold: classic steak au poivre and the seasonings found in A.1. steak sauce. (That's not so crazy; ketchup was an Indian invention, after all.) I like to serve this with Braised Romaine (page 223) and potatoes any which way.

1 teaspoon Szechwan peppercorns	2 tablespoons cumin seeds
1 tablespoon allspice berries	1 tablespoon kosher salt
3 tablespoons black peppercorns	Six 6-ounce strip loin steaks, about
2 tablespoons yellow mustard seeds	1½ inches thick
3 tablespoons coriander seeds	¾ cup canola oil

Grind the Szechwan peppercorns in an electric coffee/spice grinder until medium-fine, then put in a large bowl. Grind the allspice medium-fine in the grinder and pass through a small sieve into the same bowl. Return the coarse bits of allspice to the grinder and add the peppercorns. Grind the peppercorns medium-fine and add to the spice blend in the bowl. Grind the mustard seeds until very coarse and add to the bowl. Grind the coriander seeds until very coarse and add to the bowl. Grind the cumin seeds until very coarse and add to the bowl. Stir all the ground spices together until combined thoroughly and stir in the salt.

Dredge the steaks one at a time in the spice blend and press the coating onto the steaks firmly. Gently but firmly tie each steak around its circumference with kitchen string. Transfer the steaks to a platter and let sit, refrigerated and covered loosely with plastic wrap, for at least 2 hours. *The steaks can be prepared up to 8 hours ahead. Bring them to room temperature before cooking.*

Preheat the oven to 350°F and season the steaks with salt.

Heat half of the oil in a 10- to 12-inch skillet over moderate heat until it shimmers and sear 3 steaks on one side for 2½ to 3 minutes, or until nicely browned. (Don't rush this step; the caramelization that occurs during the searing results in deep, rich flavor.) Turn the steaks over with tongs and transfer to a baking sheet with sides. Cook the remaining steaks in the remaining oil in the same way and transfer to the baking sheet. Put the baking sheet in the middle of the oven and cook the steaks, without turning them, for 5 to 7 minutes for medium-rare meat.

Transfer the cooked steaks to a platter and let them rest for 5 to 10 minutes. Remove the kitchen string from the steaks before serving.

curry leaf–marinated flank steak

Small, glossy curry leaves come from the small, deciduous curry leaf tree, which grows both wild and cultivated in India, northern Thailand, and Sri Lanka. The tree is also cultivated in Australia, California, and Florida, so fresh curry leaves are becoming more widely available in the United States. The leaves are intensely aromatic, with a warm, citrusy herbal scent. The addition of soy sauce might seem unusual here, but there has long been a Chinese contingent in India, and soy sauce was a common ingredient in my mother's kitchen. The steak is cooked in the oven, but it is outstanding when grilled as well. I've given a relatively modest amount of meat here to be divided among six people, so combine it with Turmeric Mashed Potatoes (page 218) or plain mashed potatoes or roasted vegetables and perhaps cooked greens.

FOR THE MARINADE
1 tablespoon black peppercorns
1½ teaspoons cumin seeds
1 small dried red chile (see Glossary)
1 tablespoon sliced peeled ginger
2 large garlic cloves, sliced
About 80 fresh or frozen curry leaves

3 tablespoons soy sauce
3 tablespoons canola oil
One 2-pound flank steak, about
    ½ inch thick
⅓ cup fresh lime juice (from about
    2 limes)
Kosher salt

Finely grind the peppercorns, cumin seeds, and chile together in an electric coffee/spice grinder.

Puree the ginger, garlic, curry leaves, soy sauce, and oil in a blender or mini food processor, scraping down the side of bowl, until the mixture is a smooth paste. Combine the paste and ground spices in a large bowl and dredge the steak in the marinade until coated well. *Marinate the steak, covered and refrigerated, for at least 2 and up to 8 hours.*

Preheat the oven to 450°F.

Drizzle the steak with lime juice and put it on a rack in a baking pan or on a baking sheet with sides. Put the pan in the middle of the oven and cook the steak, without turning it, for 10 to 15 minutes for medium-rare meat.

Transfer the steak to a cutting board and let rest for 10 minutes. Cut the steak across the grain at a 45-degree angle into ¼- to ½-inch slices. Arrange the meat on a warm platter. Pour any pan juices over it and serve at once.

hamburgers

You might think hamburgers are quintessentially American, but ground-beef patties are eaten in western India as well, where they are called "cutlets." Chopped cilantro, tomatoes, onions, and fresh green chile give these burgers sparkle, and a coating of the crisp Japanese bread crumbs called *panko* give them great texture. They're a perennial favorite at Tabla.

I tablespoon coriander seeds
I tablespoon cumin seeds
I teaspoon black peppercorns
2 pounds ground beef chuck
I cup chopped white onion
I tablespoon minced peeled ginger
I tablespoon minced garlic
I tablespoon chopped mild to
   moderately hot fresh green chile

½ plum tomato, finely chopped
I egg, lightly beaten
¼ teaspoon cayenne
½ teaspoon ground turmeric
2 tablespoons chopped cilantro
I tablespoon salt
I½ cups panko
½ cup canola oil

Toast the coriander seeds in a dry small skillet over moderately low heat, shaking the skillet, until fragrant and a couple of shades darker, about 3 minutes. Transfer the seeds to a small tray or plate to cool. Toast the cumin seeds and then the peppercorns the same way, turning them out to cool on the same tray. Finely grind the toasted spices together in an electric coffee/spice grinder.

Put the ground beef, onion, ginger, garlic, and chile in a large bowl and combine. (Your freshly washed hands are the best tool for the job.) Work in the ground spices, tomato, egg, cayenne, turmeric, cilantro, and salt. Form the meat mixture into 6 equal-size patties.

Put the panko on a platter and dredge the burgers, one at a time, gently patting the coating down so it adheres to the burgers. Let the burgers sit in the panko, covered loosely, in the refrigerator for 2 hours. Before cooking the burgers, pat more panko over the burgers.

Preheat the oven to 200°F.

Heat the oil in a 12-inch skillet over moderately high heat until it shimmers. Cook the burgers, turning them once, for 10 minutes total. (They should be cooked through. If the panko coating is getting too dark, reduce the heat to moderate.)

barbecued brisket

The smoky heat from chiles meets tender, yielding meat in this barbecued brisket. If you have a stovetop or outdoor smoker at home, now's the time to use it: simply put the brisket in the smoker for an hour or so. This is delicious with corn or potatoes; it is also great in a sandwich.

FOR THE MARINADE
1 tablespoon black peppercorns
1 tablespoon cumin seeds
1 tablespoon brown mustard seeds
3 cloves
One cinnamon stick, broken in half
1 small dried red chile (see Glossary)
1 pasilla de Oaxaca chile
2 tablespoons chopped peeled ginger
9 garlic cloves, smashed and peeled
½ cup red wine vinegar
1 heaping teaspoon ground turmeric

3 cups quartered and sliced white onion
2 tablespoons jaggery or brown sugar
One 12-ounce bottle Belgian-style ale or beer
2 cups canned tomatoes, including juice
One 3¼-pound beef brisket (preferably the thinner cut), trimmed but with a thin layer of fat
Kosher salt

Finely grind the peppercorns, cumin seeds, mustard seeds, cloves, cinnamon, and chiles together in an electric coffee/spice grinder.

Puree the ginger, garlic, and vinegar in a blender.

Combine the puree, ground spices, turmeric, onion, jaggery, ale, and tomatoes and dredge brisket in the marinade. *Marinate, covered and refrigerated, for 2 to 3 days.*

Preheat the oven to 350°F. Season the brisket with salt.

Put the brisket and marinade in an ovenproof 5- to 6-quart pot (don't worry if the marinade doesn't cover the beef) and bring to a boil on top of the stove. Transfer the pot to the middle of the oven and braise, uncovered and turning the brisket every 30 minutes, for 3½ to 4 hours, or until fork-tender. (If the liquid reduces too much, simply add a little water.) Cut into ¼-inch slices and serve.

braised short ribs

Braising is an important culinary method in India and one of my favorites. The long, slow cooking creates complexity of flavor, and it works so well for the home cook. Short ribs are easily available and always popular. For the best meaty flavor and luscious texture, make them two days ahead. As with other braises, the sauce here is as important as the meat: this one has great body and depth as well as luster. Serve these ribs with Basmati Pilaf (page 259) or mashed potatoes and Kashmiri Greens (page 213).

FOR THE SPICE BLEND

2¼ teaspoons black peppercorns
2¼ teaspoons cumin seeds
2¼ teaspoons coriander seeds
2¼ teaspoons brown mustard seeds
½ cinnamon stick, broken in half
I small dried red chile (see Glossary)
I tablespoon paprika
½ teaspoon ground turmeric

FOR THE SHORT RIBS

5 pounds meaty beef short ribs
Kosher salt and freshly ground black pepper
½ cup canola oil
II unpeeled garlic cloves, cut in half crosswise
4 cups chopped white onion
I large leek, white and pale green parts, chopped and washed (about I½ cups)
2 cups chopped carrot
2½ cups chopped celery, including the leaves
I½ bay leaves
4 cloves
⅓ cup thinly sliced peeled ginger
4 cups diced seeded tomatoes (about 5 medium) or 3 cups chopped canned tomatoes, including juice
¼ cup red wine vinegar
I cup dry red wine
2 cups Chicken Stock (page 274), reduced-sodium canned chicken broth, or water
2 tablespoons jaggery or dark brown sugar
2 tablespoons Tamarind Paste (page 284)

Finely grind the peppercorns, cumin seeds, coriander seeds, mustard seeds, cinnamon, and chile in an electric coffee/spice grinder. Combine the ground spices with the paprika and turmeric in a small bowl.

Trim all but a thin layer of fat from the short ribs. (That fat will help keep the meat juicy and give the sauce body.) Generously season the short ribs with salt and pepper.

Heat the oil in a heavy ovenproof 7- to 8-quart pot over moderately high heat until it shimmers and sear the ribs in 2 to 3 batches (don't crowd the pot), until nicely browned on both sides, about 8 minutes total (don't rush this step; all that caramelization adds great flavor). Remove the short ribs and set aside.

Preheat the oven to 325°F.

Add the garlic, onion, leek, carrot, celery, bay leaves, cloves, and ginger to the pot and cook over moderately high heat until the vegetables are softened, about 10 minutes. Stir in the tomatoes, spice blend, vinegar, and wine and cook for 5 minutes. Return the short ribs to the pot, nestling them in between the vegetables, and add the stock. Stir in the jaggery and tamarind paste and season with salt. Bring the braise to a boil and simmer for 10 minutes. Tightly cover the pot with a lid or foil and cook in the middle of the oven for 2 hours. Check the short ribs periodically; if the liquid reduces so that more than the top of the meat is exposed, add enough water to just barely cover the meat. (Evaporation will vary depending on the size of the pot.)

Return the braise to the stovetop and bring to a boil. Skim the fat from the surface with a ladle. Turn off the heat and transfer the short ribs to a large bowl. (Some meat may fall off the bones, but that's okay; add it to the short ribs in the bowl.)

Strain the braising liquid through a sieve into the bowl of short ribs, pressing hard on the solids with the back of a ladle, and discard the solids. Cool the short ribs in the sauce, uncovered. *Refrigerate the short ribs in the sauce, covered, for at least 2 and up to 3 days.*

Remove and discard the congealed fat from the surface and reheat the short ribs in the sauce over moderate heat before serving.

sweet spiced oxtails

Our family used to buy oxtails from a street vendor called "Liver Andrew." They were absolutely fresh—and absolutely delicious. We loved this inexpensive cut with rich flavor and meltingly tender texture when braised for a couple of hours. Like any braised meat dish, the sauce is as important as the meat itself. Here I like to strain the sauce, reduce it, then recombine it with the braised oxtails and finish them off in the oven, basting them frequently with the reduced sauce. The sweet beefiness deepens, and the sauce gives the oxtails a beautiful sheen. Like most braises, this one is best if made ahead time.

FOR THE SPICE BLEND

6 cloves
I cinnamon stick, broken in half
I teaspoon black peppercorns
I tablespoon coriander seeds
2 tablespoons cumin seeds
I½ tablespoons brown mustard seeds
I small dried red chile (see Glossary)
½ teaspoon ground turmeric
½ teaspoon cayenne

FOR THE OXTAILS

4 pounds oxtails
Kosher salt and freshly ground black
    pepper
¼ cup canola oil

4 cups coarsely chopped white
    onion
IO unpeeled garlic cloves, cut in half
    crosswise
2 cups chopped celery
2 cups chopped carrot
¼ cup sliced peeled ginger
I cup dry red wine
¼ cup tomato paste
2 tablespoons dark brown sugar
¼ cup plus 2 tablespoons red wine
    vinegar
Six 4-inch thyme sprigs
Two 5-inch rosemary sprigs
2 bay leaves

Finely grind the cloves, cinnamon, peppercorns, coriander seeds, cumin seeds, mustard seeds, and chile together in an electric coffee/spice grinder. Combine the ground spices with the turmeric and cayenne in a small bowl.

Preheat the oven to 375° F.

Season the oxtails generously with salt and pepper and let them sit for 10 minutes.

Heat the oil in a heavy ovenproof 6- to 8-quart pot over moderately high heat until it shimmers and sear the oxtails on all sides until browned, about 18 minutes. (Don't rush through this step even though it's a bit fussy, as oxtails are oddly shaped. The caramelization is the secret to a deeply flavored braise.) If the bottom of the pot looks like it's getting too dark, reduce the heat to moderate. Transfer the oxtails to a platter.

Add the onion, garlic, celery, carrot, and ginger to the (uncleaned) pot and cook, stirring, until the vegetables are softened and the onions are lightly browned, about 10 minutes. Stir ¼ cup of the wine into the spice blend and stir that into the vegetables. Stir in the tomato paste, then cook the vegetables for 2 minutes longer. Stir in the rest of the wine and the brown sugar.

Return the oxtails and their juices from the platter to the pot and add 6 cups water. Add 1 tablespoon salt along with the vinegar, thyme, rosemary, and bay leaves.

Bring the braising liquid to a boil, then tightly cover the pot with a lid or foil. Put the oxtails in the middle of the oven and braise them for 2 to 2½ hours, or until fork-tender.

Transfer the oxtails to a large bowl. Strain the braising liquid through a sieve into the bowl, pressing hard on the solids with the back of a ladle, and discard the solids. Skim the fat from the strained liquid. You should have 1½ to 2 cups sauce left; if you have more, bring it to a boil in a 2-quart pan and reduce until you have 1½ to 2 cups. Pour the sauce over the oxtails and let them cool, uncovered. *Refrigerate the cooled oxtails, covered, for 1 day.*

Preheat the oven to 375°F.

Remove and discard any congealed fat from the braising liquid. Return the oxtails and sauce to the same (cleaned) 6- to 8-quart pot and bring to a boil. Transfer the pot to the middle of the oven. Cook the oxtails, basting them with the sauce every 5 minutes, for 25 to 30 minutes, or until the oxtails are hot and the sauce is the consistency of syrup.

roast lamb with mint—black pepper sauce

The first taste I had of lamb was in Kashmir, when I was about nineteen. Kashmir, way up in the North in the Himalayas, has long been called the land of milk and honey, for it boasts fertile soil, a temperate climate, and immense agricultural riches. It was long ruled by Muslims from central Asia who were known as Moghuls (*Moghul* means "Mongol," as in Genghis Khan and the Mongol Empire). Their Persian cooking style blended with the older Hindu traditions and evolved into a singular cuisine. Hindus who ate meat, for instance, grew fond of Persian lamb dishes, and to this day Kashmir is the main place in India where lamb is preferred.

FOR THE SPICE RUB
1½ teaspoons yellow mustard seeds
¾ teaspoon black peppercorns
4 large black cardamom pods
Leaves from one 10-inch rosemary
    sprig
3 tablespoons extra virgin olive oil

FOR THE LAMB
2½ pounds boneless leg of lamb or
    lamb loin, cut into pieces about
    4 × 2 inches
Kosher salt
½ cup extra virgin olive oil

FOR THE SAUCE
4½ tablespoons extra virgin olive oil
1½ tablespoons finely chopped
    shallot
2 packed tablespoons finely chopped
    peeled ginger
2 packed tablespoons finely chopped
    garlic
3 cups chopped plum tomatoes
½ teaspoon kosher salt
3 cups lamb stock or Chicken Stock
    (page 274), reduced to 1½ cups
    and kept warm
Sugar
Six 6-inch mint sprigs
Leaves from two 7-inch rosemary
    sprigs

Grind the mustard seeds, peppercorns, and cardamom pods in an electric coffee/spice grinder until medium-fine. Set aside half the ground spices (about 1 scant tablespoon) to make the sauce. Put the remaining ground spices in a bowl and stir in the rosemary and oil.

Coat the lamb with half of the spice rub. *Marinate the lamb, covered and refrigerated, for 4 to 8 hours.*

Prepare the sauce: Heat 4½ tablespoons oil in a heavy 4-quart pot over moderately high heat until it shimmers and cook the shallot, ginger, and garlic until the shallot is translucent, about 2 minutes. Add the scant tablespoon of ground spices, the tomatoes, and the salt and continue to cook, stirring occasionally, until the tomatoes start breaking down, about 4 minutes.

While the tomatoes are cooking, heat the reduced stock to boiling. Add the boiling stock and sugar to taste to the tomatoes and cook over high heat, stirring occasionally, until reduced by about a third, about 15 minutes. You should have about 2½ cups sauce. Remove the sauce from the heat and keep it warm.

Preheat the oven to 350°F. Season the lamb with salt.

Heat the ¼ cup of the oil in a heavy 12-inch skillet over high heat until it shimmers. Sear half of the lamb on one side until golden, about 2 minutes. Turn the lamb over and transfer to a shallow roasting pan. Sear the remaining lamb in the remaining oil the same way. Turn it over and transfer to the roasting pan.

Put the pan in the middle of the oven and roast the lamb for 5 minutes for medium-rare meat. Remove the lamb from the oven and baste thoroughly with the fat in the pan. Transfer the lamb to a platter and let it rest for 10 minutes.

Coarsely chop the mint and rosemary and add to the sauce off the heat. Let the sauce sit for 10 minutes, then strain it through a sieve into a small pan, pressing firmly on the solids. Discard the solids and gently reheat the sauce. Slice the lamb and serve with the sauce ladled over.

milk-braised lamb shanks

SERVES 6

This dish from northern India is one of the glories of Moghul cooking. The lamb is braised in a subtly flavored sauce until unctuous, and the cooking liquid is reduced, then pureed into a sauce. It is plain-looking, true, but, like pork loin braised in milk Bolognese style, it is unexpectedly sophisticated and absolutely delicious. I first had lamb braised this way at a roadside café in Kashmir. I was nineteen, and it was one of the best things I had ever tasted. Don't worry that the onion, shallot, and leek combination will be too strong; it adds both nuance and depth of flavor. The mellow "warming" spices used here—cardamom and cinnamon—are common to the cool Indian highlands. Serve the lamb shanks with Cracked Wheat Pilaf (page 265) or Basmati Pilaf (page 259).

Six 12- to 14-ounce lamb shanks
Kosher salt
2 tablespoons coriander seeds
1 tablespoon black peppercorns
8 green cardamom pods
2 black cardamom pods
1 cinnamon stick, broken into pieces
1 teaspoon ground ginger
1 bay leaf
4 cups chopped white onion (about 2 large)
1 cup chopped shallot (about 4 medium)

1 leek, white and pale green parts, chopped (about 1 cup) and washed well
4 celery stalks, including leaves, halved crosswise, or 1 small celery root, peeled and roughly chopped
1 quart Chicken Stock (page 274), reduced-sodium canned chicken broth, or lamb stock
1 quart whole or low-fat milk
1 mild to moderately hot fresh green chile, slit down 1 side

Season the lamb shanks generously with salt and let sit for 45 minutes.

Coarsely grind the coriander seeds in an electric coffee/spice grinder, then separately grind the peppercorns the same way. Coarsely crack the green and black cardamom pods in a small mortar with a pestle (or with the flat side of a large knife or the bottom of a heavy skillet).

Combine the lamb shanks, 1 tablespoon salt, all the spices, and all the remaining ingredients in a heavy 7- to 8-quart pot and bring to a boil. Reduce the heat and simmer, scraping the bottom occasionally to prevent the milk from sticking, for about 2 hours, or until the shanks are tender. (The sauce might look curdled at this stage. It's not a pretty sight, but don't worry: the end result will look fine and taste delicious.)

Take the shanks out of the sauce and put them in a large bowl. Strain the sauce through a sieve into a bowl, pressing hard on the solids with the back of a ladle, and discard the solids. If not serving the shanks right away, cool them, uncovered, in the sauce. *The shanks can be made up to this point 1 day ahead and refrigerated, covered.*

Transfer the sauce back to the (cleaned) cooking pot. Bring the sauce to a boil and boil vigorously until thickened and several shades darker, about 10 minutes. With the sauce still at a boil, reheat the shanks in sauce, basting them frequently and gently scraping underneath them with a spatula to prevent sticking. Reduce the sauce to a thick glaze, about 25 minutes.

Transfer the shanks to plates. If desired, blend the sauce until smooth with an immersion blender before napping the shanks with the sauce.

peanut sesame–crusted lamb chops with tomatoes and fresh peas

SERVES 6

In the eighteenth century, the southern region of Hyderabad developed its own distinctive cuisine. Its roots are in the northern cities of Agra and Delhi, in the palace kitchens of the Moghul (and Muslim) emperors, but it takes advantage of ingredients—peanuts, sesame seeds, coconut, and tamarind, for instance—used by local Hindus in southern India. Here I press a nutty Hyderabadi crust onto seared lamb chops and then pop them in the oven. On the plate, shards of the crust inevitably end up in the vegetables—a spicy, soupy jumble of peas and tomatoes—and it is a very happy marriage. It's important to coordinate the cooking of the meat and vegetables here; if the peas are done ahead of time, they will lose their vibrant color. Serve this with Semolina Pilaf (page 266), steamed rice, or crusty bread.

FOR THE PEANUT SESAME CRUST

½ cup grated fresh coconut (see page 283) or unsweetened desiccated coconut

½ cup sesame seeds

½ cup roasted peanuts, preferably unsalted

1 tablespoon chopped peeled ginger

2 tablespoons lime juice

2¼ teaspoons Tamarind Paste (page 284)

6 black cardamom pods

1 tablespoon black peppercorns

Kosher salt

FOR THE TOMATOES AND PEAS

3 medium tomatoes or one 28-ounce can, including juice (see Note)

¼ cup extra virgin olive oil

1 tablespoon cumin seeds

1 teaspoon nigella seeds

1 small dried red chile (see Glossary), broken into small pieces

¼ cup julienne strips peeled ginger

½ cup thinly sliced shallot

1½ teaspoons thinly sliced garlic

About 1 pound shelled fresh peas (from about 2½ pounds in pods) or frozen green peas

⅛ teaspoon Aleppo pepper or
  cayenne
1 tablespoon Tamarind Paste (page
  284)
Kosher salt and freshly ground black
  pepper
½ teaspoon sugar

Twelve 7-ounce lamb chops
1 cup canola oil

Toast the coconut in a dry 10-inch skillet over low heat, stirring and shaking the skillet frequently, until golden brown. (You can also toast it in a preheated 350°F oven for 15 to 20 minutes.) Spread the toasted coconut out on a tray or large plate to cool. Toast the sesame seeds in the skillet over low heat, stirring and shaking the skillet frequently, until light golden and fragrant, 3 to 4 minutes, and turn out on the plate with the coconut to cool. Transfer the coconut and sesame seeds to a food processor and add the peanuts and ginger. Process the mixture to a rough paste. Add the lime juice and tamarind paste and process until thick and smooth.

Finely grind the cardamom pods and peppercorns in an electric coffee/spice grinder. Add half the ground spices to the peanut-sesame paste and reserve the rest of the ground spices for seasoning the lamb chops. Season the peanut-sesame paste with salt to taste and mix together with your hands to blend well.

Preheat the oven to 500°F. Bring a large pot of water to a boil.

Core the tomatoes and cut an X in the bottom of each tomato. Blanch the tomatoes in the boiling water for 10 seconds and transfer to a bowl of ice water. While the tomatoes are cooling, sprinkle the lamb chops with the reserved spice mixture.

When the tomatoes are cool enough to handle, peel them, then cut them in half crosswise and discard the seeds. Squeeze the excess juice out of them and cut them into ½-inch dice.

Heat the olive oil in a wide 4-quart pan over moderately low heat until it shimmers. Add the cumin seeds, nigella seeds, and chile and cook, stirring, until fragrant, about 2 minutes. Add the ginger, shallot, and garlic and cook, stirring, for about 3 minutes. Add the fresh peas, if using, and cook, stirring, for another 3 minutes. Add the tomatoes, Aleppo pepper, tamarind paste, and salt to taste, and cook, stirring, for 3 minutes longer. Stir in ½ cup water if using fresh peas. If using frozen peas, add them now, along with ¼ cup water. Stir in the sugar and simmer the vegetables for 5 minutes. Season with black pepper to taste.

Meanwhile, heat ⅓ cup of the oil in a 12-inch skillet over high heat and sear 4 of the lamb chops until nicely browned, about 2 minutes on each side for medium-rare. Transfer to a large shallow baking pan. Sear the remaining chops in 2 more batches in the same way, wiping out the skillet with a paper towel between batches and adding ⅓ cup of the remaining oil to the skillet for each batch. Transfer each batch when done to the baking pan. Pat the peanut-sesame paste firmly onto the tops of the chops. Put the pan in the middle of the oven and cook the chops for 5 minutes. Serve the chops with the tomatoes and peas.

NOTE: *I prefer organic Muir Glen canned tomatoes.*

lamb meatballs stuffed with fresh figs

SERVES 6

Koftas are fried or baked spiced meatballs that are served with all sorts of rich curries. This dish is North Indian in inspiration: the meatballs are made of ground lamb and filled with an herbaceous mixture of diced fresh figs, cilantro, and mint, and the lush, emerald green sauce is based on a Punjabi preparation of spicy mustard greens and cornmeal. Its body, in part, comes from a puree of the greens with thick Greek-style (or drained regular) yogurt. Serve with flatbread such as naan or pita.

FOR THE MEATBALL MIX

2½ pounds ground lamb

3 tablespoons finely chopped garlic

½ cup finely chopped shallot

1½ teaspoons finely chopped peeled ginger

2 tablespoons finely chopped mint leaves

2 tablespoons finely chopped cilantro leaves

1 tablespoon finely chopped fresh rosemary leaves

1½ teaspoons kosher salt

Freshly ground black pepper

FOR THE MEATBALL FILLING

2 tablespoons mint chiffonade (see page 8)

2 tablespoons cilantro chiffonade (see page 8)

1 cup chopped ripe figs (about 6 large)

Kosher salt and freshly ground black pepper

FOR THE SAUCE

1 pound mustard greens, washed and leaves stripped of center rib

½ cup Greek-style plain whole-milk yogurt or regular plain whole-milk yogurt, drained (see Note)

2 cups Chicken Stock (page 274), reduced-sodium canned chicken broth, or lamb stock

2 tablespoons canola oil

2 cloves

1 teaspoon brown mustard seeds

⅓ cup thinly sliced shallot

2 tablespoons thinly sliced garlic

1 heaping tablespoon julienne strips peeled ginger

168 one spice, two spice

1 tablespoon sliced mild to
    moderately hot fresh green chile
2½ tablespoons unsalted butter
¼ cup cornmeal
Kosher salt and freshly ground black
    pepper

FOR COOKING THE MEATBALLS
AND FINISHING THE SAUCE
Pinch of cayenne
½ teaspoon salt

Blend the lamb, garlic, shallot, ginger, mint, cilantro, and rosemary in a large bowl. (Your freshly washed hands are the best tool for the job.) Season with salt and pepper to taste and refrigerate the meatball mix, covered, for 30 minutes.

Stir together the mint, cilantro, and figs in a bowl and season with salt and pepper to taste.

Divide the meatball mix into 18 equal portions. Form 1 portion into a flattened disk in the palm of your hand. Put 1 heaping teaspoon filling in the center of the disk and form a meatball around the filling. Form 17 more meatballs in the same way. *The meatballs can be formed 1 day in advance and refrigerated, covered, on a tray.*

Bring a 6- to 8-quart pot of water to a boil. Blanch the mustard greens for 20 seconds and transfer to a bowl of ice water. When the greens are cool, squeeze dry and chop roughly. Put the greens and yogurt in a blender and puree until smooth, adding ¼ to ½ cup of the stock to make a smooth puree.

Heat the oil in a 4-quart saucepan over moderately high heat until it shimmers. Add the cloves and mustard seeds and cook until the mustard seeds pop and are fragrant, about 30 seconds. Add the shallot and garlic and cook, stirring, until the shallot and garlic are just starting to color and soften, about 1 minute. Add the ginger, chile, and butter and cook, stirring, until the butter melts, about 30 seconds. Stir in the cornmeal and cook, stirring, until the sauce thickens, about 2 minutes. Add the remaining stock and salt and pepper to taste. Reduce the heat and simmer the sauce gently for 15 minutes, stirring frequently.

Preheat the oven to 500°F. Season the meatballs with salt and pepper. Put the meatballs on a baking sheet and bake in the middle of the oven, turning the meatballs halfway through baking, for 15 minutes, or until the lamb is just cooked through.

Stir the mustard green puree into the sauce. Stir in the cayenne and salt and cook, stirring, 1 minute over moderately high heat, or until heated through. Spoon the sauce onto a platter and top with the meatballs.

NOTE: *To use a non-Greek-style yogurt such as Stonyfield Farm, put it in a cheesecloth-lined sieve over a bowl and let it drain, refrigerated, overnight. It will then have the right thickness.*

lamb stew with turnips and dried apricots

SERVES 6

This stew was inspired by Bade (pronounced "buday") Miah, a master chef in Delhi, and his wonderful pairing of lamb and turnips. It's essentially a Parsi dish, incorporating ingredients common to northern India such as lamb, cardamom, and dried apricots. Indian dried apricots, by the way, come from Kashmir and look quite different from California or Turkish dried apricots—they are about the size of a cherry, contain pits, and are chewy, with a nice balance of sweetness and acidity. You can find them in Indian markets, but for this dish, use any dried apricots that are handy. I always use lamb chuck for stewing, as it results in tender, juicy meat. Try this in the early fall, when turnips are still small and sweet.

3 pounds lamb chuck, cut into
  1½-inch cubes
Kosher salt and freshly ground black
  pepper
1 cinnamon stick
4 green cardamom pods, cracked
  with the flat side of a large knife
4 black cardamom pods, cracked
  with the flat side of a large knife
1 piece mace
2 cloves
2 tablespoons coriander seeds
1 teaspoon cumin seeds
1½ teaspoons black peppercorns
½ teaspoon ground turmeric
¼ cup canola oil
1 cup coarsely chopped carrot
1 cup coarsely chopped celery or
  peeled celery root

2 cups coarsely chopped white onion
8 garlic cloves, smashed and peeled
1½ tablespoons thinly sliced peeled
  ginger
1¾ cups chopped tomato
2 bay leaves
1 cup dry white wine
1 quart Chicken Stock (page 274),
  reduced-sodium canned chicken
  broth, or lamb stock
1 cup diced dried apricots
6 uncooked lamb leg bones, cut into
  pieces by butcher (optional; see
  Notes)
1¼ pounds baby turnips, greens
  reserved for another use, tops
  trimmed, ½-inch of stem left
  intact, and cut in half if large (see
  Notes)

one spice, two spice

Season the lamb generously with salt and pepper.

Finely grind the cinnamon, cracked cardamom pods, mace, cloves, coriander seeds, cumin seeds, and peppercorns in an electric coffee/spice grinder. Put the ground spices on a small tray or plate and add the turmeric.

Heat 3 tablespoons of the oil in a heavy 6- to 8-quart saucepan over moderately high heat until it shimmers. Sear about half of the lamb, turning it with tongs, until lightly browned, about 8 minutes total. Transfer the lamb to a tray or platter and sear the rest of the lamb in the same way. (Do not add more oil between batches.)

Add the remaining tablespoon of the oil to the pot if needed and add the carrot, celery, onion, garlic, and ginger. Cook over moderately high heat for 3 minutes, until the vegetables are just starting to color, and add the ground spices, tomato, bay leaves, and a pinch of salt. Stir in the meat, wine, stock, apricots, and, if using, the lamb bones. Reduce the heat until the stew is simmering gently. Cover the pot and simmer the stew for 1 hour.

Add the turnips to the stew. If it looks like the liquid has reduced too much (it shouldn't have, if it's been at a gentle simmer), add some water to bring it back to a stewlike consistency. Simmer the stew for another 15 to 20 minutes, or until the turnips and lamb are very tender. Skim the fat.

Discard the lamb bones if you used them and season the stew with salt and a generous amount of pepper before serving.

NOTES: *If you can easily get a few lamb leg bones from the butcher, add them to the stew while it's simmering. They will add flavor and rich gelatin to the dish.*

If you can find only large turnips, cut them into bite-sized pieces and add them to the stew a little earlier; they will take longer to cook than baby turnips.

goan spiced roast pork tenderloin

When the Portuguese seized Goa, marriages between Portuguese men and local women were encouraged, and over the centuries a unique culture was created—Catholic, Portuguese-speaking, and with its own cuisine. Every summer, when my great-grandmother had the season's pig (always named Chikulaw) slaughtered, it was always a nasty shock to us children. Looking back, though, I can be philosophical about it. We didn't waste a thing—we ate every part of that pig and were grateful. Don't brown this pork tenderloin before roasting it, because the spice mixture in the marinade tends to burn. Serve this dish with Braised Cabbage (page 201) or Braised Romaine (page 223), along with some sort of chutney (pages 229–40). It also makes a great sandwich.

1 teaspoon black peppercorns
1 tablespoon cumin seeds
½ cinnamon stick
3 cloves
½ teaspoon ground turmeric
5 garlic cloves, peeled
1 heaping tablespoon roughly chopped peeled ginger

⅓ cup apple cider
1 tablespoon cider vinegar
Kosher salt and freshly ground black pepper
2 pork tenderloins, about 2¼ pounds total

Finely grind the peppercorns, cumin seeds, cinnamon, and cloves together in an electric coffee/spice grinder. Combine the ground spices with the garlic, ginger, cider, vinegar, 1 tablespoon salt, and pepper to taste in a blender and puree until smooth. Generously pat the tenderloins all over with the marinade. *Marinate the tenderloins, covered and refrigerated, for at least 6 and up to 8 hours.*

Preheat the oven to 425°F. Bring the tenderloins to room temperature.

Sprinkle the tenderloins with salt and roast on a rack in a roasting pan in the middle of the oven for 30 minutes, or until an instant-read thermometer registers 140°F.

Let the tenderloins rest in the pan at room temperature for 10 minutes. (The temperature should rise to 155°F after resting.) Transfer the tenderloins to a cutting board and cut them against the grain on the bias into ½-inch-thick slices. Arrange the pork on a warm platter and serve at once.

stuffed pork chops with mustard shrimp sauce

SERVES 6

In India and Southeast Asia, dried shrimp are used much the way anchovies are in Western cooking—to give a deep, resonant backnote of flavor. Don't be put off by the smell of the uncooked dried shrimp; they won't be the least bit fishy or overbearing in the finished dish. Every time I open a bag of dried shrimp and toast them, their smell takes me back to my childhood. In our local fishing village, people would spread their shrimp catches out on coconut palm mats to dry in the sun, and the entire village reeked for days.

FOR THE STUFFING

3 tablespoons dried baby shrimp

2 dried New Mexico chiles, broken into pieces, including seeds

2 small dried red chiles (see Glossary), broken into pieces, including seeds

1½ tablespoons paprika

1 teaspoon kosher salt

½ teaspoon Aleppo pepper or cayenne

2 tablespoons chopped garlic

1 thick cilantro root (pale green and white parts only) or 3 cilantro stems, chopped

Six 9-ounce bone-in center-cut pork chops, 1¼ to 1½ inches thick

FOR THE SAUCE

1 teaspoon cumin seeds

1 tablespoon canola oil

1 teaspoon brown mustard seeds

1 teaspoon yellow mustard seeds

1 tablespoon unsalted butter

1 cup beef stock, Chicken Stock (page 274), or reduced-sodium canned chicken or beef broth

1 teaspoon minced peeled ginger

1 tablespoon minced garlic

¼ cup red wine vinegar

1 tablespoon jaggery or molasses

Kosher salt

1 cup canola oil

Toast the dried shrimp and chiles in a dry 10- to 12-inch skillet over moderately low heat, shaking the skillet occasionally, until the mixture is fragrant and the chile seeds are a couple of shades darker, about 3 minutes. Let the mixture cool, then finely grind it in an electric coffee/spice grinder. Combine the ground spices with the paprika, salt, Aleppo pepper, garlic, and cilantro root and mash into a dry paste in a mortar or a mini food processor.

Make a deep horizontal pocket (wide enough to fit a tablespoon measure) in each pork chop (opposite the bone and not on the flat side of each chop) with a small knife, making room for the stuffing.

Reserving ⅓ cup of the stuffing for the sauce, loosely pack each pork chop with about 1 tablespoon stuffing. Tie the perimeter of each chop with kitchen string, making one loop around the bone to help hold it in place. *Stuff the pork chops at least 1 and up to 8 hours ahead and refrigerate.*

Grind the cumin seeds in a mortar with a pestle (it's the easiest way with only a teaspoon of seeds) or in an electric coffee/spice grinder.

Heat the oil in a 6-inch skillet or a 1½-quart saucepan over moderately high heat until it shimmers and toast the brown and yellow mustard seeds until they pop and are fragrant, about 30 seconds. Add the butter and cook, stirring, until the butter smells nutlike, about 1 minute longer. Add the stock, ginger, and garlic and cook for 1 minute, stirring. Add the reserved stuffing mixture, ground cumin, and vinegar and cook for 2 minutes longer. Add the jaggery and cook just until it is incorporated, about 30 seconds.

Preheat the oven to 350°F. Generously season the pork chops with salt.

Heat ½ cup of the oil in the 10- to 12-inch skillet over moderate heat until it shimmers and sear half of the chops on one side until nicely browned, about 5 minutes. Turn the chops over and transfer to a shallow roasting pan. Sear the remaining chops in the same way, wiping out the skillet with paper towels and adding the remaining oil to the skillet. Put the pan in the middle of the oven and cook for 8 to 10 minutes, or until the chops are just done (they will still be pink inside). Serve the chops with the sauce.

slow-roasted spareribs with cider jus

SERVES 6

This dish has its roots in a typical Goan spit-roasted suckling pig. For the best flavor, marinate the ribs for a day. They can be cooked on the grill, although you might miss the tangy cider jus.

7 cloves
½ cinnamon stick, broken in half
1½ tablespoons brown mustard seeds
1 teaspoon black peppercorns
3 small dried red chiles (see Glossary)
½ teaspoon Aleppo pepper or
   cayenne
1½ tablespoons paprika

6 large garlic cloves, peeled
3 tablespoons sliced peeled ginger
¼ cup tequila
½ cup cider vinegar
1 tablespoon kosher salt
2 racks pork spareribs (about
   7 pounds)
2 cups apple cider

Finely grind the cloves, cinnamon, mustard seeds, peppercorns, chiles, and Aleppo pepper in an electric coffee/spice grinder. Turn the ground spices out into a medium bowl and stir in the paprika.

Puree the garlic, ginger, tequila, and vinegar in a blender until smooth. Add the garlic puree to the ground spices and mix well to form a loose paste. Stir in the salt.

Trim the excess fat from the ribs and pull the membrane off the underside of the racks. Slather the spice paste on both sides of the rib racks. Put the rib racks in a shallow baking pan and pour the apple cider over them. (You could also divide the racks and cider between 2 very large heavy-duty resealable plastic bags.) *Marinate the ribs for at least 6 and up to 24 hours.*

Preheat the oven to 375°F.

Put 1 cup of water in a 13 × 9-inch roasting pan and wedge the racks into the pan (they will shrink during cooking). Add the liquid from the pan they've been sitting in. Roast the ribs in the middle of the oven for about 1 hour and 45 minutes, or until they are tender, turning them once about halfway through. Serve the ribs with the jus from the bottom of the pan.

braised veal roulade

Veal shoulder and breast, two underappreciated cuts of meat, take well to braising. (Either cut will work here; simply have your butcher roll and tie it for you.) The long, slow cooking breaks down all the connective tissue and renders the meat fork-tender and unctuous. The braising liquid is reduced to give it more body and then served as a sauce. For six people, two roulades (the rolled, tied meat) are easier to handle—and take less time to cook—than one big one. And if you want to turn this into a hearty stew, dice the aromatic vegetables—the carrots, celery, and onion—and keep them in the sauce rather than straining them out. This dish deepens in flavor if made at least one day ahead.

Two 1½-pound boneless veal
   shoulder roasts or veal breasts,
   rolled and tied into roulades
Kosher salt and freshly ground black
   pepper
½ cup canola oil

FOR THE BRAISING LIQUID
1½ tablespoons cumin seeds
1½ tablespoons coriander seeds
1½ tablespoons brown mustard seeds
1 tablespoon black peppercorns
1 heaping teaspoon ground turmeric
4 cloves
One 2-inch cinnamon stick
3 medium carrots, cut into
   ¼-inch-thick slices

2 large celery stalks, roughly
   chopped
1 pound white onions, roughly
   chopped (about 4 cups)
2½ tablespoons sliced peeled ginger
1 cup finely grated fresh coconut (see
   page 283) or unsweetened
   desiccated coconut
1 cup dry white wine
24 coriander stems and/or roots
2 large rosemary sprigs
Kosher salt
5 cups Chicken Stock (page 274) or
   reduced-sodium canned chicken
   broth

Pat the roulades dry and season generously with salt and pepper. Heat the oil in a wide heavy ovenproof 6- to 8-quart pot over moderately high heat until it shimmers and sear the roulades, turning them with tongs, until well browned on all sides, about 12 minutes. (Lower the heat if the bits stuck to the bottom of the pot are getting too dark.) Transfer the roulades to a plate. (Do not clean the pot.)

Finely grind the cumin seeds, coriander seeds, mustard seeds, and peppercorns in an electric coffee/spice grinder. Transfer the ground seeds to a small bowl and stir in the turmeric. Add the cloves, cinnamon, carrots, celery, and onions to the (uncleaned) pot and cook over moderately high heat, stirring, for 2 minutes. Stir in the ginger, coconut, ground spices, wine, coriander stems/roots, rosemary, and salt to taste and cook, stirring, for 2 minutes. Return the roulades to the pot, along with the stock and any meat juices that have accumulated on the plate, and bring the braising liquid to a boil. Tightly cover the pot with a lid or foil and transfer the pot to the oven. Braise the roulades, turning them a few times, for about 2 hours, or until the veal is fork-tender.

Transfer the roulades to a large bowl and, if desired, strain the braising liquid through a sieve, pressing hard on the solids with the back of a ladle, over the roulades. Discard the solids left in the sieve. If serving the vegetables, remove and discard the cloves, rosemary, and cilantro stems/roots. Transfer the vegetables to the bowl containing the roulades. *The roulades (and vegetables) can be made up to this point 2 days ahead and cooled, uncovered, before being refrigerated, covered.*

Preheat the oven to 350°F. Remove the roulades, and vegetables if using them, from the braising liquid and skim the fat from the liquid. Bring the liquid to a boil in the cleaned pot or a heavy ovenproof 12-inch skillet until thickened, about 10 minutes. Remove the strings from the roulades and cut into 1½-inch-thick slices. Add the veal to the sauce and tightly cover the pot with a lid or foil. Transfer the pot to the middle of the oven and cook until the veal is heated through, 20 to 25 minutes. Serve the veal with the sauce spooned over it.

veal chops stuffed with hominy and lemon chutney

I first tasted hominy—cooked dried white corn kernels from which the hull has been removed—in the hearty New Mexican stew called posole. It is enormously satisfying, and a great vehicle for carrying flavors. Lemon Chutney (page 235) adds brightness and acidity. I stuff veal chops here, but you could also do a whole loin. The chops work beautifully on the grill too.

I cup drained white hominy from
    one 15-ounce can
I cup Lemon Chutney (page 235)
I teaspoon freshly ground black pepper
¼ cup finely chopped cilantro

¼ cup finely chopped chives
Six I-inch-thick bone-in veal rib
    chops
Kosher salt
⅔ cup canola oil

Preheat the oven to 400°F.

Put the hominy and chutney in a food processor and pulse until finely chopped (or use a knife). Put the hominy mixture in a bowl and stir in the pepper, cilantro, and chives.

Make a pocket in a long side of each chop (opposite the bone) by cutting a 1-inch-long horizontal incision with a small knife and pivoting the knife back and forth inside each chop to make a 3-inch-long pocket.

Transfer the filling to a large resealable plastic bag and cut a hole in one end to rig a pastry bag. (Or, if you happen to own a real pastry bag, now's the time to use it.) Squeeze a sixth of the filling into the pocket of each chop. Season the chops all over with salt.

Heat half of the oil in a 12-inch skillet over high heat until it shimmers and sear 2 chops for about 3 minutes on each side. Transfer them to a shallow roasting pan large enough to hold all 6 chops. Heat the remaining oil until it shimmers and sear 2 more chops in the same way. Transfer them to the roasting pan. There will be enough oil remaining in the skillet to sear the last 2 chops in the same way. Transfer them to the roasting pan as well. Roast the chops in the middle of the oven until just cooked through, 18 to 20 minutes. The chops should be slightly pink inside.

seared veal chops
with tomato kut

The kingdom of Hyderabad, in southern India, was one of the cultural centers of Muslim India, rising to prominence as the Moghul empire declined in the early eighteenth century. The Muslim chefs there served the same elaborate dishes they did farther north, but incorporated such local ingredients as the curry leaves, mustard seeds, and chile you'll see below. This recipe is inspired by Bade Miah, a Hyderabadi chef I worked for in Delhi. I was scared to death of him. Fierce and enormously fat, he would sit in the restaurant's kitchen and smoke cigarettes as his cooks scurried around. I could swear he had eyes in the back of his head, because he never missed a thing. And Delhi was unfamiliar to me, so I was homesick as well. The main thing I remember from that time in my life, though, was that my unhappiness was tempered by the fact that I got to cook—and eat—the most amazing food. Every time I make tomato *kut*—a chunky tomato purée that has a deep, rich spiciness—I think of Bade Miah and that kitchen in Delhi. Try the sauce with pasta or as a topping for bruschetta or pizza.

FOR THE TOMATO *KUT*

10 medium tomatoes (about
    4¾ pounds) or 6 cups roughly
    chopped canned whole tomatoes,
    juice reserved
¼ cup extra virgin olive oil
1 teaspoon brown mustard seeds
½ teaspoon nigella seeds
1 teaspoon cumin seeds
1 small dried red chile
    (see Glossary)
20 fresh curry leaves
8 garlic cloves, thinly sliced

1 cup sliced shallot
2 tablespoons chopped peeled ginger
2 bay leaves
¼ teaspoon ground turmeric
1 tablespoon Aleppo pepper or
    cayenne or 1½ teaspoons hot red
    pepper flakes
1½ tablespoons Tamarind Paste
    (page 284)
Kosher salt
Sugar

FOR THE VEAL CHOPS

Six 1¼- to 1½-inch-thick veal rib chops, 13 to 14 ounces each, tied around the perimeter with kitchen string and bones frenched by butcher if desired

Kosher salt and freshly ground black pepper
½ cup canola oil
½ cup loosely packed chopped cilantro

Fill a 4- to 6-quart saucepan with water and bring to a boil. Have a bowl of ice water ready.

If using fresh tomatoes, cut out the cores and score an X in the bottoms of the tomatoes. Blanch half of the tomatoes for 15 seconds, counting from the moment the tomatoes are slipped into the boiling water. Transfer the tomatoes to the ice water and blanch the rest of the tomatoes in the same way. Discard the water from the saucepan and dry the saucepan when it's cool enough to handle. Peel the tomatoes, cut in half crosswise, and squeeze the juice and seeds into a bowl. Strain the juice (you should have about 1⅔ cups) into another bowl and discard the seeds. Roughly chop the tomatoes (you should have about 6 cups).

Heat the olive oil in the saucepan over moderately low heat until it shimmers and cook the mustard seeds until they pop and are fragrant, about 30 seconds. Add the nigella seeds and cumin seeds. Break the chile in half and add to the saucepan, along with the curry leaves, garlic, and shallot. Cook the mixture, stirring occasionally, until the shallot has a little color, about 8 minutes, then add the ginger, bay leaves, turmeric, cayenne, and Aleppo pepper. Stir in the tomatoes, strained juice (or the canned tomatoes and reserved juice), tamarind paste, and 1 teaspoon salt. Bring the *kut* to a simmer and cook, covered, for 5 minutes.

Remove the lid and simmer for 25 minutes longer, until most of the liquid has evaporated. (It should be the consistency of a chutney.) Adjust the seasoning, adding a little more salt if desired and a little sugar if the *kut* is too acidic. Remove the *kut* from the heat and set aside.

Preheat the oven to 350°F. Pat the chops dry and generously season with salt and pepper. Let them sit for 5 minutes.

Heat ¼ cup of the canola oil in an ovenproof 12- to 14-inch skillet over high heat. Sear 3 chops for about 4 minutes, or until golden brown. Turn the chops over, sear the other side for 2 minutes, then transfer the chops to a shallow roasting pan. Sear the remaining chops in the remaining oil in the same way and transfer them to the roasting pan. Roast the chops in the oven for 15 to 20 minutes, depending on their thickness, for medium meat.

Stir the cilantro into the tomato *kut* and spoon onto a warm platter. Remove the string from the chops and arrange the chops on top of the *kut*. Drizzle the chops with the pan juices and serve immediately.

goan pot-au-feu with jeera meera broth

Like the French classic, this pot-au-feu is restorative on many different levels, and it is a good reason to keep homemade beef or veal stock in the freezer. A pot-au-feu generally contains more than one type of meat, but not this one. I suggest using veal tongue in addition to veal loin; you will be rewarded with a broth that is soulfully rich in flavor. The roots of this dish lie in the beef curry made by our cook, Ermine, when I was growing up. (You could substitute New York strip for the veal if you like.) I wasn't crazy about it at the time, but it turned out to be one of the things I missed most after I left home. *Jeera* means "cumin" in the west Indian language of Konkani, by the way, and *meera* means "pepper." If you make this in the summer, leave out the mace—it's an intense "heating" spice and would never be used during hot months in India. One last thing: the broth is even more delicious if made a day ahead, but once you poach the veal, you will want to serve this dish right away; otherwise the meat will dry out.

1 teaspoon black peppercorns

1 tablespoon cumin seeds

1 teaspoon ground turmeric

2½ tablespoons canola oil

6 cloves

½ cinnamon stick

1 piece mace

1 cup thinly sliced shallot

¼ cup thinly sliced garlic

¼ cup julienne strips peeled ginger

1 bay leaf

Kosher salt and freshly ground black pepper

¼ cup white port

2 quarts veal stock or beef stock, or 4 quarts reduced-sodium canned beef broth boiled until reduced by half

1 tablespoon Tamarind Paste (page 284)

2 pounds veal loin, cut across the grain into 12 even pieces

2 cups fingerling potatoes, cut in half crosswise

12 baby turnips, cut in half lengthwise

12 baby carrots or young small bunch carrots, cut in half crosswise

One 5-inch rosemary sprig

Eight 4-inch-long cilantro stems and/or roots, tied together with kitchen string	1 cup cilantro leaves

Finely grind the peppercorns and cumin seeds together in an electric coffee/spice grinder. Add the turmeric.

Heat the oil in a 6- to 8-quart pot over moderately high heat until it shimmers and add the cloves and cinnamon. Cook until fragrant, about 1 minute. Add the mace, shallot, garlic, ginger, bay leaf, and a generous pinch of salt. Cook the mixture, stirring, for 2 minutes, then add the ground spices. Cook the mixture for another 2 minutes, then stir in the white port, stock, and tamarind paste. *The broth can be made 1 day ahead and cooled to room temperature, uncovered, before being refrigerated, covered.*

Season the veal with salt and pepper and let sit for 20 minutes.

While the veal is sitting, add the potatoes to the broth and bring to a simmer. Simmer the broth until the potatoes are about half cooked, about 10 minutes. Add the turnips, carrots, rosemary, and bundle of cilantro stems with roots. Add the veal to the broth and bring to a boil. Reduce the heat and poach the veal, covered, at a bare simmer for 5 minutes. Let the pot sit, covered, for about 4 minutes. Remove and discard the cloves, cinnamon, bay leaf, rosemary, and bundle of cilantro stems/roots.

Divide the cilantro leaves among 6 bowls or soup plates and ladle the pot-au-feu over them.

sweetbread
chile fry

Frying things up in a robust, spicy blend of garlic, ginger, chiles, and the tart dried fruit called *kokum* is common in Goa. I sauté the chile fry ingredients quickly in two batches. (If you crowd the pan, they will not cook properly.) I don't soak, blanch, and weight sweetbreads before cooking them because I love their loose texture, but many people prefer them firmer. I give both methods here. If you plan to soak them, plan to start a day before you want to serve the dish. The chile fry mixture is endlessly versatile; have fun experimenting with mushrooms, steak, chicken, shrimp, or calamari.

FOR THE CHILE FRY

3 tablespoons canola oil

1 teaspoon brown mustard seeds

12 fresh curry leaves

1 small dried red chile (see Glossary), broken in half

6 cups thinly sliced red onion

Kosher salt

2 heaping tablespoons minced peeled ginger

2 heaping tablespoons thinly sliced garlic

1 fresh red chile, cut into ⅛-inch-thick slices

12 pieces kokum (labeled "wet kokum"), sliced (about 1½ tablespoons)

FOR THE SWEETBREADS

1 pound veal sweetbreads

Kosher salt

¼ cup canola oil

½ cup chopped cilantro

Heat 1½ tablespoons of the oil in a heavy 10-inch skillet over moderately high heat until it shimmers and add ½ teaspoon of the mustard seeds, 6 curry leaves, and half of the dried chile, crumbled. Cook the spice mixture, stirring, until the mustard seeds pop and are fragrant, about 30 seconds. Add half of the onion, salt to taste, and half of the ginger, garlic, fresh chile, and kokum. Sauté, stirring and shaking the skillet, until the onion is just softened, then transfer to a bowl.

Heat the remaining oil in the skillet and cook the remaining chile fry ingredients in the same way.

If you're *not* soaking and weighting the sweetbreads, preheat the oven to 350°F. Pat the sweetbreads dry and season them with salt.

Heat the oil in a heavy ovenproof 10- to 12-inch skillet over moderately high heat until it shimmers and sauté the sweetbreads, turning them once, until crisp and golden brown, about 3 minutes on each side. Transfer the skillet to the middle of the oven and cook the sweetbreads for 5 minutes longer. Return the skillet to the stovetop and, if the sweetbreads have lost some of their crispness, sauté them over moderately high heat, turning once and basting with the fat in the skillet, until crisp all over. Transfer the sweetbreads to a warm platter.

Wipe the fat out of the skillet with a paper towel and add the chile fry and cilantro. Reheat the chile fry over moderately high heat, stirring occasionally, for about 3 minutes and serve immediately with the sweetbreads.

If you *are* soaking and weighting the sweetbreads, soak them in a large bowl of water to cover in the refrigerator for 8 hours. Change the water twice during soaking.

Drain the sweetbreads and put in a 3- to 4-quart saucepan. Add enough water to cover them by 2 inches, then bring to a boil. Reduce the heat and simmer for 3 minutes. Transfer the sweetbreads to a bowl of fresh water.

Trim any fat and pull as much connective tissue as you can from the sweetbreads. Put them in a baking dish, then cover with plastic wrap and a plate. Put a couple of soup cans on the plate and refrigerate for at least 4 and up to 8 hours.

Preheat the oven to 350°F. Pat the sweetbreads dry and season with salt.

Heat the oil in a heavy ovenproof 10- to 12-inch skillet over moderately high heat until it shimmers and sauté the sweetbreads, turning them once, until crisp and golden brown, about 3 minutes on each side. Transfer the skillet to the middle of the oven and cook the sweetbreads for 5 minutes longer. Return the skillet to the stovetop and, if the sweetbreads have lost some of their crispness, sauté over moderately high heat, turning once and basting with the fat in the skillet, until crisp on all sides. Transfer the sweetbreads to a warm platter.

Wipe the fat out of the pan with a paper towel and add the chile fry and cilantro. Reheat the chile fry over moderately high heat, stirring occasionally, for about 3 minutes and serve immediately with the sweetbreads.

stewed kid goat with cardamom and turnips

After a good steak, I think my favorite meat is kid (baby) goat. My children love it, too. The texture is almost like that of veal shoulder—tender, delicate, gelatinous. Goat, perhaps the most commonly eaten meat in India, is available in North America at Indian, Caribbean, and Middle Eastern markets and by special order from most butchers. You can add goat bones to the stew for extra flavor or make a stock with them. This stew is based on one that my mother-in-law, Guddi, used to make. Like other stews and braises, it's at its best if made the day before and reheated. All you need is good bread as an accompaniment.

2 pounds boneless kid goat shoulder, trimmed of excess fat and cubed
Kosher salt
1½ tablespoons coriander seeds
1½ teaspoons black peppercorns
2 medium white onions, quartered and thinly sliced
¼ cup canola oil
4 cloves
6 black cardamom pods
10 green cardamom pods, cracked
1½ teaspoons fennel seeds, preferably Lucknow
1½ teaspoons cumin seeds

18 to 20 fresh curry leaves
8 garlic cloves, sliced lengthwise
⅓ cup julienne strips peeled ginger
1 mild to moderately hot fresh green chile, slit down 1 side
2 bay leaves
5 cups water, Chicken Stock (page 274), or reduced-sodium canned chicken broth
About 16 baby turnips (about the size of limes), trimmed and cut in half
1 cup plain whole-milk yogurt

Season the goat with salt and let sit for about 20 minutes.

Finely grind the coriander seeds and peppercorns together in an electric coffee/spice grinder.

Bring a pot of water to a boil and blanch the onions for 3 minutes. Drain the onions.

Heat the oil in a 6- to 8-quart pot over moderate heat until it shimmers. Add the cloves, cardamom pods, fennel seeds, and cumin seeds and cook, stirring, for 2 minutes, or until the spices are fragrant. Reduce the heat to low and stir in the curry leaves and garlic. Cook for 1 to 2 minutes longer, stirring (don't let the garlic color). Stir in the ginger and ground spices and cook for 1 minute. Add the blanched onions, chile, goat, bay leaves, water, and a generous pinch of salt. Increase the heat and bring the stew to a boil. Reduce the heat and simmer the stew, covered, for 1¼ hours. Add the turnips and simmer the stew, uncovered, for 10 minutes longer. *The stew can be made to this point 1 day ahead. Cool the stew, uncovered, completely before refrigerating, covered. Reheat the stew to simmering before finishing the recipe.*

Just before serving, put the yogurt in a bowl and whisk until smooth, then whisk in a little of the simmering liquid. Stir the yogurt mixture slowly into the stew and return it to a simmer. Remove the cloves, cardamom pods, and bay leaves before serving.

goat
haleem

This cold-weather dish, rich with cardamom and mace, comes from Hyderabad, in central India. Similar in texture to pulled pork, it was originally a way to use up pieces of meat that weren't the choice cuts. The pot was put on the embers of the kitchen fire and the thick stew gently bubbled all night long. The onions are cooked slowly until very brown, a time-honored step in making a traditional red or brown curry. Cracked wheat (bulgur) thickens the stew almost imperceptibly. Many people assume goat will be tough and gamy, but I use tender kid goat (available at Indian, Caribbean, and Middle Eastern markets and by special order at most butchers) here—it is unctuous, delicate, and hearty all at once. I serve this as a stew, but it makes a delicious dip for flatbread as well.

1 heaping tablespoon coriander seeds
½ teaspoon black peppercorns
½ teaspoon cumin seeds
1½ small dried red chiles (see Glossary)
5 green cardamom pods
3 black cardamom pods
1 piece mace
2 pounds boneless kid goat shoulder, trimmed of excess fat and cubed
Kosher salt
⅓ cup *masoor dal* (pink lentils), washed and drained
⅓ cup *moong dal* (hulled split mung beans), washed and drained
2 tablespoons *chana dal* (hulled split yellow Indian chickpeas), washed and drained

⅓ cup canola oil
2 heaping cups quartered and thinly sliced white onion
1½ tablespoons minced garlic
2 tablespoons julienne strips peeled ginger
3 bay leaves
½ teaspoon ground turmeric
2 cups chopped fresh or canned tomatoes
1 quart water or reduced-sodium canned chicken broth
1 cup 1-inch pieces peeled Delicata or butternut squash or sugar or cheese pumpkin (about 5 ounces)
⅓ cup cracked wheat (bulgur), washed and drained
1 cup finely chopped cilantro

Finely grind the coriander seeds, peppercorns, cumin seeds, chiles, cardamom pods, and mace together in an electric coffee/spice grinder.

Season the goat with salt and let sit for about 20 minutes.

Put the *dals* in a bowl and cover with water by 2 inches. Soak them for 20 minutes.

Meanwhile, heat the oil in a 6- to 8-quart pot over moderate heat until it shimmers. Add the onion and cook, stirring occasionally, for 20 to 25 minutes, or until very brown and fragrant. (Reduce the heat if the onion starts to burn.) Add the garlic and ginger and cook, stirring, over moderate heat for 1 minute. Add the bay leaves, ground spices, and turmeric and cook, stirring, for 1 minute longer. Add the tomatoes and a generous pinch of salt to the onions and cook, stirring, for 8 minutes. Add the goat, water, squash, and a pinch of salt. Bring the stew to a simmer and simmer, covered, for 45 minutes.

Drain the *dals* and add to the stew. Add salt to taste and return the stew to a simmer, covered. Simmer the stew for 10 minutes. Stir in the cracked wheat and simmer, uncovered and stirring often to help break up the meat, for 10 minutes longer. *The stew can be made to this point 1 day ahead. Cool it completely before putting it in the refrigerator, covered.*

Remove the stew from the heat and stir in the cilantro before serving.

rabbit and spring vegetable stew

SERVES 6

This is a play on a bistro standard, but instead of relying on whole-grain mustard, I use mustard seeds. I'm fond of the shallots in this dish; because they are kept whole, they become amazingly tender and full of a subtle shalloty essence. Serve this with a loaf of good bread.

6 whole fresh or thawed frozen rabbit
   legs
Kosher salt and freshly ground black
   pepper
1 tablespoon cumin seeds
2 tablespoons coriander seeds
2 tablespoons brown mustard seeds
2 tablespoons canola oil
4 cloves
1 cup cubed slab or thick-sliced
   bacon (about 5 ounces)
12 small whole shallots, peeled
2 sprigs fresh curry leaves
2 heaped cups quartered and thinly
   sliced white onion
6 large garlic cloves, sliced lengthwise
6 small young carrots, cut into
   1½-inch pieces if on the large side

¼ cup julienne strips peeled ginger
1 mild to moderately hot fresh green
   chile, slit halfway down 1 side
1 teaspoon ground turmeric
1 cup dry white wine
6 cups Chicken Stock (page 274),
   reduced-sodium canned chicken
   broth, or water
Two 5-inch rosemary sprigs
8 cilantro stems and/or roots, tied in
   a cheesecloth bundle
12 baby or small turnips, trimmed
   and halved if on the large side
2 tablespoons cider vinegar
Pinch of sugar
¼ cup finely chopped cilantro

Season the rabbit with salt and pepper and let sit for 20 minutes.

Coarsely grind the cumin seeds, coriander seeds, and 1 tablespoon of the mustard seeds together in an electric coffee/spice grinder.

Heat the oil in a 6- to 8-quart pot over moderately high heat until it shimmers and add the cloves and the remaining tablespoon of mustard seeds. When the mustard seeds pop and are fragrant, about 30 seconds, add half the bacon and 3 of the rabbit legs. Sear the rabbit until golden brown on both sides, 6 to 8 minutes. (Don't rush this step; the caramelization will add great flavor.) Transfer the rabbit to a platter. Sear the remaining rabbit legs in the spiced oil. When you turn them over, add the shallots and lightly brown those as well. Transfer the rabbit legs to the platter.

Lower the heat to moderate and add the sprigs of curry leaves, onion, garlic, carrots, ginger, chile, and ground spice mixture to the pot. Stir in the turmeric and ½ cup wine and cook, stirring and scraping up the caramelized bits stuck to the bottom of the pot. (They are packed with flavor.) Cook, stirring, until dry looking, 3 to 5 minutes, and add the remaining ½ cup wine, seared rabbit legs, stock, rosemary, cilantro bundle, and a generous pinch of salt.

Bring the stew to a boil, then reduce the heat and simmer, covered, for 20 minutes. Add the turnips, vinegar, and sugar and cook, covered, for about 30 minutes longer, or until the rabbit is cooked through. Season the stew with salt to taste and serve garnished with cilantro.

venison steaks
with coriander

My mother loved to tell stories about her grandfather, who worked for the East India Company. Every time the army blokes would go hunting, he would come home with venison for his family. It wasn't, strictly speaking, venison, but *nilgai*—the largest Asian antelope, found at the base of the Himalayas. I've never eaten it but have heard about it all my life. I use farm-raised venison (see the back of the book for a mail-order source). The recipe calls for steaks cut from a leg of venison, but loin, tenderloin, or even chops would work as well. If grilling outside isn't an option, use a ridged cast-iron grill pan. Try this with a turnip puree.

2 heaping tablespoons coriander
    seeds
1½ tablespoons black peppercorns
1 tablespoon cumin seeds
2 small dried red chiles
    (see Glossary)
2 heaping tablespoons chopped garlic

¼ cup chopped peeled ginger
1½ tablespoons dark brown sugar
4½ tablespoons extra virgin olive oil
Twelve 4-ounce venison steaks from
    the leg, 1½ to 2 inches thick
Kosher salt

Coarsely grind the coriander seeds, peppercorns, cumin seeds, and chiles in an electric coffee/spice grinder. Put the ground spices in a large bowl and add the garlic, ginger, brown sugar, and oil, mixing well. (Your freshly washed hands are the best tool for the job.) Dredge the venison in the spice mixture. *Marinate the venison, covered and refrigerated, for at least 8 and up to 12 hours.*

Prepare a charcoal fire or a gas grill and season the steaks with salt.

When the coals are medium hot, put the steaks on the grill rack. Cook the steaks on all sides for 6 to 8 minutes total, depending on the thickness of the meat, for medium-rare meat.

venison chili

SERVES 6

This chili is a product of my "waste not, want not" philosophy in the kitchen, and it is a staff favorite. It's just the thing for a blustery winter evening or Super Bowl Sunday. All you need is a pan of corn bread on the side. I use *kala chana*, the black chickpeas of India, in this recipe. They have an earthy, nutty flavor and are al dente in texture when thoroughly cooked. Substitute regular chickpeas if you prefer. The base of the chili is a puree made from tomatoes and deeply browned onions. Make a double batch of the puree and freeze half of it so you have an instant sauce for a spur-of-the-moment curry or chicken stew.

Heaping ½ cup *kala chana* (Indian chickpeas) or regular dried chickpeas

½ large carrot, peeled

½ large white onion plus 2 cups halved and thinly sliced

½ celery stalk

4 bay leaves

½ cup canola oil

3 cups chopped fresh or drained canned tomatoes

4 large garlic cloves

2 tablespoons thinly sliced peeled ginger

1 tablespoon coriander seeds

1 tablespoon cumin seeds

1½ teaspoons black peppercorns

½ teaspoon ground turmeric

1 tablespoon paprika

½ teaspoon cayenne

Kosher salt

6 green cardamom pods, cracked

6 black cardamom pods, uncracked

2 pounds ground venison

Four 3-inch thyme sprigs

One 5-inch rosemary sprig

1 cup finely chopped cilantro

Soak the *kala chana* or regular chickpeas in water to cover, refrigerated, for at least 8 hours. (You can also use the quick-soak method: Put them in a pan and cover with water by 2 inches. Bring to a boil and boil for 2 minutes. Remove from the heat and let stand, covered, for 1 hour.) Drain the chickpeas.

Put the drained chickpeas in a 3-quart pot and cover with water by 2 inches. Add the carrot, ½ onion, celery, and 1 bay leaf to the pot and bring to a boil. Reduce the heat and simmer the chickpeas until tender but still firm, about 40 minutes. (If you used the quick-soak method for the chickpeas, they will take about 1½ hours to cook.)

Drain the chickpeas. Dice the vegetables cooked with the chickpeas and set them aside.

While the chickpeas are simmering, heat ¼ cup of the oil in a 10-inch skillet over moderate heat until it shimmers. Add the sliced onion and cook, stirring occasionally, until evenly dark brown but charred in places, about 30 minutes. Transfer the onion to a blender and add the tomatoes, garlic, ginger, and ¼ cup water. Puree until smooth.

Finely grind the coriander seeds, cumin seeds, and peppercorns together in an electric spice/coffee grinder. Add the turmeric, paprika, and cayenne. Add the spice mixture to the puree along with a pinch of salt.

Heat the remaining ¼ cup oil in a 6- to 8-quart pot over moderate heat until it shimmers and add the cardamom pods. Cook for 1 minute. Add the puree and remaining 3 bay leaves and cook, stirring occasionally, for 15 minutes. (A spatter guard will come in handy.)

Add the venison, breaking it up with a wooden spoon, and increase the heat to moderately high. Cook, stirring and breaking up the ground meat, for 5 minutes.

Tie the thyme and rosemary together with kitchen string. Stir the drained cooked chickpeas, the cut-up vegetables, bundle of herbs, ½ cup water, and salt to taste into the chili. Reduce the heat and simmer the chili for about 20 minutes. *The chili can be made 1 day ahead and cooled completely, uncovered, before being refrigerated, covered.*

Garnish the chili with cilantro before serving.

vegetables

sautéed asparagus
and morels

Asparagus and morels are two of my favorite foods for spring. Both fresh and dried morels are available at fancy food shops (see the back of the book for a mail-order source). You could substitute oyster mushrooms or chanterelles—any flavorful mushroom that isn't too overpowering. (I wouldn't use shiitake or porcini, for instance.) Black, or royal, cumin seeds (*shah jeera*) have a real affinity for mushrooms. They are smaller and darker than regular cumin seeds and have a more complex aroma and flavor. They give this dish a deep savoriness.

I pound fresh morels or ¼ pound
   dried, cleaned (see page 197)
I pound pencil-thin asparagus
I tablespoon canola oil
¼ teaspoon black cumin seeds
2 teaspoons chopped shallot
I tablespoon chopped peeled ginger
I tablespoon chopped mild to
   moderately hot fresh green chile

I½ to 2 tablespoons unsalted butter
Kosher salt and freshly ground black
   pepper

FOR GARNISH (OPTIONAL)
I tablespoon chopped chives
I tablespoon chopped cilantro

Trim the morels if you're using fresh morels. Whether using fresh or dried, cut the mushrooms in half lengthwise.

Wash the asparagus and cut on the bias into 2-inch lengths.

Heat the oil in a large heavy skillet over moderately high heat until it shimmers and cook the black cumin seeds, shallot, ginger, and chile for 30 seconds, or until the cumin seeds are fragrant and the shallot and ginger are softened. Add the asparagus and sauté for 4 to 5 minutes. Add the butter and morels and season with salt and pepper. Sauté for 3 to 4 more minutes, or until the asparagus and morels are tender. Garnish the vegetables with chives and cilantro if desired.

cleaning morels and asparagus

Some of the meaty flavor of fresh morels is lost during washing, so I always brush them instead. Trim the end of the stems as well. If you are using dried morels, soak them in warm water for 20 minutes. Then squeeze the excess water out, rinse to remove any remaining grit, and squeeze dry. (Add the excess water, sans grit, to whatever you are cooking; it is full of flavor.) Morels should never be eaten raw; they contain tiny amounts of helvellic acid, which is toxic but destroyed by cooking.

Asparagus, like morels, can be sandy and gritty. To clean thin asparagus, trim the bottoms and swish in a bowl of water as you would leeks. For thicker stalks (which are a different variety, not simply more mature specimens), bend each one and snap it off where it breaks naturally before rinsing. Peel the lower part of the thick stalks so it will be as tender as the tops.

fricassee of
summer beans

Green beans and wax beans are a pretty combination for a summer table. I get mine from a farm called Berried Treasure in Roscoe, New York. Here I've added blanched peeled edamame (Japanese soybeans), but you could also substitute blanched peeled fava beans. The addition of *urad dal*—skinned and split black lentils—gives an earthy flavor and slight crunch to the dish.

3 tablespoons canola oil

1½ teaspoons *urad dal* (split black lentils), skinned

2 tablespoons brown mustard seeds

1 small dried red chile (see Glossary), broken and seeds discarded

10 to 12 fresh curry leaves

½ cup thinly sliced shallot

1 tablespoon julienne strips peeled ginger

½ pound green beans, cut crosswise into ½-inch pieces

½ pound wax beans, cut crosswise into ½-inch pieces

2 cups Chicken Stock (page 274), reduced-sodium canned chicken broth, or water

Kosher salt

1 cup blanched shelled edamame

Heat the oil in a 3- to 4-quart sauté pan over moderately low heat until it shimmers. Cook the *urad dal*, shaking the pan, until pale golden, about 2 minutes. Working quickly, add the mustard seeds, chile, curry leaves, shallot, and ginger. Remove the pan from the heat and stir everything together.

Return the pan to the stove, increasing the heat to moderate, and cook, stirring, until the shallot is softened, about 2 minutes. Add the green and wax beans and cook, stirring, for 1 minute. Increase the heat to high and add the stock, then salt to taste. Cook until the beans are still firm but beginning to get tender, about 6 minutes. Add the edamame and cook for 2 to 3 minutes longer, until all the beans are tender but still firm. Season with salt and serve immediately.

pan-roasted brussels sprouts and chanterelles

SERVES 6

Brussels sprouts, cooked just until tender, will surprise you with their mild, nutty flavor. This dish will add spice and color to your Thanksgiving table.

I pound Brussels sprouts, trimmed and cut into quarters, halved if small

6 ounces slab bacon, cut into ¼-inch dice

2 tablespoons canola oil

I teaspoon brown mustard seeds

½ pound chanterelle mushrooms, trimmed and quartered lengthwise (including stems), or halved if small

½ cup thinly sliced shallot

2 tablespoons thinly sliced garlic

I heaping tablespoon chopped peeled ginger

I cup loosely packed grated fresh coconut (see page 283) or unsweetened desiccated coconut

2 tablespoons chopped mild to moderately hot fresh green chile

½ teaspoon black cumin seeds

Kosher salt and freshly ground black pepper

I heaping tablespoon sliced chives

I heaping tablespoon chopped cilantro

Bring a large pot of generously salted water (it should taste like the ocean) to a boil and blanch the Brussels sprouts until barely tender, about 2 minutes. Transfer to a bowl of ice water. When the sprouts are cool, drain them and set aside.

Cook the bacon in a 10- to 12-inch skillet over moderately high heat until crisp, about 5 minutes. Drain the bacon on paper towels and reserve 2 tablespoons of the fat in a small bowl.

Heat the oil in the skillet over moderately high heat until it shimmers. Add the mustard seeds and cook until they pop and are fragrant, about 30 seconds. Add the mushrooms, shallot, garlic, ginger, coconut, chile, black cumin, blanched sprouts, bacon, bacon fat, and salt and pepper to taste.

Cook the sprouts and mushrooms over moderately high heat, stirring, until both are tender, about 3 minutes. Sprinkle the sprouts and mushrooms with the chives and cilantro before serving.

braised cabbage

This preparation, bright with chile and ginger, is simple. Try it with pork.

1½ pounds Savoy cabbage (about
    ½ large head)
¼ cup plus 1 tablespoon canola oil
2 whole cloves
1 tablespoon brown mustard seeds
2 sprigs fresh curry leaves
1 bay leaf
2 heaping tablespoons finely chopped
    shallot
2 teaspoons finely chopped garlic
2 tablespoons julienne strips peeled
    ginger

2 tablespoons thinly sliced mild to
    moderately hot fresh green chile
1 cup chopped fresh or canned
    tomato
1½ cups Chicken Stock (page 274) or
    reduced-sodium canned chicken
    broth
Two 4-inch thyme sprigs
One 6-inch rosemary sprig
Kosher salt

Cut the cabbage into 6 wedges, leaving most of the core intact to hold each wedge together during the braising. Heat ¼ cup of the oil in a wide heavy 6- to 8-quart pot over moderate heat until it shimmers. Add the cabbage and sear until lightly caramelized, turning once with tongs, about 3 to 5 minutes. Transfer to a plate.

Heat the remaining tablespoon oil in the (uncleaned) pot over moderately low heat until it shimmers. Add the cloves, mustard seeds, curry leaves, bay leaf, shallot, and garlic and cook, stirring, for 1 minute. Add the ginger, chile, tomato, stock, thyme, rosemary, and salt to taste. Bring to a boil and add the cabbage, tightly fitting it together in the bottom of the pot. Braise the cabbage, covered, until tender, about 10 minutes, turning it over halfway through the cooking time. Remove the cloves, curry leaf stems, and bay leaf before serving.

cauliflower puree
with chestnuts

SERVES 6

The inspiration for this dish was a trip to a market, where heaps of creamy-colored white cauliflower and glossy brown chestnuts were being sold right next to one another. Who could resist? Cauliflower is used widely in India; it takes to spices beautifully. And we don't waste the core, or *danda* ("stick" in Hindi). Simply trim the tough outer part away and cook the crisp, tender inside with the florets. I like to puree it after cooking, but you can simply leave the florets whole. Try this dish with the Seared Sea Scallops with Lime Jaggery Glaze (page 106).

FOR THE CAULIFLOWER PUREE

2½ pounds cauliflower

¼ cup canola oil

1 tablespoon cumin seeds

1 small dried red chile (see Glossary), broken in half

1 cup thinly sliced shallot

¼ cup thinly sliced garlic

Scant ¼ cup thinly sliced peeled ginger

Scant ¼ cup thinly sliced mild to moderately hot fresh green chile

¼ teaspoon ground turmeric

1 scant cup diced plum tomato

Kosher salt and freshly ground black pepper

1 cup Vegetable Stock (page 282), Chicken Stock (page 274), or water

FOR THE CHESTNUTS

2 tablespoons unsalted butter

2 tablespoons thinly sliced peeled ginger

¼ pound bottled roasted whole chestnuts, halved crosswise and sliced (about 10)

Kosher salt

¼ cup chopped chives

¼ cup chopped cilantro

Break the cauliflower into large florets. Trim off and discard the tough outer layer of the core, then cut the tender inside into 1½-inch pieces.

Heat the oil in a heavy 6-quart pan over moderate heat until it shimmers. Add the cumin seeds and dried red chile and cook, shaking the pan, for 1 minute. Add the shallot, garlic, ginger, and fresh green chile and cook, stirring, for 30 seconds. Stir in the turmeric, tomato, and salt to taste.

Stir in the cauliflower and stock and cover the pan. Simmer gently until the cauliflower is tender, 15 to 20 minutes. (It's important that the cauliflower cook slowly; otherwise, the liquid will evaporate too quickly, you'll have to add more, and the cauliflower will turn soggy.)

Puree the cauliflower mixture in a food processor in 2 batches until smooth. Season to taste with salt and pepper.

Melt the butter in a 10-inch skillet over high heat and sauté the ginger for 30 seconds. Add the chestnuts, stirring and shaking the skillet, and season with salt. Sauté the ginger and chestnuts until golden and caramelized and a little crisp around the edges, about 2 minutes. Transfer the ginger and chestnuts to paper towels to drain.

Reheat the puree over low heat and stir in the chives and cilantro. Serve the puree topped with the sautéed ginger and chestnuts.

cauliflower
caldin

A *caldin* is a classic Goan coconut curry. This one is light, with a bright burst of heat. When buying the coconut, look for one that's heavy for its size. Coconuts sold wrapped in plastic are usually fresher. In India, this would also be made with fresh coconut milk, but here in the States I use Chaokoh brand canned unsweetened coconut milk—it's found on most supermarket shelves. For a heartier dish, stir a half pound of medium shrimp, peeled and deveined, into the cauliflower when you add the tamarind paste (see Note). Serve with Plain Basmati Rice (page 258).

2 cups grated fresh coconut (see page 283), thawed frozen coconut, or 1½ cups unsweetened desiccated coconut soaked in 1½ cups hot water

3 garlic cloves, peeled

1 small onion, halved lengthwise and thinly sliced lengthwise

1 tablespoon cumin seeds

1 tablespoon canola oil

1 teaspoon ground turmeric

1 fresh red chile, halved lengthwise with stem intact

1 large head of cauliflower (about 2½ pounds), cut into 1-inch florets

1 heaping tablespoon Tamarind Paste (page 284)

One 13- to 14-ounce can unsweetened coconut milk, stirred well

1 tablespoon cider vinegar

Kosher salt

Puree the coconut, garlic, half the onion, and ½ cup water in the blender until it becomes a paste.

Finely grind the cumin seeds in an electric coffee/spice grinder.

Heat the oil in a heavy 4- to 5-quart pot over moderate heat until it shimmers and cook the remaining onion, stirring, until softened, about 5 minutes. Add the coconut paste, ground cumin, turmeric, and chile and cook at a bare simmer, uncovered, for 3 minutes. (Don't let the curry boil, or the coconut sauce will separate.) Stir in 2 cups water and cook at a bare simmer, uncovered, for 15 minutes. Add the cauliflower and cook at a bare simmer, uncovered and stirring occasionally, until just tender, 15 to 20 minutes.

Stir the tamarind paste, coconut milk, and vinegar into the cauliflower mixture. Return the curry to a bare simmer and season with salt to taste.

NOTE: *If adding shrimp, toss it with ½ teaspoon salt in a small bowl and let sit for 5 minutes while the cauliflower is cooking. After stirring the shrimp into the curry, return it to a bare simmer and cook until the shrimp are just done, about 3 minutes.*

chickpeas with coconut and tamarind

SERVES 6

This side dish is delicious with lamb or chicken or spread on bruschetta. Tamarind paste plays a large part here, for the balance of sweet and sour is all-important. Either dried chickpeas or canned ones will do the trick in this recipe, but if you're starting from scratch with dried, you'll have to begin the night before.

1¼ cups loosely packed grated fresh coconut (see page 283), thawed frozen coconut, or unsweetened desiccated coconut

1 mild to moderately hot fresh green chile, roasted, peeled, and seeded (see page 9)

¼ cup Tamarind Paste (page 284)

1½ tablespoons coriander seeds

1 tablespoon black peppercorns

2 tablespoons canola oil

Pinch of asafetida

1 pound dried chickpeas, cooked (see Note), or 6 cups drained and rinsed canned chickpeas

⅓ cup packed jaggery or dark brown sugar

Kosher salt

¼ cup chopped cilantro

Toast the coconut in a dry 10-inch skillet over low heat, stirring and shaking the skillet frequently, until golden brown, 10 to 12 minutes. Spread the toasted coconut out on a tray or large plate to cool. Set ¼ cup of the toasted coconut aside for garnish.

Puree the toasted coconut, chile, ½ cup water, and tamarind paste in a blender until smooth. Add another ¼ cup water if necessary to make a smooth puree.

Finely grind the coriander seeds and peppercorns together in an electric coffee/spice grinder.

Heat the oil in a heavy 6-quart pan over moderately high heat until it shimmers and add the asafetida. Cook for 15 seconds and add the puree and ground spices. Simmer the mixture until the oil separates out, about 4 minutes. Stir in the chickpeas, 2 cups water, and the jaggery. Vigorously simmer the chickpeas over high heat, coarsely mashing about 10 percent of the chickpeas with a potato masher to help break them down. It should take about 5 minutes to thicken the mixture. (It should still be slightly wet.) Season with salt to taste. Serve the chickpeas garnished with cilantro and the reserved toasted coconut.

NOTE: *Cover the dried chickpeas with 2 inches of water and soak overnight. Then drain them, put them in a pot with fresh water to cover generously, and bring to a boil. Reduce the heat and simmer the chickpeas until tender, 1 to 1 ¼ hours.*

corn on the cob with lime

This takes me back to the street food of Bombay—one of life's great pleasures as far as I'm concerned. It's also a great way to dress up corn on the cob for a party. The corn is boiled in spiced water, but you could use plain water if you prefer. After cooking, the corn is slathered with butter made tangy with lime juice and the spice blend called *chaat masala*. The flavors are a sophisticated contrast to the summer sweetness of the corn.

1 cinnamon stick
4 cloves
1 tablespoon black peppercorns
1 tablespoon coriander seeds
1 small dried red chile (see Glossary)
2 star anise
Kosher salt and freshly ground black pepper

½ teaspoon ground turmeric
6 ears corn, shucked and broken in half
¼ cup lime juice
1 tablespoon unsalted butter, cut into small pieces
¼ teaspoon cayenne
¾ teaspoon chaat masala

Fill a 6-quart pot about two-thirds full of water. Add the cinnamon, cloves, peppercorns, coriander seeds, chile, and star anise, then bring to a boil. Reduce the heat and simmer for 2 to 3 minutes to infuse the water with the spices. Season the water with enough salt so that it tastes like the ocean, then add the turmeric.

Return the water to a boil and add the corn. Cook the corn for about 5 minutes, or until tender yet still crisp.

Put the lime juice in a large bowl. Transfer the corn with tongs to the bowl, along with the butter, cayenne, chaat masala, and salt and pepper to taste. The best tool for slathering the corn with the spice mixture is your (scrupulously clean) hands.

roasted eggplant puree

This thick eggplant puree is based on *bharta*, a mashed eggplant dish, which I've always found a little heavy with spices and oil. I've lightened it up considerably, but plenty of smoky, roasted eggplant flavor still comes through. Traditionally the eggplants are roasted in a covered skillet (rather like a Dutch oven) or over an open cooking fire. This dish is a natural with lamb, but it also makes a great bed for roasted cod or bass or an excellent dip or spread for bruschetta.

2 large shallots, sliced, plus
   1½ teaspoons finely chopped
2 large garlic cloves, sliced, plus
   I teaspoon finely chopped
2 teaspoons fresh thyme leaves
¼ cup extra virgin olive oil
Kosher salt and freshly ground black
   pepper
2 large eggplants (1¾ pounds total),
   halved lengthwise

1½ teaspoons cumin seeds
I tablespoon chopped peeled ginger
I teaspoon chopped fresh red chile
   with seeds
½ to I teaspoon hot red pepper flakes
1½ tablespoons lime juice
2 plum tomatoes, diced
¼ cup salted roasted peanuts,
   roughly chopped

Preheat the oven to 350°F. Line a baking sheet with sides with parchment paper.

Scatter the sliced shallots and garlic and the thyme on the baking sheet. Drizzle with half of the oil and sprinkle with salt and pepper before laying the eggplant, cut sides down, on top. Put the baking sheet in the middle of the oven and roast the eggplant until it is soft to the touch, about 1 hour. When the eggplant is cool enough to handle, scoop out the flesh into a bowl and mash with a fork or potato masher.

Heat the remaining oil in a 2-quart saucepan over moderately high heat. Add the cumin seeds and cook for 30 seconds, then add the chopped shallot and garlic, ginger, fresh chile, and red pepper flakes. Cook, stirring, for 2 minutes, or until the garlic just begins to turn golden brown. Add the eggplant and salt to taste and cook over moderate heat, stirring occasionally, until thick and creamy (the eggplant fibers should break up almost completely), about 12 minutes.

Stir in the lime juice, tomatoes, peanuts, and salt and pepper to taste and serve.

braised baby
root vegetables

These gently cooked young, tender root vegetables—earthy and delicate all at the same time—are a tribute to early autumn at the farmers' market. Trim all but a quarter inch of the greens from the turnips and carrots so they look beautiful on the plate. White poppy seeds (see Sources), which are used in India as a thickener, are stirred in at the last minute to provide a satisfying textural contrast, and a pasilla de Oaxaca chile adds a little smoky heat.

4 unpeeled garlic cloves
Extra virgin olive oil
Kosher salt
¼ cup white poppy seeds
¼ cup canola oil
1 tablespoon cumin seeds
1 dried pasilla de Oaxaca chile
2 large shallots, thinly sliced
    lengthwise
¼ cup julienne strips peeled ginger

10 baby turnips, trimmed and
    halved, quartered if large
24 baby carrots, trimmed and cut in
    half lengthwise if large
½ pound fingerling potatoes, cut
    into ½-inch slices
¼ pound cipollini onions, peeled
    and quartered, or cut into eighths
    if large
2 to 3 tablespoons chopped cilantro

Preheat the oven to 350°F. Put the garlic cloves on a piece of foil. Drizzle the garlic with the olive oil and season with salt. Wrap the garlic tightly in the foil and roast in the middle of the oven for 30 to 35 minutes, or until the garlic is soft. Slip the skins off the garlic cloves.

Toast the poppy seeds in a dry medium skillet over moderately low heat, shaking the skillet, until the seeds are fragrant and a couple of shades darker, about 3 minutes. Transfer the poppy seeds to a small bowl.

Heat the canola oil in a heavy 4- to 6-quart pan over moderately high heat until it shimmers and add the cumin seeds. Cook for 30 seconds and add the chile, shallots, roasted garlic, ginger, vegetables, 1 cup water, and salt to taste. Bring the mixture to a simmer. Cover the pan tightly and braise the vegetables over low heat until tender, about 15 minutes.

Stir the toasted poppy seeds into the vegetables and garnish with the cilantro to serve.

kashmiri greens

I first visited Kashmir, up in the mountains of northern India, when I was in my late teens, and the food made a huge impression. Although the cuisine is most famous for its meat dishes (such as the Milk-Braised Lamb Shanks on page 163) and Persian-inspired rice pilafs, the treatment of greens is exceptional as well. In Kashmir, this dish is made with kohlrabi greens in season, but it is equally delicious when made with any hearty braising greens such as collards, chard (the colored varieties are very pretty), mustard greens, and/or turnip greens. Bok choy and pea shoots are good additions to the mix. Serve this with steak, chicken, or fish.

4 pounds braising greens
1 tablespoon canola oil or olive oil
¼ teaspoon asafetida
2 teaspoons cumin seeds
2 large shallots, sliced
½ cup julienne strips peeled ginger

1 small dried red chile (see Glossary), broken in half (see Note)
Kosher salt and freshly ground black pepper

Discard the tough stems from the greens. Chop the tender stems and set aside, then roughly chop the leaves.

Heat the oil in a 4-quart pot over moderately high heat until it shimmers and add the asafetida and cumin seeds. Cook, stirring, until the spices are fragrant, about 1½ minutes. Add the shallots, ginger, and chile and cook, stirring, until the shallots are translucent, about 3 to 4 minutes. Add the stems of the greens and salt to taste, then cook, stirring, for 1 minute. Add the greens and cook, tossing occasionally with tongs, until just tender, 15 to 20 minutes. Discard the chile and season with salt and pepper to taste.

NOTE: *If you want a spicier dish, break the chile into smaller pieces.*

stewed pink lentils with spinach and coconut

This is incredibly satisfying on its own or served with grilled fish, shrimp, or chicken.

¾ cup *masoor dal* (pink lentils)
3 tablespoons canola oil
3 cloves
1½ tablespoons cumin seeds
1 heaping cup thinly sliced shallot
3 tablespoons thinly sliced garlic
3 tablespoons julienne strips peeled ginger
2 tablespoons sliced mild to moderately hot fresh green chile
1½ cup packed grated fresh coconut (see page 283) or thawed frozen coconut

1½ cups Chicken Stock (page 274), reduced-sodium canned chicken broth, or Vegetable Stock (page 282)
Kosher salt and freshly ground black pepper
1½ pounds spinach, tough center ribs removed
3 tablespoons julienne strips kokum (labeled "wet kokum")

Wash the lentils in a bowl of cold water, swishing them around with your hand. Pour the water out and repeat until the water loses its murkiness and remains clear. Cover the lentils with fresh water by 2 inches and soak for 1 hour.

Heat the oil in a wide 6-quart pan over moderate heat until it shimmers and add the cloves and cumin seeds. Cook, stirring, until the cumin seeds are fragrant and a couple of shades darker, about 2 minutes. Add the shallot, garlic, ginger, and chile and cook, stirring, for 1 minute. Add the coconut and cook, stirring, until the coconut takes on a little color, about 2 minutes. Add the lentils, stock, and salt and pepper to taste and cook for 2 minutes longer. Stir in the spinach and kokum and cover the pan. Cook until the lentils and spinach are tender, about 15 minutes.

mushroom chickpea cakes with tomato sauce

SERVES 6

Here the deep savor of tomatoes meets the meatiness of mushrooms, which I season with a little black cumin—it is duskier and more foresty than regular cumin. Sometimes I smoke the tomatoes in a stove-top smoker or on the grill. Based on a very traditional *shami* kebab, which is made with lamb, it makes an enormously satisfying vegetarian main course. You could also make the cakes smaller and serve them as an hors d'oeuvre, with Asian chile sauce.

FOR THE MUSHROOM CHICKPEA CAKES

- ½ cup *chana dal* (hulled split yellow Indian chickpeas)
- I tablespoon coriander seeds
- ¼ cup canola oil
- I teaspoon black cumin seeds (*shah jeera*)
- I¼ pounds shiitake or white button mushrooms, stems discarded
- ½ cup thinly sliced shallot
- Scant ¼ cup thinly sliced peeled ginger
- ¼ cup thinly sliced garlic
- Kosher salt and freshly ground black pepper
- ¼ teaspoon ground turmeric
- ¼ teaspoon Aleppo pepper or cayenne
- 12 tarragon leaves, chopped
- ¼ cup cilantro leaves, chopped
- I heaping tablespoon chopped chives
- 3 tablespoons chickpea flour (*besan*), sifted

FOR THE TOMATO SAUCE

- I½ pounds tomatoes, cored and halved crosswise
- 3 tablespoons extra virgin olive oil
- ½ teaspoon mustard seeds
- One I-inch piece dried pasilla de Oaxaca chile
- 12 to 15 fresh curry leaves, thinly sliced crosswise
- ¼ cup sliced shallot
- 2 garlic cloves, sliced lengthwise into julienne strips
- Kosher salt
- ¼ cup julienne strips peeled ginger
- ¼ teaspoon black cumin seeds (*shah jeera*)

1 cup chickpea flour (*besan*)
½ cup canola oil

Put the *chana dal* in a 2-quart pan and add 1 quart water. Bring to a boil and reduce to a simmer. Simmer the *chana dal* until tender yet still firm, about 30 minutes. Drain the *chana dal* in a sieve and spread on a tray or plate to cool.

Very coarsely grind the coriander seeds in an electric coffee/spice grinder.

Heat the oil in a 12-inch skillet over moderately high heat until it shimmers and add the ground coriander seeds and the whole black cumin seeds. Add the mushrooms and reduce the heat to moderate. Add the shallot, ginger, and garlic and stir to coat everything with oil and spices. Stir in ¼ teaspoon salt and ¼ teaspoon pepper and continue to cook, stirring and breaking up the mushrooms, for 10 minutes. Stir in the turmeric, Aleppo pepper, cooled *chana dal*, and ½ cup water. Stir to scrape all the browned bits (they are full of flavor) off the bottom of the skillet. Continue to cook for about 3 minutes, or until the mixture is on the dry side. Spread the mushroom mixture on a tray or platter to cool.

Transfer the cooled mushroom mixture to a food processor and add the tarragon, cilantro, and chives. Pulse until finely ground.

Transfer the mushroom mixture to a bowl and work in the chickpea flour, 1 teaspoon salt, and ½ teaspoon pepper. (Your freshly washed hands are the best tool for the job.) Form the mushroom mixture into 6 hamburger-shaped cakes about 3½ inches wide (a scant ½ cup each).

Puree the tomatoes in a blender or food processor until smooth and strain them through a sieve into a bowl. Discard the solids in the sieve.

Heat the olive oil in a 10-inch skillet over high heat until it shimmers and cook the mustard seeds until they pop and are fragrant, about 30 seconds. Add the piece of chile, curry leaves, shallot, garlic, and salt and cook for 2 minutes, stirring. Add the ginger, black cumin, and tomato puree. Bring the mixture to a boil and reduce to a simmer. Simmer the sauce until cooked down and slightly thickened, about 20 minutes.

Lightly dredge the cakes in chickpea flour.

Heat the oil in a 12-inch skillet over moderately high heat until it shimmers and fry the cakes until golden, about 2 minutes on each side. Serve the cakes on top of the sauce.

grilled
okra

I have my brother Bryan to thank for this dish, in which an ever-popular Indian vegetable meets an all-American suburban backyard grill. You will need medium to large okra pods if you are going to use a charcoal or gas grill, because small pods will fall through the grill rack. If you use a ridged cast-iron grill pan, however, any size will do. No matter what method you use, don't be afraid to get a little char on the okra; that roasted-toasted flavor really knocks this one out of the park. This is delicious with roasted chicken or lamb.

I pound medium to large okra, caps trimmed
3 tablespoons olive oil
½ teaspoon brown mustard seeds
½ teaspoon cumin seeds
I teaspoon minced peeled ginger

I teaspoon minced mild to moderately hot fresh green chile
I teaspoon lime juice
½ teaspoon chaat masala
Kosher salt and freshly ground black pepper

Preheat a charcoal or gas grill.

Toss the okra with 1 tablespoon of the oil in a bowl. Grill the okra over moderate heat on the grill, turning it occasionally, until charred in places and tender yet still firm, about 8 minutes.

Heat the remaining oil in an 8- to 10-inch skillet over moderately high heat until it shimmers and add the mustard seeds. When the mustard seeds pop and are fragrant, after about 30 seconds, add the cumin seeds, ginger, chile, and okra. Cook the okra, stirring and tossing it to coat, for about 30 seconds and transfer to a bowl. Stir in the lime juice, chaat masala, and salt and pepper to taste.

turmeric mashed potatoes

These potatoes have a nutty sweetness that goes well with Marinated Hanger Steak (page 148) or roast chicken. They're inspired by the filling for *dosas*—the South Indian rolled pancakes that are crisp-crunchy on the outside but slightly spongy inside. I really love them because they bring back great memories: Mom would pile the family in the car and take us out for a *dosa* dinner twice a month.

2¾ pounds equal-size boiling
    potatoes such as Yukon Gold
3 tablespoons canola oil
1½ tablespoons *chana dal* (hulled
    yellow split chickpeas)
1 medium red onion, thinly sliced
1½ tablespoons unsalted butter
Heaping ¼ teaspoon ground
    turmeric

¾ cup heavy cream
¾ cup milk
1½ teaspoons dry mustard
1½ tablespoons honey
Kosher salt and freshly ground black
    pepper

Peel the potatoes and cut them in half crosswise (quarter them if large). Cover them with cold water by 2 inches in a 3-quart saucepan and simmer until just tender, 15 to 20 minutes, depending on the size of the potatoes. Drain in a colander and return to the pan to let them dry slightly, about 2 minutes. While they are still warm, mash the potatoes using a potato masher or a ricer and keep them warm, covered.

Heat the oil in a 10-inch skillet over moderate heat until it shimmers. Add the *chana dal* and sauté until light golden, about 1 minute. Add the onion, butter, and turmeric and cook the mixture, stirring, until the onion is translucent, about 3 minutes. Add the cream and milk and cook until the mixture is reduced by half, about 7 minutes.

Meanwhile, whisk together the dry mustard and honey in a small bowl. Whisk in about ¼ cup of the cream mixture, then whisk the honey mixture, salt, and pepper into the reduced cream mixture.

Heat the mashed potatoes over low heat until warmed through and add the cream mixture, stirring until well combined. Season with salt and pepper.

ramps with spinach and bacon

Ramps—essentially small leeks that grow wild in much of America's woodlands—are one of spring's most fleeting joys, so when you see them at a farmers' market, pounce. Ramps have a rough, untamed garlicky streak in them that I love, especially when finessed with smoky nuggets of bacon cooked crisp and a slick of flavorful drippings. Make this early in the season, when the ramp bulbs are small and fairly mild. (The more mature they get, the stronger they become in flavor and aroma.) A few handfuls of spinach round out this dish.

1 pound ramps
1 tablespoon canola oil
1 teaspoon brown mustard seeds
1 teaspoon cumin seeds
14 ounces lean bacon, cut into
   ¼-inch dice
1 teaspoon chopped peeled ginger

½ teaspoon chopped mild to
   moderately hot fresh green chile
Kosher salt and freshly ground black
   pepper
1½ pounds spinach, tough stems
   discarded and leaves torn into
   large pieces

Trim the root ends from the ramps. Cut the bulbs from the leaves. If the bulbs are small, simply smash them with the back of a large heavy knife. If large, cut them crosswise into thin slices.

Heat the oil in a 10-inch skillet over moderately high heat until it shimmers. Add the mustard seeds and cook, stirring, until they pop and are fragrant, after about 30 seconds. Add the cumin seeds and cook, stirring, for 30 seconds. Add the bacon and cook until it starts to turn color, about 2 minutes. Stir in the ramp bulbs, ginger, and chile and cook for 1 minute. Add the ramp leaves and pepper to taste and cook, stirring, for 2 minutes. Add the spinach and salt to taste and cook until the spinach is wilted, about 2 minutes longer.

ratatouille

Ratatouille is often code for "eggplant mush," which is why I loathed it in my cooking school days. I never gave the dish a second thought until I spied the most gorgeous eggplants and tomatoes at the Union Square Greenmarket, where we do much of the restaurant's shopping. We buy eggplant grown by Cherry Lane Farms in southern New Jersey. When serving this with lamb, I garnish it with julienne strips of mint. If I'm serving it as a vegetarian main course, though—with Cracked Wheat Pilaf (page 265) or rice—I add chopped cilantro and chives just before serving. Blanching the eggplant first prevents it from absorbing too much oil while being roasted. In the height of summer, go all out with heirloom tomatoes and fresh, young garlic. This makes a great hors d'oeuvre or sandwich filling.

FOR THE RATATOUILLE

4 small purple and/or white Italian or Japanese eggplants (about 1½ pounds), quartered lengthwise and cut into ⅛-inch-thick slices (about 7 cups)

¼ cup extra virgin olive oil

1 teaspoon brown mustard seeds

1 teaspoon nigella seeds

4 garlic cloves, thinly sliced

1½ cups roughly chopped red onion

1 tablespoon chopped shallot

2 small zucchini, halved and cut into ⅛-inch slices (about 3 cups)

2 small yellow squash, halved and cut into ⅛-inch slices (about 3 cups)

3 tablespoons thinly sliced fresh red chile with seeds

2 teaspoons julienne strips peeled ginger

5 plum tomatoes, seeded and roughly chopped (about 2 cups)

Kosher salt

Bring a large pot of generously salted water to a vigorous boil. Blanch the eggplant, stirring often, in batches (it's important not to crowd the pot) for 2 to 2½ minutes, or until just softened. Remove the eggplant with a slotted spoon and drain on paper towels.

Preheat the oven to 375°F.

Heat the oil in a heavy ovenproof 12- to 14-inch skillet over moderately high heat until it shimmers and add the mustard seeds. When they start to pop and are fragrant, after about 30 seconds, add the nigella seeds and cook until they are fragrant, about 5 to 10 seconds.

Add the garlic, onion, and shallot and cook over high heat, stirring, for 2 minutes, or until the onion is translucent. Then add the zucchini, squash, chile, ginger, and 1¼ teaspoons salt and cook, stirring, for about 3 minutes, or until the zucchini is barely tender. Stir in the tomatoes, eggplant, and salt to taste, then roast in the middle of the oven for about 10 minutes, or until the eggplant is tender.

braised romaine

Here hearts of romaine are braised to a delicate crunch, and a pasilla de Oaxaca chile from Mexico gives them a smoky kick. This is a sophisticated accompaniment to the Coriander-and-Mustard-Crusted Strip Loin (page 149). It's enormously versatile and easy to make, though, and can be used to give finesse to almost any meal.

1½ tablespoons extra virgin olive oil
½ teaspoon thinly sliced dried pasilla de Oaxaca chile (see Note)
1 teaspoon brown mustard seeds
2 tablespoons chopped shallot
1 small carrot, finely chopped
3 hearts of romaine (about ¾ pound), cut in half lengthwise and cores scored

1 tablespoon thinly sliced kokum (labeled "wet kokum")
Kosher salt and freshly ground black pepper
1 cup Chicken Stock (page 274) or reduced-sodium canned broth

Heat the oil in a heavy 6- to 8-quart pot over moderately high heat until it shimmers and add the chile, mustard seeds, shallot, and carrot. Cook, stirring, for 2 minutes, or until the shallot begins to soften.

Add the romaine halves to pot, flat sides down and wedging them tightly together. (They will wilt, so don't worry if they don't fit perfectly to begin with.) Sprinkle the kokum over the romaine and season generously with salt and pepper. Pour the stock over the romaine and cover the pot tightly with a lid or foil. Braise the romaine until just tender, about 10 minutes. Remove the lid and boil until almost all the liquid is evaporated, about 3 minutes longer.

NOTE: *If the chile is dry to the point of brittleness, soak it in a small amount of water for a few minutes to make it pliable again. Don't waste the soaking water; add it to the pot.*

roasted acorn squash with maple syrup and lime

After my two sons, Justin and Peter, and I made maple syrup one spring up in New England, this dish became part of our Sunday cooking repertoire. It eventually landed on the menu at Tabla. I use duck fat here because I always have it on hand at the restaurant, but bacon fat gives its own delicious flavor. This is fantastic with pork chops or pork tenderloin.

1 tablespoon extra virgin olive oil

2 star anise

3 cloves

1 small dried red chile (see Glossary), broken in half

3 tablespoons duck fat, bacon fat, or unsalted butter

2 bay leaves

5 large garlic cloves, sliced lengthwise

Scant ¼ cup thinly sliced peeled ginger

One 5-inch rosemary sprig

½ large white onion, cut in half crosswise and thinly sliced

2½ pounds acorn or Delicata squash (about 2), peeled, cut in half, seeded, and cut into 1-inch pieces about ¼ inch thick

½ cup lime juice (from 2 large limes)

Kosher salt and freshly ground black pepper

¼ cup pure maple syrup

Preheat the oven to 375°F.

Heat the oil in a wide ovenproof 6-quart pot over moderately high heat and add the star anise and cloves. Cook, stirring, for 30 seconds. Add the chile, duck fat, bay leaves, garlic, ginger, rosemary, and onion. Cook, stirring, until the onion has softened, about 5 minutes. Add the squash and lime juice, stirring to coat the squash with the lime juice, and season with salt and a generous amount of pepper.

Roast the squash, uncovered, in the middle of the oven, stirring occasionally, until the squash is tender, about 30 minutes. Stir in the maple syrup and salt and pepper to taste. Remove the star anise, cloves, chile, bay leaves, and rosemary before serving.

braised silk squash and long squash

This recipe is reason alone to head for your nearest Asian market. Silk squash—also called *Chinese okra* or *angled loofah*—is eaten all over Asia. It originated in India, though, and it's one of my all-time favorite vegetables. Crisp-tender and mild, it picks up other flavors like a sponge. (Another variety, in fact, *is* a sponge—the loofah that you use in the bath.) Long squash—also known as *bottle gourd, calabash, cucuzza,* and *upo*—is eaten all over the world, from India to Italy, from the Caribbean to China. It has a lovely firm texture that's reminiscent of cucumber and zucchini. You could substitute winter melon. You could also substitute zucchini for both or either squash; the texture will be different but it will still be delicious.

1½ pounds long squash

1½ pounds silk squash

3 tablespoons canola oil

1½ teaspoons brown mustard seeds

1½ teaspoons cumin seeds

2 tablespoons finely chopped shallot

1 tablespoon finely chopped garlic

2 tablespoons unsalted butter

2 tablespoons finely chopped mild to moderately hot fresh green chile

2 tablespoons finely chopped peeled ginger

Kosher salt and freshly ground black pepper

1 cup Chicken Stock (page 274) or reduced-sodium canned chicken broth

1½ teaspoons finely chopped sage leaves (about 4)

¼ cup chopped chives

¼ cup chopped cilantro

Peel the long squash and cut it in half lengthwise. Scoop out the spongy-looking, seedy core and discard it. Cut the flesh into chunks about 1 inch long and ¼ inch thick. Peel the silk squash and cut it in half lengthwise. Cut the flesh into the same-size chunks.

Heat the oil in a wide heavy 6-quart pot over moderate heat until it shimmers and cook the mustard seeds, cumin seeds, shallot, and garlic, stirring, for 1 minute. Add the butter and cook until the shallot and garlic are lightly caramelized, about 2 minutes longer. Stir in the chile, ginger, and then the long squash. Season with salt to taste and add the stock. Cover the pot, bring the braise to a boil, and simmer for 5 minutes. Add the silk squash and simmer, covered, for 5 minutes longer. Stir in the sage.

Serve the vegetables seasoned with salt and pepper to taste and garnished with chives and cilantro.

condiments: chutneys, pickles, raitas, and dressings

about chutneys and pickles

In India chutneys and pickles are used as condiments to brighten up curries and other dishes with small, intense bursts of flavor and heat. There is no incorrect way to eat them: you can dollop them directly onto foods or use them as a dip, either as is or stirred into yogurt or sour cream. Their appeal is endless, so don't limit your thinking to the recipes in this book. They can give grilled meat, vegetables, sandwiches—even the Thanksgiving turkey—a new twist.

Making chutney is similar to making jam, except that it's much more forgiving. The longer a chutney sits in the refrigerator, the better—the flavors will ripen and mellow into something that will turn a plain roast chicken or piece of salmon into something special.

Pickling, a way of preserving seasonal vegetables and fruits the world over, relies on an acid such as vinegar as well as salt. Proportions are important in giving crispness and flavor to the end result. Like making chutney, making an Indian pickle is a relaxed proposition, a nice thing to do on a Sunday afternoon while you are puttering around the kitchen.

apple
chutney

This chunky chutney is delicious with roast pork or seared foie gras. The dried pomegranate seeds are one of the many souring agents used in India; here they provide a welcome bit of fruity astringency. The black salt, which is mined in India, has a smoky aroma and a briny tang. Both ingredients can be found at Indian markets or by mail order (see Sources).

FOR THE SPICE SACHET
5 cloves
1 cinnamon stick, broken in half
2 star anise
1 bay leaf

FOR THE CHUTNEY
1½ teaspoons black peppercorns
2 tablespoons dried pomegranate
    seeds
4½ pounds apples (such as Empire,
    McIntosh, or Gala; not Granny
    Smith), peeled, cored, and cut
    into 1-inch pieces

3 cups apple cider
⅓ cup julienne strips peeled ginger
½ cup cider vinegar
Scant ½ cup jaggery or dark brown
    sugar
1 cup golden raisins
1 tablespoon yellow mustard seeds
½ dried pasilla de Oaxaca chile
½ teaspoon ground turmeric
¼ teaspoon black salt
½ teaspoon Aleppo pepper or
    cayenne
2¼ teaspoons kosher salt

Wrap the cloves, cinnamon, star anise, and bay leaf together in cheesecloth and tie with kitchen string.

Finely grind the peppercorns and dried pomegranate seeds together in an electric coffee/spice grinder.

Put the apples in a wide heavy 6- to 8-quart pot. Add the apple cider, ginger, vinegar, jaggery, raisins, sachet, mustard seeds, chile, and ground peppercorns and pomegranate seeds, then bring to a boil.

Add the turmeric, black salt, Aleppo pepper, and salt and return to a boil. Simmer the mixture, uncovered, stirring occasionally, until the apples are tender, about 40 minutes. Remove the sachet and chile before serving. *The chutney keeps in an airtight container in the refrigerator for 2 weeks.*

cherry
chutney

The idea for this chutney was inspired by the ducks I get from Stone Church Farms, in upstate New York. It's also delicious with game, foie gras, and pork.

I tablespoon mustard oil
I tablespoon canola oil
¼ cinnamon stick
2 cloves
2 star anise
One I-inch piece dried pasilla de
    Oaxaca chile
I tablespoon chopped peeled
    ginger

I½ pounds pitted fresh or frozen
    sweet cherries
¼ cup ruby port
I½ tablespoons red wine vinegar
I piece dried ginger or ½ teaspoon
    ground ginger
½ teaspoon black peppercorns
I teaspoon sugar
Kosher salt

Heat the mustard oil in a 4-quart pan over moderately high heat until it smokes, then remove the pan from the heat. (Mustard oil is very pungent, so don't breathe it in when it's smoking.) Add the canola oil and heat until it shimmers. Add the cinnamon, cloves, star anise, chile, ginger, cherries, port, and vinegar.

Grind the piece of dried ginger if using in an electric coffee/spice grinder and add ½ teaspoon to the cherry mixture. Finely grind the peppercorns and add them to the cherry mixture. Stir in the sugar and salt to taste and simmer for 15 to 20 minutes, or until the cherries are soft but not completely broken down. (If using frozen cherries, cook them about 5 minutes longer, until glazed.)

Let the chutney cool completely and discard the cinnamon, cloves, star anise, and chile. *The chutney keeps in an airtight container in the refrigerator for 2 weeks.*

coconut coriander chutney

Try this green chutney with roast leg of lamb or with fish such as the mahimahi on page 87. It's also the mainstay of a street sandwich that was a staple of my college days: slices of cucumber, onion, boiled potato, and tomato on white bread. Almost every movie house and college had a stand with a guy making that sandwich. This recipe calls for both a food processor and a blender but results in a satiny texture.

½ pound cilantro, roughly chopped

2 cups packed grated fresh coconut (see page 283)

1 mild to moderately hot fresh green chile, roughly chopped

5 large garlic cloves, peeled

2 tablespoons thinly sliced peeled ginger

2 cups roughly chopped white onion

2 tablespoons extra virgin olive oil

3 tablespoons lime juice

2 tablespoons Mango Chutney (page 237) or store-bought

Kosher salt and freshly ground black pepper

Pulse the cilantro, coconut, chile, garlic, and ginger in a food processor until finely chopped.

Puree the onion, olive oil, lime juice, and cilantro mixture in a blender until smooth. (Put the onion, oil, and lime juice into the bottom of the blender and put everything else on top; that way, there will be enough liquid to puree the mixture. If necessary, add 2 to 4 tablespoons water.) Add the mango chutney and puree until very smooth. Season the chutney with salt and pepper and transfer it to a bowl. *Refrigerate the chutney, covered, for 2 hours so that the flavors meld. The chutney keeps in an airtight container in the refrigerator for 1 week.*

Before serving, taste the chutney and adjust the seasonings.

dried-fruit chutney

MAKES 6 CUPS

Every year at Diwali, the Hindu New Year, my father was given boxes of dried fruit as gifts. One Thanksgiving, I was reminded of that tradition when I was given some organic dates and decided to make this chutney instead of cranberry sauce for our holiday table. Try it with duck, venison, or turkey, or as an accompaniment to a cheese platter.

¼ cup extra virgin olive oil
½ cinnamon stick
3 star anise
2 cloves
½ teaspoon brown mustard seeds
¼ dried pasilla de Oaxaca chile
2 cups orange juice
2 cups apple cider
1 cup dried sour cherries
2 cups sliced dates

1 teaspoon packed grated orange zest
¼ cup julienne strips peeled ginger
2 cups quartered dried apricots
2 cups fresh cranberries
1½ tablespoons fennel, preferably Lucknow
1 teaspoon yellow mustard seeds
¼ cup cider vinegar
Kosher salt

Heat the oil in a heavy 6-quart pot over moderately high heat until it shimmers and cook the cinnamon, star anise, and cloves for 1 minute. Add the brown mustard seeds and chile. When the seeds pop and are fragrant, after about 30 seconds, remove the pan from the heat and carefully add the orange juice and apple cider. Bring the mixture to a boil and add the cherries, dates, zest, ginger, apricots, cranberries, fennel, yellow mustard seeds, and vinegar. Briskly simmer the mixture, uncovered, stirring occasionally, until the liquid is reduced and the fruits are softened and tender, about 1½ hours. Stir in salt to taste.

Let the chutney cool completely before serving. *The chutney keeps in an airtight container in the refrigerator for 1 week.*

mint coriander chutney

Every street food stand in India serves a version of this smooth, brilliantly green chutney with its food; each one is distinct and very good. Indian markets in North America sell it in jars, but it lacks the sparkle and depth of one that is freshly made. This rendition is especially good with lamb and potatoes.

I cup chopped white onion
I cup plain whole-milk yogurt
2½ cups packed mint leaves (about
    5½ ounces)
2½ cups packed cilantro leaves
    (about 5½ ounces), roughly
    chopped

2 tablespoons thinly sliced peeled
    ginger
½ green bell pepper, roughly
    chopped
I tablespoon sugar
Kosher salt
¼ cup lime juice

Put the onion, yogurt, mint, cilantro, ginger, and bell pepper in a blender and puree until smooth.

Transfer the chutney to a bowl and whisk in the sugar, salt to taste, and lime juice. *The chutney keeps, its surface covered with plastic wrap, in the refrigerator for 2 days, or in an airtight container in the freezer for 4 to 6 weeks.*

lemon chutney

MAKES 7½ CUPS

The first step in this chutney—preserving the lemons—takes two weeks, but the end result is bright with flavor. I use it in the Veal Chops Stuffed with Hominy (page 179), but it is also delicious stirred into a risotto or chopped and put into the dressing for a bean salad. You can substitute Key limes or any other thin-skinned limes for lemons in this chutney.

FOR THE PRESERVED LEMONS
12 lemons
5 to 6 cups kosher salt

1 cup sugar
1 cup white wine vinegar

1 teaspoon coriander seeds
1 mild to moderately hot fresh green chile
1 teaspoon nigella seeds
1 teaspoon fennel seeds
1 teaspoon yellow mustard seeds

Cut the ends off of the lemons. Cut each lemon lengthwise into 6 wedges and remove the seeds.

Put about ½ cup of the salt into the bottom of a 6- to 8-quart glass or plastic container and top with a layer of lemon wedges. Continue to layer the salt and lemon wedges, ending with a layer of salt. (The lemon wedges should be completely submerged in the salt.) Cover the container and leave the lemons in the refrigerator for 14 days.

Rinse the lemons in several changes of water, swishing them around with your hand, and let them soak in a fresh change of water overnight. Make sure the lemons are covered with about 4 inches of water.

Rinse the lemons well and soak them in a fresh change of water for one more night. Drain the lemons.

Put the sugar, vinegar, and 2 cups water in a deep 12-inch skillet and bring to a boil over high heat. Cook just until the sugar is dissolved.

Coarsely grind the coriander seeds in a mortar with a pestle or in an electric coffee/spice grinder. Add the drained lemons, chile, and coriander seeds to the hot liquid, along with the unground nigella seeds, fennel seeds, and mustard seeds. Bring the mixture to a boil. Reduce the heat to moderate and simmer the chutney for 15 to 20 minutes. Let the chutney cool completely before serving. *The chutney keeps in an airtight container in the refrigerator for 2 weeks.*

mango chutney

MAKES 10 CUPS

The Sanskrit word for mango is *amra*, which means "of the people," and mangoes, a cultivated crop in India for thousands of years, are indeed an integral part of the food, culture, and religion there. I can't imagine life without them. Mango chutneys are made from green (unripe) mangoes, and they go with just about everything.

1½ cups sugar

1½ cups white wine vinegar

2 tablespoons paprika

1 tablespoon nigella seeds

1½ teaspoons mustard *dal*

½ teaspoon cayenne

1 teaspoon ground turmeric

4 medium green (unripe) mangoes
   (about 4 pounds), pitted and
   roughly cut into 1-inch pieces (see
   page 8)

12 garlic cloves, smashed and peeled

¾ cup julienne strips peeled ginger

1 cup raisins, preferably golden

1½ cups dates, cut in half crosswise
   and pitted

Kosher salt

Put the sugar in a heavy 6- to 8-quart pot and add 1 quart water. Heat the mixture over moderately high heat until the sugar is dissolved and add the rest of the ingredients. Bring the mixture to a boil. Reduce the heat and simmer briskly for 1 hour, or until the mango is softened and the mixture is thickened. (Cover the pot if the mixture reduces too quickly and starts to dry out.)

Let the chutney cool to room temperature and season with salt to taste. *The chutney keeps in an airtight container in the refrigerator for up to 1 year.*

tamarind
chutney

You'll find different versions of this chutney on street food carts all over India, as it's an important component of *chaats*—snacks sprinkled with a tantalizing hot and sour seasoning. With just the right balance of fruity sweetness and tang, it's delicious with just about anything.

2 tablespoons fennel seeds

1 tablespoon coriander seeds

1 teaspoon cumin seeds

1 teaspoon black peppercorns

2 black cardamom pods, uncracked

2 green cardamom pods, cracked

2 star anise

1 cinnamon stick, broken into pieces

1 small dried red chile (see Glossary), broken into pieces

3 pieces dried ginger or 1 teaspoon ground ginger

17 ounces jaggery or dark brown sugar (about 2¾ cups)

4 cups Tamarind Paste (page 284)

Kosher salt

Toast the fennel seeds in a dry heavy 8-inch skillet over moderately low heat, shaking the skillet, until fragrant and a couple of shades darker, about 2 minutes. Turn the seeds out onto a small tray or platter to cool. Toast the coriander seeds in the same way and turn them out on the tray or platter. Toast the cumin seeds in the same way, turning them out to cool, and then toast the peppercorns, turning them out to cool as well. Put the cardamom pods in the skillet and add the star anise, cinnamon, chile, and dried ginger. (If using ground ginger, do not add it at this point.) Toast the mixture in the same way and cool on the tray or platter. Finely grind all the toasted spices together in an electric coffee/spice grinder. If using ground ginger, add it now.

Put 3 cups water and the jaggery in a heavy 6- to 8-quart pot and bring to a boil. Once the jaggery has melted, stir in the tamarind paste. Bring the mixture to a simmer and add the ground spices and salt to taste. Simmer the mixture over moderate heat until thickened, about 15 minutes. (When cool, the chutney will be a spreadable consistency.)

Remove the chutney from the heat and let cool. *The chutney keeps in an airtight container in the refrigerator for 4 to 6 weeks.*

warm tomato
chutney

This sweet-spicy tomato chutney, called *kalonji*, is a staple at Tabla. It makes a good dip for bread and is a great complement to roasted meats, especially veal.

Two 28-ounce cans whole or chopped tomatoes (see Note)
¼ cup canola oil
1 teaspoon yellow mustard seeds
1 teaspoon brown mustard seeds
1 teaspoon cumin seeds
1 teaspoon nigella seeds
2 tablespoons finely chopped garlic
3 tablespoons finely chopped peeled ginger

1 cup finely chopped white onion
2 small dried red chiles (see Glossary), crumbled
Kosher salt and freshly ground black pepper
2 tablespoons Tamarind Paste (page 284)
1 tablespoon sugar

Roughly puree the tomatoes to a medium-coarse consistency in batches in a blender or food processor.

Heat the oil in a 4- to 6-quart pot over moderately high heat until it shimmers. Add the mustard seeds, cumin seeds, and nigella seeds, shaking the skillet, and when they pop and are fragrant, after about 30 seconds, quickly add the garlic, ginger, onion, and chiles. Immediately reduce the heat to moderate, and cook, stirring, until the garlic and onion have softened. (Don't let them color.) Stir in a pinch of salt and the tomato puree. Bring the mixture to a boil, then reduce the heat and simmer for 1 hour.

Stir in the tamarind paste, sugar, and salt and pepper to taste, then remove the chutney from the heat. Serve the chutney warm. *The chutney keeps in an airtight container in the refrigerator for 2 weeks or in the freezer for 1 month.*

NOTE: *I prefer Muir Glen organic tomatoes, either plain or, for a little more kick, the "Fire-Roasted" variety.*

mango
water pickle

My dad used to tell us that when he was growing up his family was so poor that a meal often consisted of nothing more than rice and mango water pickle (so-called because it's pickled in water). Looking back, I think that story was just a way to teach us to appreciate the bounty on our table. It worked. I never look at mango water pickle without feeling grateful, and with a jar of it in the refrigerator I feel ready for anything. Mango water pickle couldn't be easier to make, and its tart sweetness and crisp texture goes well with vegetables or fish. Make sure the mango is very hard and unripe. Slice up mango water pickle and toss it in a salad, dice it and add it to Pan-Roasted Cod and Clams with Basmati Kanji (page 71), or scatter it over a bowl of rice and be thankful.

½ cup kosher salt

1 cup sugar

½ cup cider vinegar

1 mild to moderately hot fresh green
    chile, slit down 1 side

5 garlic cloves

2 tablespoons thinly sliced peeled
    ginger

3 medium green (unripe) mangoes
    (about 2 pounds), peeled, pitted,
    and quartered (see page 8)

Put the salt, sugar, vinegar, and 5 cups water in a 6-quart pot and heat over high heat, stirring, until hot. Add the chile, garlic, and ginger and bring to a boil, stirring, until the salt and sugar are completely dissolved.

Put the green mango in a very clean 3-quart plastic or glass container with a tight-fitting lid and pour the liquid over it. Let the pickle cool completely, uncovered, and refrigerate, covered, for at least 6 hours. *The mango pickle keeps in the refrigerator for 1 month.*

garlic pickle

Before Tabla opened, I went back to India for a three-week research trip. I found a garlic pickle similar to this one in the southern city of Bangalore and knew I wanted to re-create it at our restaurant. In India, garlic pickle is used, like any other pickle, as a condiment, but I also use it as an ingredient—in braises and curries (such as the Duck Orange Curry on page 139), for instance. It is an easy way to add interest and complexity to a dish.

3 large heads of garlic (about 12 ounces), separated into cloves and peeled
½ cup plus 1 tablespoon canola oil
1½ teaspoons brown mustard seeds
2 cloves
1 fresh mild to moderately hot fresh green chile, slit down 1 side

1 bay leaf
1½ tablespoons packed jaggery or dark brown sugar
1 cup white wine vinegar
¼ teaspoon ground turmeric
1 teaspoon kosher salt

Preheat the oven to 350°F.

Put the garlic cloves and 1 tablespoon of the oil in a shallow roasting pan and toss the garlic until well coated with the oil. Roast the garlic in the middle of the oven for about 25 minutes, or until light golden.

Heat the remaining ½ cup oil in a 2-quart pan over moderate heat until it shimmers and toast the mustard seeds and cloves until the seeds pop and the spices are fragrant, about 30 seconds. Add the chile, bay leaf, and jaggery and cook for 1 minute. Turn the chile over to toast the other side and carefully add the vinegar, turmeric, and roasted garlic (the mixture will spatter). Cook the mixture, stirring, for 1 minute longer and remove from the heat. Discard the cloves and add the salt.

When the garlic pickle is completely cool, transfer it to a very clean jar with a tight-fitting lid. *The garlic pickle keeps in the refrigerator for 1 month.*

pickled
ramps

Ramps are small, strong-smelling garlicky leeks that grow wild from the southern Appalachians up to Canada and as far west as Minnesota, and their appearance every spring inspires harvest festivals and menu specials across the land. At Tabla, we preserve hundreds of pounds of ramps every year, to see us through until the following spring. The pickling juice that remains once the ramps are gone is a great seasoning for vinaigrettes. For this recipe, you need the white bulb and the lower part of the red stem, but save the smooth, pointed lilylike leaves for sautéing (see Note).

½ pound ramps, washed well
Kosher salt
1 cup sugar
2 cups Champagne vinegar or
    white wine vinegar
1 teaspoon mustard *dal*

1 teaspoon fennel seeds
1½ teaspoons coriander seeds
1 small dried red chile (see Glossary)
¼ teaspoon fenugreek seeds
1 teaspoon brown mustard seeds
2 cloves

Trim the green leaves and root ends from the ramps. Save the greens for another use (see Note) and discard the root ends. Have a bowl of ice water ready. If the bulbs are young and small, blanch in a pot of well-salted boiling water for 20 seconds and transfer to the ice water. If it is later in the season and the bulbs are larger, blanch for an extra 10 seconds. When bulbs are cold, drain and them pat dry.

Put all the remaining ingredients in a 2-quart pot and bring to a boil. Simmer, stirring, until the sugar is completely dissolved, 2 to 5 minutes. Remove from the heat.

Transfer the blanched ramps to a very clean jar and pour the pickling liquid over them. Seal with a tight-fitting lid. *The pickled ramps keep in the refrigerator for 1 month.*

NOTE: *The greens are delicious cut in half crosswise, sautéed, and served over pasta. Blanch them first so that they will be sweet and mild.*

about raita

Yogurt is a vital and delicious component of Indian cooking. Most obviously, it defuses the heat from chiles and hot spices. Rich in protein, calcium, and B vitamins, among other things, and easily digestible, it's often eaten in the form of raita (WRY-tah), yogurt whisked until smooth and flavored with—well, practically anything, as you'll see in the recipes that follow.

A raita is really more than an accompaniment; it's considered an integral part of many meals. In India, a raita is generally a loose, soupy sauce, but I prefer it thicker, so that it has a certain lushness. The type of yogurt used is key. I prefer Stonyfield Farm; it has a great consistency, great flavor—tangy and well balanced—and it's available nationally. Greek yogurt is also delicious, and if you are lucky enough to live in a place where you can get it, use that instead, but adjust the acid in the recipes by adding about a tablespoon of lime juice. And you can use either whole-milk or low-fat yogurt, but avoid the nonfat variety.

Raitas are enjoyed all over India, but the spices used differ according to region. In North India, toasted spices such as cumin are the rule; in the South, raitas are frequently finished with a tarka, a sizzling-hot topping of spiced oil.

Want something thick enough to be scooped up with pita chips? Start a day ahead and place the yogurt in a sieve lined with a coffee filter or cheesecloth and let most of the whey collect in a bowl. You will be rewarded with yogurt that is the texture of the freshest cheese imaginable.

Raitas are best served chilled, so refrigerate them after they are made for at least an hour. That way the flavors will have time to bloom and deepen. Before serving, taste your raita and adjust the seasoning so that the dish is rounded and well balanced—don't be afraid to add another pinch of salt, for instance, or jack up the heat with a bit more cayenne.

apple
walnut raita

MAKES 3 CUPS

Apples and walnuts are common ingredients in Kashmir. This raita is delicious with pork or poultry.

½ tablespoon unsalted butter
½ cup walnut halves
¼ teaspoon sugar, plus more to taste
¼ teaspoon cayenne
Kosher salt and freshly ground black
    pepper
1½ cups grated peeled apples such as
    Empire, McIntosh, or Gala
1 tablespoon lime juice

1 tablespoon chopped mild to
    moderately hot fresh green chile
About 20 mint leaves, cut into
    chiffonade (see page 8; about
    1 tablespoon)
1½ cups plain whole-milk or low-fat
    yogurt
⅛ teaspoon chaat masala

Melt the butter in a small heavy skillet over moderately low heat and add the walnuts, ¼ teaspoon sugar, cayenne, and a pinch of salt. Toast the walnuts, stirring to coat with the butter and spices, for about 2 minutes, until the nuts are fragrant and browned. Drain the nuts on paper towels and chop them.

Stir the apples, lime juice, chile, and mint together in a small bowl.

In a larger bowl, whisk the yogurt to lighten it. Stir in the apple mixture, chaat masala, walnuts, and salt and pepper to taste. *Cover the raita and refrigerate for at least 1 hour and up to 3 days.*

Taste the raita and adjust the seasonings if necessary before serving.

lemon chive raita

Try this with smoked salmon or any other smoked fish or as a dressing for a tuna sandwich.

1 teaspoon cumin seeds

2 lemons

1½ cups plain whole-milk or low-fat yogurt

2 tablespoons finely chopped fresh chives

¼ cup finely chopped red onion

2 tablespoons chopped drained bottled capers (see Note)

1 teaspoon sugar

Pinch of cayenne

Kosher salt and freshly ground black pepper

Toast the cumin seeds in a dry small skillet over moderately low heat, shaking the skillet, until fragrant and a couple of shades darker about 3 minutes. Coarsely crush them with a mortar and pestle or a rolling pin.

Zest 1 lemon (you should have about 1 packed teaspoon grated zest). Cut the lemon into individual segments as you would a grapefruit or orange and discard the seeds (you should have about 2 level tablespoons lemon segments).

Put the yogurt in a medium bowl and whisk it to lighten. Whisk in the lemon zest, lemon segments, chives, onion, capers, sugar, cayenne, and salt and pepper to taste. *Cover the raita and refrigerate for at least 1 hour and up to 3 days.*

Taste the raita and adjust the seasonings if necessary before serving.

NOTE: *You can also use capers packed in salt, but you should rinse them and soak them in 4 to 5 cups water for at least 2 hours and up to overnight. Rinse them again and pat them dry before chopping.*

cucumber raita with
tiny chickpea puffs

MAKES 1⅓ CUPS RAITA WITH 1¾ CUPS BHOONDI

This raita is made with *bhoondi*, addictive little crisp-fried orbs of chickpea batter. They are available at Indian markets (see Sources), but they are easy to make at home; you simply pour the batter through the holes of a slotted spoon into hot oil and fry them until they are crisp and golden. You could also use a spaetzle maker if you have one, although the end result will be free-form instead of round. *Bhoondi* keep for weeks in an airtight container and are delicious added to soups or salads as well as in raita. I flavored these *bhoondi* with cilantro, but have fun experimenting with other herbs—rosemary, for example.

FOR THE CHICKPEA BATTER

½ cup chickpea flour (*besan*)

I scant tablespoon minced mild to moderately hot fresh green chile

Kosher salt and freshly ground black pepper

Pinch of cayenne

¼ teaspoon cumin seeds

I scant tablespoon minced cilantro

2 cups canola oil

FOR THE RAITA

¼ pound cucumbers, preferably a mixture of seedless and Kirby (see Note)

1¼ teaspoon cumin seeds

I cup plain whole-milk or low-fat yogurt

I tablespoon minced mild to moderately hot fresh green chile

⅛ teaspoon cayenne

I teaspoon lime juice

¼ teaspoon sugar

Kosher salt

Whisk the flour, chile, and ¼ cup plus 2 tablespoons water in a bowl. Whisk in ⅛ teaspoon salt, ⅛ teaspoon pepper, cayenne, cumin seeds, and cilantro. Let the batter sit for 15 minutes.

Heat the oil in a heavy 2-quart pot over moderately high heat until the oil shimmers.

Whisk the batter and pour a small amount through a slotted spoon into the oil. The *bhoondi* will bob to the surface almost immediately, but continue to deep-fry them until they are golden and crisp, about 1 minute. Transfer the *bhoondi* with another slotted spoon to paper towels to drain and sprinkle with salt. Make more *bhoondi* with the remaining batter in the same way. *Bhoondi keep in an airtight container for 2 weeks.*

If using Kirby cucumbers, peel and grate them into a medium bowl. If using seedless cucumbers, leave the peel on and grate into the bowl. (A mixture of peeled and unpeeled cucumbers makes for a very pretty raita.) Squeeze excess moisture out of the cucumber with your hands and discard the liquid. (You should have a packed ⅓ cup grated, squeezed cucumber.)

Toast the cumin seeds in a dry small skillet over moderately low heat until fragrant and a couple of shades darker, about 3 minutes. Coarsely crush them with a mortar and pestle or a rolling pin.

Whisk the yogurt into the cucumber. Whisk in the chile, cumin seeds, cayenne, lime juice, sugar, and salt to taste. *Cover the raita and refrigerate for at least 1 hour and up to 2 days.*

Taste the raita and adjust the seasonings if necessary.

Divide the *bhoondi* among 6 small bowls and stir together with a generous amount of raita.

NOTE: *I tend to avoid regular cucumbers because they can be very seedy and watery.*

horseradish ginger raita

I like to serve this raita drizzled over Marinated Hanger Steak (page 148). It's also a great dressing for a sandwich. It doesn't keep well—the ginger juice will turn bitter—so use it lavishly.

One 1-inch piece peeled ginger
1 cup plain whole-milk or low-fat
    yogurt
1 tablespoon grated fresh horseradish
    (see Note) or drained bottled
    horseradish

Kosher salt and freshly ground black
    pepper
½ teaspoon sugar

Grate the ginger on the small teardrop holes of a box grater and squeeze it through a garlic press or cheesecloth. (You should have 1 tablespoon packed grated ginger and 1 tablespoon ginger juice.)

Fold together the yogurt, ginger juice, horseradish, ½ teaspoon salt, sugar, and a generous amount of pepper in a bowl with a rubber spatula just until combined. (It will get loose if you whisk it or beat it with a fork.) *Cover the raita and refrigerate for at least 1 hour and up to 2 days.*

Taste the raita and adjust the seasonings if necessary before serving.

NOTE: *Use the small teardrop holes on a box grater.*

pickle
raita

MAKES 2 CUPS

I call this a pickle (*aachar*) raita because it incorporates Indian pickling spices such as fennel seeds, nigella seeds, mustard seeds, and asafetida. It's finished with a tarka—a traditional Indian technique in which whole spices are cooked briefly in sizzling oil and immediately swirled into a dish. It's a great way to add depth and nuance to something simple.

About ½ cup quartered and very thinly sliced red or Vidalia onion
½ cup very thinly sliced radishes, halved if large (about 6)
1 tablespoon minced peeled ginger
1 tablespoon sliced mild to moderately hot fresh green chile
½ teaspoon nigella seeds
½ teaspoon fennel seeds
1 cup plain whole-milk or low-fat yogurt
¼ teaspoon sugar

Pinch of cayenne
Kosher salt and freshly ground black pepper

FOR THE TARKA
2 tablespoons canola oil
1 teaspoon brown mustard seeds
Pinch of asafetida

1 tablespoon cilantro chiffonade (see page 8)

Stir together the onion, radishes, ginger, and chile in a medium bowl.

Toast the nigella and fennel seeds in a dry small skillet over moderately low heat until fragrant and a couple of shades darker, about 3 minutes. Coarsely crush them with a mortar and pestle or a rolling pin.

Stir the crushed spices and yogurt into the onion mixture. Stir in the sugar, cayenne, and salt and pepper to taste. *Cover the raita and refrigerate for at least 1 hour and up to 2 days.*

Heat the oil in a heavy small pan over moderately high heat until it shimmers. Add the mustard seeds and cook, shaking the pan, until they pop and are fragrant, about 30 seconds. Add the asafetida and cook for 15 seconds. Immediately stir the tarka into the raita.

Stir the cilantro into the raita and adjust the seasonings if necessary before serving.

cider
vinaigrette I

Apple cider isn't used in India at all, even though we have fantastic apples from Kashmir. I became interested in it as an ingredient after I started using cider vinegar—one of the workhorses of my kitchen. I serve this vinaigrette with raw tuna at Tabla. It's also delicious with grilled fish, pork, even a green salad.

2 cups apple cider
1 tablespoon finely chopped shallot
1 teaspoon finely chopped ginger
1 teaspoon brown mustard seeds
¼ teaspoon chaat masala

¼ teaspoon kosher salt
¾ teaspoon freshly ground black
  pepper
1 tablespoon cider vinegar
¼ cup canola oil

Bring the cider, shallot, and ginger to a boil in a heavy saucepan over moderately high heat until the mixture is reduced to a thick, syrupy glaze (about ½ cup), about 20 minutes. Pour the glaze into a bowl and wipe out the pan.

Toast the mustard seeds in the pan over moderately low heat until they pop and are fragrant, about 30 seconds.

Add the mustard seeds, chaat masala, salt, and pepper to the glaze, then whisk in the cider vinegar and oil. *The vinaigrette keeps, covered and chilled, for about 2 weeks.*

cider
vinaigrette 2

MAKES ABOUT 1 CUP

Apple cider has a great fruity balance of sweet and sour. I love cider vinaigrettes, and I'm always coming up with new ones. I wasn't thrilled with this one until I added some walnut oil at the end—and what a difference it made in the depth of flavor. Walnut oil is available at fancy food shops and some supermarkets. It turns rancid very quickly, so taste it before you use it—and if you are not satisfied, take it back. Once it's opened, keep it in the refrigerator and let it come to room temperature before using it.

2 cups apple cider
I teaspoon chopped peeled ginger
I teaspoon yellow mustard seeds
I tablespoon cider vinegar
I teaspoon chopped fresh red chile

½ cup canola oil
I tablespoon walnut oil
Kosher salt and freshly ground
   black pepper

Bring the cider, ginger, and ½ teaspoon of the mustard seeds to a boil in a heavy saucepan over moderately low heat until the mixture is reduced to a thick, syrupy glaze (about ½ cup), about 20 minutes.

Coarsely crush the remaining ½ teaspoon mustard seeds in a mortar and pestle or with a rolling pin, then put them in a bowl. Whisk in 1 teaspoon of the glaze, the cider vinegar, chile, and the remaining glaze. Then whisk in the canola oil, walnut oil, and salt and pepper to taste. *The vinaigrette keeps, covered and chilled, for about 2 weeks.*

252 one spice, two spice

curry leaf
lime vinaigrette

This is one of the first things I came up with when I started working at Tabla; the flavors are based on a South Indian chicken curry that I love. It's good on greens, cucumbers, and roasted summer vegetables. And you can play around with different herbs. Substitute about a half cup of Thai basil leaves for the curry leaves and you have a great dressing for August tomatoes. Or substitute a half cup of tarragon leaves for a Green Goddess effect and drizzle it over fish or chicken.

5 garlic cloves

I tablespoon chopped peeled ginger

30 fresh curry leaves

I tablespoon chopped mild to
    moderately hot fresh green chile

¼ cup lime juice

½ teaspoon sugar

Kosher salt and freshly ground black
    pepper

⅔ cup canola oil

Blanch the garlic in boiling water for 20 seconds 3 times, using fresh water each time. (This mellows the garlic and makes it easier to digest.)

Put the garlic, ginger, curry leaves, chile, lime juice, sugar, and salt and pepper to taste, and half of the oil in a blender and puree, slowly adding the rest of the oil to form an emulsion, until very smooth. *The vinaigrette keeps, covered and chilled, for up to a week.*

boodie's ketchup

This, one of my favorite condiments, is delicious on almost anything. I tried to re-create the ketchup made by my mother (nicknamed "Boodie" by my father), who made vast quantities—enough to last a year—at a time. This recipe makes a generous amount; stored in the refrigerator, it keeps for ages.

⅓ cup canola oil
5 cloves
3 bay leaves
One 2-inch cinnamon stick, broken
   in half
¾ cup minced shallot
½ cup minced garlic
⅓ cup minced peeled ginger

Three and a half 28-ounce cans
   whole tomatoes with juice (see
   Note)
2 teaspoons cayenne
2 tablespoons kosher salt
¼ cup plus 2 tablespoons red wine
   vinegar
¼ cup sugar

Heat the oil in a wide heavy 8-quart pot over moderately high heat until it shimmers and add the cloves, bay leaves, and cinnamon. Cook, stirring, for 30 seconds. Reduce the heat to moderate. Add the shallot, garlic, and ginger and cook until the shallot and garlic have softened, about 3 minutes. Stir in the tomatoes with juice, cayenne, and salt, then simmer, uncovered, stirring occasionally and smashing the tomatoes, for 1½ hours, or until most of the liquid is gone. Remove the cloves, bay leaves, and cinnamon and reserve them.

Puree the hot tomato mixture in batches in a blender. (Be careful—it's hot.) Transfer the puree as blended to a bowl.

Return the puree to the (uncleaned) pot and add the reserved cloves, bay leaves, and cinnamon. Bring the puree to a simmer. Stir in the vinegar and sugar and simmer for 10 minutes longer.

Strain the puree through a sieve into a large bowl, pressing hard on the solids with the back of a ladle, and discard the solids. Let the ketchup cool completely. *The ketchup keeps in an airtight container in the refrigerator for at least 1 month.*

NOTE: *I like Muir Glen organic tomatoes; they have a well-rounded flavor that is not too acidic.*

rice and
the like

plain
basmati rice

I like to cook basmati like pasta, in lots of generously salted boiling water. I think it makes the rice fluffier. Don't rush the steps of washing and soaking the rice; it makes a big difference in the end result. You want to remove all the milling powder and the unmistakable, almost musty, smell of the burlap bag it's often kept in, and a nice soak in lukewarm water helps prevent the rice from breaking in the boiling water. Another tip for ensuring long, unbroken grains is to refrain from stirring the rice too vigorously while it's cooking. Stir it gently once or twice and then just leave it alone to do its thing.

2 cups white basmati rice
Kosher salt

Put the rice in a large bowl and fill the bowl with cold water from the tap. Swish the grains around gently with your hand, then pour off the water. Wash the rice about 7 more times in this way, or until the washing water loses its murkiness and remains clear. Cover the rice in the bowl with lukewarm water from the tap and let soak for 20 minutes. Drain the rice in a sieve.

Put 10 cups water in a 5- to 6-quart pot and add a generous amount of salt (the water should taste like the ocean).

Bring the water to a boil and add the drained rice. Cook the rice, stirring gently once or twice and skimming off the foam that appears on the surface, until the grains are just tender, about 10 minutes. Drain the rice in a sieve and set it on top of the pot. Let it sit for 5 minutes before serving.

basmati pilaf

This pilaf is simple yet sophisticated. My wife, Barkha, likes to sprinkle black, or royal, cumin seeds over the finished dish to give it a slightly mysterious fragrance. When cooking basmati for a pilaf, I always use the absorption method, instead of cooking it like pasta in a large amount of water, which is the way I make plain basmati. That's why the size of the pot is important: the quantity of cooked rice should never fill less than half the pot and never more than three-quarters of the pot. And I always measure both rice and liquid by volume, so I use a dry-measuring cup.

2 cups white basmati rice

2½ cups Vegetable Stock (page 282), Chicken Stock (page 274), or water

3 tablespoons canola oil

One 1-inch piece cinnamon stick

3 cloves

1 cup finely chopped white onion

2 bay leaves

Generous pinch of kosher salt

½ teaspoon black cumin seeds (*shah jeera*) (optional)

Put the rice in a large bowl and fill the bowl with cold water from the tap. Swish the grains around gently with your hand, then pour off the water. Wash the rice about 7 more times in this way, or until the washing water loses its murkiness and remains clear. Cover the rice in the bowl with lukewarm water from the tap and let soak for 20 minutes. Drain the rice in a sieve.

Heat the stock in a small pot over moderately high heat until hot.

Heat the oil in a 4-quart pot (see headnote) over moderate heat until warmed through and add the cinnamon and cloves. Cook for about 1 minute, or until the spices are fragrant. Add the onion and cook, stirring, until softened (don't let it color), about 3 minutes. Add the bay leaves and drained rice, stirring to coat the rice with the oil.

When the rice starts sticking to the bottom of the pot, which will take about 1 minute, add the hot stock and salt. Bring the mixture to a boil. Fold the rice over with a rubber spatula and cover the pot. Reduce the heat to low so that the mixture simmers very gently. Simmer for 5 minutes, or until most of the stock has been absorbed. Turn off the heat and let the pilaf sit, covered, for 15 minutes.

Fluff the pilaf with a fork and sprinkle the black cumin over if desired.

basmati pilaf with mung beans and lentils

SERVES 6

Hulled split mung beans (*moong dal*) are a very digestible source of protein, and so they're often cooked with rice and ghee and served to people who are ill. This classic comfort food is called *kichidi* and shouldn't be confused with kedgeree, the fish-and-rice dish created by British colonials in India. Here I've added pink lentils (*masoor dal*) for extra richness.

⅓ cup *moong dal* (hulled split mung beans), hulled

⅓ cup *masoor dal* (pink lentils)

1½ cups white basmati rice

3 tablespoons canola oil

3 cloves

4 green cardamon pods, cracked

One 1-inch piece cinnamon stick

1 teaspoon cumin seeds

1 teaspoon black peppercorns

3 large garlic cloves, sliced lengthwise

1 cup chopped white onion

2 heaping tablespoons julienne strips peeled ginger

2 tablespoons unsalted butter

1 quart Vegetable Stock (page 282), Chicken Stock (page 274), or water

Kosher salt

Put the *moong dal* in a bowl and fill it with cold water from the tap. Swish the beans around with your hand, then pour off the water. Wash the beans 5 more times in this way, or until the washing water loses its murkiness and remains clear. Cover the *moong dal* with lukewarm water from the tap and let soak for 30 minutes.

Wash the *masoor dal* in the same way, in 5 changes of water.

Drain the *moong dal*, add the washed *masoor dal*, and soak in more lukewarm water for 20 minutes.

Wash the rice in the same way, in about 7 changes of water. Cover the rice in the bowl with lukewarm water from the tap and let soak for 20 minutes. Drain the *dals* in a sieve and set aside in a bowl. Drain the rice in the sieve and set aside in a separate bowl.

Heat the oil in a 6-quart pot over moderate heat until warm and add the cloves, cracked cardamom pods, and cinnamon. Cook until the spices are fragrant, about 1 minute. Add the cumin seeds, peppercorns, garlic, and onion and cook, stirring, for 1 minute. Add the ginger and butter and cook, stirring, until the onion is golden brown, 5 to 8 minutes. (Don't rush this step; all that caramelization adds great flavor.)

Add the stock, drained *dals*, drained rice, and salt to taste. Bring the mixture to a simmer and reduce the heat to low. Simmer the mixture, covered, stirring occasionally, for about 10 minutes. Remove from the heat and let sit, covered, for 5 minutes. Remove the cloves, cardamom pods, and cinnamon before serving, but leave the peppercorns in.

tapioca
pilaf

Tapioca is made from the New World starchy root called variously *yuca* (YOO-ca), *cassava,* or *manioc.* It probably came to India with the Portuguese through Goa, which came into Portuguese hands in the early sixteenth century. The Portuguese had already conquered Brazil by then and took tropical staples like yuca and cacao to Africa and India, where tapioca is commonly eaten in savory preparations rather than sweet ones. This pilaf, considered a breakfast dish in Bombay, is delicious with the Sweet Spiced Oxtails (page 159) as well as other meat and hearty fish dishes. You'll want to soak the tapioca overnight, so this recipe requires a little forethought.

1½ cups pearl tapioca
¼ cup canola oil
1½ tablespoons brown mustard seeds
1½ teaspoons cumin seeds
1 small dried red chile (see Glossary), broken into 3 pieces
¾ cup salted peanuts, coarsely crushed
3 tablespoons finely chopped shallot

1½ tablespoons finely chopped peeled ginger
4 tablespoons unsalted butter
¾ cup chopped daikon
3 cups grated boiled baking potato (about 2 potatoes)
Kosher salt
3 tablespoons chopped chives
3 tablespoons cilantro chiffonade (see page 8)

Put the tapioca in a bowl and wash in several changes of cold water from the tap until the water loses its murkiness and remains clear. *Soak the tapioca in fresh cold water to cover for 8 hours.*

Drain the tapioca in a sieve and spread on a tray lined with a clean kitchen towel. *Refrigerate the drained tapioca for at least 1 hour and up to 2 days.*

Heat the oil in an 8-quart pot over moderately high heat until it shimmers and cook the mustard seeds until they pop and are fragrant, about 30 seconds. Add the cumin seeds and chile, stirring. Add the peanuts, shallot, and ginger and increase the heat to high. Cook the mixture, stirring, for 1 minute. Stir in the butter and, when melted, add the daikon, potato, tapioca, and salt to taste. Cook until the tapioca is heated through, 1 to 2 minutes.

Turn off the heat and cover the pot. Let the pilaf sit for 5 minutes. Just before serving, stir the chives and cilantro into the pilaf and season with salt.

cracked wheat pilaf

Cracked wheat, or bulgur, has a nutty, sweet taste that I love. In India, it's eaten with milk and sugar for dessert, but I like to serve it as a savory pilaf. I use Chicken Stock for added richness and flavor, but you can substitute Vegetable Stock (page 282) if you want to. And, depending on what else you are serving with the pilaf, feel free to embellish with chopped fresh chiles, cilantro, and/or mint.

2 teaspoons canola oil
2 cloves
One ¼-inch piece cinnamon stick
½ teaspoon cumin seeds
1 bay leaf
½ teaspoon ground turmeric
   (optional)

½ small white onion, finely chopped
1 tablespoon minced peeled ginger
2 cups Chicken Stock (page 274) or
   reduced-sodium canned chicken
   broth
2 cups cracked wheat (bulgur)
Kosher salt

Heat the oil in a 2-quart saucepan over moderate heat until it shimmers and cook the cloves, cinnamon, cumin seeds, bay leaf, and turmeric (if using), stirring and shaking the pan, until the spices are fragrant, 2 to 3 minutes. Add the onion and ginger and cook until the onion is translucent, 2 to 3 minutes longer. Add the chicken stock, then bring to a boil over high heat. Stir in the cracked wheat and 1½ teaspoons salt and return the mixture to a boil.

Remove from the heat and let the pilaf stand for 30 minutes. Remove the cloves, cinnamon, and bay leaf and fluff the pilaf with a fork and season with salt to taste before serving.

semolina
pilaf

Think of this side dish, called *upma* ("OOP-ma"), as southern India's answer to a creamy-style polenta. It's delicious with just about everything, including the Sweetbread Chile Fry (page 184). It's even great on its own, as a simple, restorative supper in a bowl. In place of Indian semolina, I rely on my American standby, Cream of Wheat. *Upma* doesn't keep well, so make it and serve it right away. Sometimes I add peas and diced steamed carrots.

2 tablespoons canola oil

I teaspoon brown mustard seeds

I teaspoon cumin seeds

¼ cup thinly sliced scallion, white and pale green parts only, dark green parts reserved

2 tablespoons finely chopped shallot

I tablespoon thinly sliced garlic

I tablespoon julienne strips peeled ginger

1½ cups quick-cooking Cream of Wheat

3 tablespoons unsalted butter

3 cups Chicken Stock (page 274) or reduced-sodium canned chicken broth

2 cups canned coconut milk, stirred well

Kosher salt and freshly ground black pepper

2 tablespoons chopped chives

2 tablespoons cilantro chiffonade (see page 8)

Heat the oil in a 4-quart pot over moderate heat until it shimmers and cook the mustard seeds until they pop and are fragrant, about 30 seconds. Add the cumin seeds, white and pale green parts of the scallion, and shallot. Cook, stirring, for 1 minute. Add the garlic and ginger and cook, stirring, for 1 minute longer. Add the Cream of Wheat and butter and cook, stirring frequently, until the Cream of Wheat is toasted and fragrant, 8 to 10 minutes. Add the stock and 1 cup of the coconut milk and cook, whisking frequently (to prevent lumps from forming), until the mixture is smooth and begins to thicken, about 2 minutes. Whisk in the remaining coconut milk and salt and pepper to taste. Increase the heat to moderately high and whisk until the pilaf is thick, about 1 to 2 minutes longer. Whisk in the chives, cilantro, and dark green parts of the scallions and serve.

barley
risotto

This dish is based on a classic preparation called "tomato rice" from South India. The barley here is on the al dente side—it has a wonderful, satisfying chew that way. You also want it to be a little soupy. I often add some heat, in the form of half of a fresh green chile, chopped. You can substitute canned chopped tomatoes if you like.

3 to 4 large tomatoes, chopped
    (about 4 cups)
Kosher salt and freshly ground black
    pepper
2 tablespoons canola oil
2 cloves
½ cinnamon stick
1½ teaspoons brown mustard seeds
1½ teaspoons cumin seeds
½ cup finely sliced shallot
One 2-inch piece peeled ginger,
    halved and sliced crosswise

1 tablespoon chopped garlic
2 tablespoons extra virgin olive oil
½ pound barley
One 5-inch rosemary sprig
1 bay leaf
2 cups Chicken Stock (page 274),
    reduced-sodium canned chicken
    broth, or Vegetable Stock (page
    282)

Put the tomatoes and 1 teaspoon salt in a 4- to 5-quart pot and cook, covered, over moderately low heat until the tomatoes are broken down, about 20 minutes. Strain the tomatoes through a sieve into a bowl, pressing down on the solids with the back of a ladle, and discard the solids.

Heat the canola oil in a 5-quart pot over moderate heat until it shimmers and add the cloves and cinnamon. Cook, stirring, until the spices are fragrant, about 2 minutes. Add the mustard seeds, and when they pop and are fragrant, after about 30 seconds, add the cumin seeds. Cook, stirring, until the cumin is fragrant and a couple of shades darker, about 2 minutes. Add the shallot, ginger, and garlic and cook, stirring, for 1 minute. Add the olive oil and cook for a few minutes longer, stirring, until the shallot is translucent. Add the barley and cook, stirring to coat the grains with spiced oil, for 2 minutes. Add the strained tomato juice, a generous pinch of salt, and the rosemary and bay leaf. Increase the heat and bring the mixture to a boil.

Reduce the heat so that the mixture is simmering and cook, uncovered, stirring occasionally, until the liquid is absorbed, 12 to 14 minutes. Add 1 cup of the stock and continue to cook, uncovered, stirring, for 5 minutes. Add ½ cup of the remaining stock and cover the pot. Cook for 20 minutes undisturbed.

Stir the risotto and add the last ½ cup stock and salt and pepper to taste. Remove the pot from the heat until ready to serve. Remove the cloves, cinnamon, rosemary, and bay leaf before serving.

fennel gnocchi

SERVES 6

These gnocchi are easy to make and very soft and tender. If you toss them in a sauce, they will break, so serve them with a sauce you can pour over them. Try them with the Clams with Anise and Pepper (page 123) or a simple, summery uncooked tomato sauce. I strongly prefer Lucknow fennel seeds here because they are more refined and delicate in flavor than regular fennel seeds. They're available at Indian markets or by mail order (see Sources).

6 baking potatoes (3¾ pounds)
1 tablespoon fennel seeds, preferably Lucknow
1½ teaspoons coriander seeds
1½ teaspoons black peppercorns
Kosher salt

1 whole egg
2 egg yolks
1 cup all-purpose flour, plus flour for dusting
1 tablespoon Pernod (optional)

Preheat the oven to 400°F. Prick the potatoes with a fork and bake in the middle of the oven on a tray lined with parchment paper until tender, about 1 hour. When the potatoes have cooled slightly, peel them and push them through a ricer or a food mill into a large bowl.

Toast the fennel seeds in a dry small skillet over moderately low heat, shaking the skillet, until fragrant and a couple of shades darker, about 3 minutes. Turn them out on a small tray or plate to cool. Toast the coriander seeds in the same way and turn them out on the tray or plate. Toast the peppercorns in the same way, turning them out to cool as well. Finely grind the spices together in an electric coffee/spice grinder.

Add the ground spices, 2 teaspoons salt, whole egg, yolks, ½ cup of the flour, and Pernod if desired to the potatoes and blend with your hands.

Gradually work in ½ cup more flour and gently knead the dough on a work surface dusted with flour for about 1 minute, just enough time to get the gluten working. (If you knead the dough too much, the gnocchi will be tough.) If the dough begins to stick, dust the work surface with a little more flour.

Gently work the dough into a ball and cut it into 8 pieces. Keeping the dough you are not working with covered with plastic wrap, form each piece into about a 1-foot-long log about 1 inch thick, then cut each log into 1-inch-long pieces. Continue to flour the work surface generously to keep the dough from sticking and dip your knife into flour if it begins to stick to the dough. Make a dimple in each gnoccho with a floured forefinger. *Refrigerate the gnocchi on a tray, covered lightly with plastic wrap, for at least 4 hours and up to 1 day.*

Bring a 4- to 6-quart pot of generously salted water to a boil. Working in batches, cook the gnocchi until they float, then cook for 1 minute longer. Transfer them as done to a large shallow bowl with a slotted spoon. Serve immediately.

basics

chicken stock

You'll find that having homemade chicken stock on hand will change your life as a cook. This one is very gently spiced and incredibly versatile. You can get bones from your butcher or simply save the carcasses from that Sunday night roast chicken and freeze them in resealable plastic bags. Sometimes when I buy a whole chicken, I peel off the skin, cut off the wing tips and necks, and freeze those; then one day when I have enough, I make this stock.

2¼ pounds assorted chicken bones (including wings, backs, plenty of skin, and, if possible, the gelatin-rich feet)

2 cups chopped celery

1 carrot, peeled and cut in half crosswise

3 cups chopped white onion

1 medium leek, roughly chopped and washed well

1 head of garlic, loose papery skin discarded and the (unpeeled) cloves roughly chopped

½ cup thickly sliced unpeeled ginger

2 bay leaves

4 cloves

1 tablespoon black peppercorns

Put the chicken bones and 6 quarts water in a large stockpot and slowly bring to a boil, uncovered. Skim the froth. Put the celery, carrot, onion, leek, garlic, ginger, bay leaves, cloves, and peppercorns into the pot and return to a boil. Reduce the heat and simmer the stock, uncovered, for 2 to 3 hours.

Pour the stock through a sieve into a large bowl. Discard the bones and other solids. Cool the stock, uncovered, completely. *The stock keeps in an airtight container in the refrigerator for 2 days or in the freezer for 1 month.*

white fish stock

Fish stock is really one of the quickest stocks to make, and it freezes beautifully. I use it in a number of recipes, including Spiced Shellfish Nage (page 54), Poached Halibut in Coriander Broth (page 64), Seared Wild Striped Bass with Warm Tomato Salad and Balsamic Sauce (page 74), and Poached Wild Striped Bass with Ginger Broth (page 78). The bones of any white fish will do—bass, cod, and/ or halibut, for instance—but I'm partial to black bass with the collagen-rich skin on. The resulting stock will be mild and well balanced in flavor, and not too fishy, so it is very versatile. When buying bones from your fishmonger, ask for the heads as well; they are rich in flavor.

3 tablespoons canola oil

3 cups chopped white onion

4 celery stalks, including leaves, chopped

2 large leeks, roughly chopped and washed well

4 large unpeeled garlic cloves, cut in half crosswise

2 bay leaves

6 cloves

4 pounds fish bones and heads (see above), cut into pieces and soaked in cold water for 1 hour

2 cups dry white wine

Two 6-inch rosemary sprigs

Four 4-inch thyme sprigs

About twelve 3-inch cilantro stems with roots (optional)

Heat the oil in a heavy 8- to 9-quart pot over moderately high heat until it shimmers. Add the onion and cook, stirring, until softened (don't let it color), about 3 minutes. Stir in the celery, leeks, and garlic and cook until the celery and leeks have softened, about 5 minutes. Add the bay leaves, cloves, and fish bones (not the heads) and increase the heat to high. Lightly sweat the bones, stirring so that they color just a bit, about 5 minutes. Add the fish heads, wine, 4 quarts water, rosemary, thyme, and cilantro stems with roots if using and bring the stock to a boil.

Reduce the heat and simmer gently, uncovered, for 1½ hours, skimming the froth occasionally.

Remove the fish bones, then strain the stock through a sieve lined with cheesecloth or a coffee filter into a large bowl. Discard the bones and other solids. Cool the stock completely, uncovered. *The stock keeps in an airtight container in the refrigerator for 2 days or in the freezer for 1 month.*

roasted fish stock

I use the same fish bones—bass, cod, and or halibut—for this stock as I do for the White Fish Stock (preceding recipe), but roasting the fish bones gives the stock a deeper, richer flavor and color. A little tomato paste also adds color as well as acidity. This stock is used very effectively in the Pan-Roasted Red Snapper with Roasted Chile Sauce (page 69), Seared Striped Bass with Lime Jaggery Gastrique (page 76), and the Sautéed Black Sea Bass with Mustard Curry (page 80).

3 tablespoons canola oil, plus oil to coat the bones

4 pounds fish bones (see headnote), cut into pieces and soaked in cold water for 1 hour

2 large onions, chopped

4 celery stalks, chopped

2 medium leeks chopped and washed well

4 large unpeeled garlic cloves, cut in half crosswise

2 bay leaves

6 cloves

2 tablespoons tomato paste or 4 cups chopped fresh tomatoes

2 medium carrots, sliced

2 cups dry white wine

Two 6-inch rosemary sprigs

Four 4-inch thyme sprigs

About twelve 3-inch cilantro stems with roots (optional)

Preheat the oven to 400°F and line a baking sheet with parchment paper.

Oil the paper and spread the fish bones on the paper, turning them to coat with the oil. Roast the bones in the middle of the oven for 40 minutes, or until the bones are light golden.

Heat 1½ tablespoons oil in an 8- to 9-quart pot over moderately high heat until it shimmers. Add the onions and cook, stirring, until softened (don't let them color), 5 to 7 minutes. Stir in the celery, leeks, and garlic and cook until the celery and leeks have softened, about 5 minutes. Add the bay leaves, cloves, tomato paste, carrots, and roasted bones and cook, stirring, for 5 minutes longer. Add the wine, 18 cups water, rosemary, thyme, and cilantro stems with roots if using and bring the stock to a boil.

Reduce the heat and simmer gently, uncovered, for 40 minutes to 1 hour, skimming the froth occasionally.

Ladle the stock from over the bones into a sieve lined with cheesecloth or a coffee filter set over a large bowl. (If you simply pour the stock with the bones into the sieve, the bones will break up, and the finished stock will be cloudy.) Discard the bones and other solids. Cool the stock completely, uncovered. *The stock keeps in an airtight container in the refrigerator for 2 days or in the freezer for 1 month.*

lobster stock

Lobster carcasses (the head, body, and small legs) have a tremendous amount of flavor and make a great stock that enriches the sauce for the Lobster Coconut Curry with Eggplant and Cabbage (page 115). You can also use it for any number of seafood sauces or soups.

Carcasses from about six 1-pound
  blanched lobsters (see page 117)
2 tablespoons canola oil
3 celery stalks, roughly chopped
1 large carrot, roughly chopped
1 large white onion, roughly chopped
6 garlic cloves, cut in half crosswise
¼ cup dry white wine

¼ cup brandy
1 teaspoon black peppercorns
1 bay leaf
2 cloves
2 quarts Chicken Stock (page 274),
  reduced-sodium canned chicken
  broth, or water

Remove the carapaces of the lobster carcasses and discard the grain sac (often called the *stomach*, it is filled with grit). Keep the green liverlike tomalley or any roe; the roe will give the finished stock a lovely pink lobster color. Cut the carcasses into small pieces with kitchen shears.

Heat the oil in a 6- to 8-quart pot over moderately high heat until it shimmers and cook the celery, carrot, onion, and garlic, stirring, until the vegetables are softened. Add the cut-up lobster carcasses and brown over high heat for 5 to 8 minutes. Add the wine, brandy, peppercorns, bay leaf, cloves, and chicken stock and bring to a simmer. Gently simmer the stock, uncovered, for 45 minutes.

Strain the stock, pressing hard on the solids, and discard the solids. *The stock can be made 1 day ahead. Cool completely, uncovered, and refrigerate, covered. The stock keeps in an airtight container in the refrigerator for 2 days or in the freezer for 1 month.*

shrimp
stock

If you live in a place where you can get shrimp with the heads on, buy them, for they are the freshest thing going. The heads add fat and will infuse the stock with great flavor. Otherwise, use the shells—the more the better—and feel free to add crab or lobster shells for extra richness. The combination of white port (available at wine shops and liquor stores) and brandy, by the way, is one I learned from chef Gray Kunz at Lespinasse—it has the perfect balance of sweetness and tang. This stock comes in handy for a number of recipes, including Crispy Shrimp with Toasted Spice Curry (page 97), Panfried Shrimp with Roasted Coconut Curry (page 99), and Scallops with Silk Squash, Eggplant, and Dried Shrimp (page 108).

½ cup canola oil

4 cups chopped white onion

2 cups chopped leek, washed well

2 cups chopped carrot

3 cups chopped celery

5 tablespoons chopped garlic

6 cloves

4 bay leaves

Shells and heads (if possible) from
    4 pounds shrimp

4 cups chopped tomato

¼ teaspoon salt

1 cup white port

⅔ cup brandy

4 quarts Chicken Stock (page 274) or
    reduced-sodium canned chicken
    broth

Four 4-inch thyme sprigs

Two 6-inch rosemary sprigs

Heat the oil in a heavy 8- to 9-quart pot over moderately high heat until it shimmers. Add the onion, leek, carrot, celery, garlic, cloves, and bay leaves and cook, stirring, until the aromatic vegetables have softened (don't let them color), about 5 minutes. Add the shrimp shells and heads and cook, stirring, for 5 minutes. Add the tomato and salt, and cook, stirring and breaking up the tomato as it softens, 2 minutes. Add the white port, brandy, chicken stock, thyme, and rosemary and bring the mixture to a simmer. Simmer the stock for 30 minutes.

Strain the stock through a sieve into a large bowl, pressing on the solids with the back of a ladle. Discard the solids. Cool the stock completely, uncovered. *The stock keeps in an airtight container in the refrigerator for 2 days or in the freezer for 1 month.*

vegetable stock

A good homemade vegetable stock is easy to put together and infinitely preferable to the commercial ones available. The key is getting the right balance. You don't want one ingredient—carrot or celery, for example—to overwhelm the other flavors. I don't put mushroom stems in my stock at the restaurant because some people are allergic to mushrooms, but I add them if I'm cooking for my family.

2 pounds white onions, roughly chopped (about 5 cups)

1 bunch celery, including leaves, chopped

3 large carrots, halved and sliced ½ inch thick

½ head garlic, roots and excess papery skin discarded, cut in half crosswise

1 large fennel bulb, stalks and fronds roughly chopped (about 4 cups)

1 large leek, roughly chopped and washed well

2 cloves

1½ teaspoons black peppercorns

One 6-inch rosemary sprig

Two 4-inch thyme sprigs

4 parsley sprigs

½ cup dry white wine

1 tablespoon kosher salt

2 bay leaves

Put all the ingredients in an 8-quart heavy pot. Add 3 quarts water and bring to a boil. Reduce the heat and simmer for 45 minutes.

Strain the stock through a sieve into a large bowl, pressing on the solids with the back of a ladle. Discard the solids. Cool the stock completely, uncovered. *The stock keeps in an airtight container in the refrigerator for 2 days or in the freezer for 1 month.*

to crack and peel fresh coconut

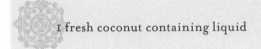

Cracking and peeling a fresh coconut is second nature to anyone who has grown up in the tropics, but it can be daunting if you don't know a few basics. If you bake the coconut for about 15 minutes before you attempt to crack it, the procedure is a snap—you just need a screwdriver and a hammer. The clear liquid inside the nut is not the coconut milk you buy in a can but is called *coconut water*. It's a refreshing drink just as it is, although you can also incorporate it into a soup or rice dish.

1 fresh coconut containing liquid

Preheat the oven to 400°F.

Find the softest eye of the coconut and pierce it with a screwdriver. Pour the coconut water into a bowl and taste it: if it's sweet, you know you have a fresh coconut; if it tastes oily, the coconut is "off" and should be discarded.

Bake the coconut in the middle of the oven for about 15 minutes. If the coconut doesn't crack in the oven, break the shell with a hammer and take out the meat with the point of a sturdy knife. Remove any brown skin with a vegetable peeler.

to make tamarind paste

Tamarind, the fruit of a tree that can reach up to eighty feet in height, is indispensable to Indian cuisine. With a deep, mellow sweet-tart tang, it is a more complex acid than lime or lemon. For culinary purposes, tamarind pulp is partially dried and pressed into semipliable rectangular blocks that are packaged in cellophane. The pulp must be soaked in hot water and strained free of seeds and fibers to form a glossy, dark brown paste before being used. Also available in Indian and Asian markets is tamarind concentrate—processed pulp in a jar. It's convenient, true, but the flavor is horrible compared to homemade. Leftover tamarind paste keeps well, in the refrigerator and the freezer.

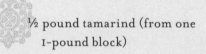 ½ pound tamarind (from one
1-pound block)

Tear off chunks of the tamarind pulp and put them in a 1-quart pan. Add 3 cups water and simmer for 30 to 35 minutes, mashing the pulp against the side of the pan with the back of a wooden spoon occasionally to help it soften.

Let the tamarind sit in the water off the heat for 30 minutes.

Strain the tamarind through a ricer or sieve into a bowl, pressing hard on the solids with the back of the wooden spoon.

Use your fingers to work the pulp free of seeds and fibers. Transfer the strained pulp back to the pan, taking care to include the pulp clinging to the underside of ricer or sieve. Add 2 cups water and bring the mixture to a vigorous boil.

Cool the paste completely and transfer to a glass jar or plastic tub. *The tamarind paste keeps in the refrigerator for 1 month or in the freezer for 3 months.*

glossary

Some of the ingredients called for in my recipes might be unfamiliar to you. They can be found at Indian (and sometimes Asian) markets and fancy food shops; many are in the spice section of the grocery store. When buying spices, choose whole ones, store them in airtight containers away from heat and light, and grind them fresh. Commercially ground preparations lose their potency almost immediately.

AJWAIN SEEDS

The small, ridged seeds of the plant *Trachyspermum ammi* (aka bishop's weed) look rather like celery seeds. They belong to the same fragrant Umbelliferae family as coriander, cumin, celery, lovage, and fennel. When ground, ajwain seeds smell and taste like thyme, but are more intense, with a peppery backnote. Ajwain is generally used with fish in North India.

ALEPPO PEPPER

These rusty-red chile pepper flakes are from the Middle East (they're named after Aleppo, in Syria) and have a mild, lightly smoked flavor and aroma. Use cayenne as a substitute.

ASAFETIDA

The spice, made from the resin of the giant fennel (*Ferula*), has a strong, disagreeable smell from sulfur compounds, so a little goes a long way. Its flavor after cooking is like the mildest, mellowest garlic you've ever had, and it does wonders for the digestion, which is why it's often used in legume dishes. Asafetida (pronounced as-a-feh-TEE-dah; from the Latin *foetidus*, "fetid") is sold in lump and ground form. The ground version is the easiest to deal with; I like Vandevi brand. Store the tin in a *very* tightly sealed container.

BANANA LEAVES

Banana leaves are a common wrapper (and plate) for foods in India. Although inedible, they give an earthy flavor to what's cooked inside them. They can be found in one-pound packages in the freezer section of Indian, Asian, and Latin American markets. Let the package thaw completely before unfolding the leaves so they don't crack. In Florida and California, you can get them fresh, but wash them before using.

BASIL

This is not a common kitchen herb in India—it's considered a sacred plant in Hindi households—so I rarely use it. When I do, I prefer Thai holy basil or pungent, tiny-leafed bush basil. **Basil seeds (takamaria)** are used in cold drinks, though, as a garnish because they're considered to have cooling properties and because they turn a beautiful blue when soaked in water. I love them against the pale green of chilled cucumber soup.

BASMATI RICE
See **Rice.**

BAY LEAVES

These woodsy, sweet leaves (*Laurus nobilis*) are probably already in your spice cabinet. I prefer the rounded Turkish leaves to the long, narrow pointy leaves from California; they have a gentler flavor. Indian bay leaves actually come from the cassia tree; they are about four inches long and have a faint hint of cinnamon. Always remove bay leaves from a dish before pureeing or serving.

BEANS
See **Legumes.**

BLACK CUMIN
See **Cumin Seeds.**

BLACK PEPPERCORNS
See **Peppercorns.**

BLACK SALT
See **Salt.**

CARDAMOM

Green and black cardamom play separate roles in Indian cooking, so don't substitute one for the other. **Green cardamom** (*Elettaria cardamomum*), a warming and sweet spice, is from a plant in the ginger family and is used widely in both sweet and savory dishes in India. Its aroma and flavor are mellow and intense all at once, with hints of lemon and camphor. **Black cardamom** (*Amomum* and *Aframomum* species) is a larger, ribbed seed pod. It has an earthier, smokier, almost pinelike aroma and flavor. It works well with lamb, goat, and game. Both green and black cardamom are best bought whole and kept in airtight containers.

CHAAT MASALA

This is the only commercial ground-spice blend I use. It's a tangy (and addictive) hot-sour mix that includes black salt, green mango powder, cumin, coriander, chiles, asafetida, and ajwain. It makes a plain sliced fresh apple taste out of this world. Look for MDH brand; I think it is the best quality.

CHICKPEA FLOUR (*besan*)

This protein-rich flour, made of ground dried Indian chickpeas, is used widely to make batters and breads.

CHILES, DRIED

When I call for a "small dried red chile," I mean the **cayenne** type, about 2 inches long. Avoid the tiny Thai or bird chiles; they are too fiery. I also use dried **pasilla de Oaxaca** chiles, familiar to devotees of Mexican and American Southwest cooking: their mellow smokiness reminds me of the smoked chiles that hung over the woodstove in my grandmother's kitchen. If I can't find pasillas de Oaxaca, I use a mix of **New Mexico** and **chipotle chiles.** If you ever see **Kashmiri chiles**, grab them—they are a true taste of India.

CHILES, FRESH GREEN

My favorite is about four to six inches long with a smooth, shiny green skin; it's full of sweetness and moderate heat. The variety is Calistan, and many growers on the West Coast and in New Mexico raise it. (Many stores on the East Coast call it a "finger hot," and it comes in either green or red.) Because growers sell to packagers/shippers, what you may get at the market is a mix of look-alike, taste-alike varieties. Anaheims or green cayennes are a fine substitute, so don't worry about it. Fresh chiles don't keep well; buy them as needed. In general, chiles are high in vitamin C; they are an appetite stimulant and aid digestion. They're considered a cooling spice because they cause the body to perspire and thus cool down.

CHILES, FRESH RED

I like to use cayennes (sometimes labeled "cayenne thick"). As a general rule, the smaller the chile, the hotter it is, so avoid the tiny red Thai or bird chiles; they are too potent.

CILANTRO

See **Coriander.**

CINNAMON

This is the thin, rolled inner bark of an evergreen tree (*Cinnamomum zeylanicum*) grown in southern India and Sri Lanka. It is the "true" cinnamon, as opposed to cassia, the inner bark of a related tree. In my recipes, the two can be used interchangeably.

CLOVES

These are the unopened flower buds of a small evergreen (*Syzygium aromaticum*) native to the Spice Islands of Indonesia. In the West, cloves are used in sweets, but in India, they are used primarily in rice and bean dishes, as well as in the spice mixture called *garam masala.*

COCONUT

I often substitute **frozen grated fresh coconut** (available at Southeast Asian or Indian markets) or **unsweetened flaked (desiccated) coconut** for fresh, depending on the dish. (Avoid the sweetened shredded coconut found in grocery stores; it's intended for baking.) **Coconut milk** isn't the thin, refreshing liquid (known as *coconut water*) that sloshes around inside a fresh coconut, but the intensely aromatic liquid made from pressed grated coconut. You can make your own, but there are good canned brands available such as Chaokoh brand. Canned coconut milk usually has a layer of cream on top, so shake the can well before using. **Coconut vinegar** (sometimes called *palm vinegar*) is made from coconut sap that's tapped from the trees, then fermented. The vinegar is low in acidity. You'll see it in the food of the Philippines as well.

CORIANDER

In India, all parts of the coriander plant (*Coriandrum sativum*)—a leafy herb that's found all over the tropical world—are used. The fresh leaves, with their intense aroma, are common to Mexican cooking and so are known in the United States by their Spanish name, **cilantro.** Buy it with the roots attached if possible; it will stay fresh longer. The large, pale green **coriander seeds** found in Indian markets have a citrusy fragrance and flavor; I prefer them to the rounder seeds from Morocco. They're considered a body-strengthening and cooling spice. Even **cilantro stems with roots** are used, as they are in Southeast Asia, either ground into curry pastes or used to flavor stocks and broths. Wash well before using.

CUMIN SEEDS

These small, elongated, oval ridged seeds from the plant *Cuminum cyminum* are native to Egypt's Nile Valley but have long been grown in many hot climates, including India, North Africa, and Latin America. Cumin seeds have a distinctive, pungent, slightly bitter flavor that gives depth and complexity to Indian cooking. **Black cumin** (royal cumin or *shah jeera*) has a more complex musky, herbal flavor. It's most often used in Moghul-style meat dishes. Cumin seeds are high in thymol, a natural antiseptic.

CURRY

As Indian migrants traveled—both voluntarily and involuntarily—all over the world, they took culinary traditions with them. These days you'll find different kinds of curries in Singapore, Indonesia, Thailand, Japan, Britain, South Africa, Kenya, and Trinidad, just to name a few countries. The word *curry* is thought to come from the Tamil (southern Indian) word *kari,* which means "sauce," or from the word *karhai,* a type of Indian cooking pot. Essentially, *curry* means an Indian-style dish with an aromatic, flavorful sauce. It can be very brothy or thick and stewlike; hot or mild; creamy with coconut milk or yogurt or fruity with kokum or tamarind. One thing they all have in common is that they incorporate a variety of spices.

CURRY LEAVES

Curry leaves come from a bushy shrub (*Murraya koenigii*) native to southern India; they look like tiny bay leaves and are very aromatic. Their flavor, spicy and citrusy, is prevalent in southern Indian food, although they aren't always an ingredient in curries. They are often sold on the stem and are available fresh and frozen at Indian and Asian markets, where they might be labeled *meetha neem* or *kari patta.* Avoid dried curry leaves; they are virtually tasteless. Kept wrapped up well in plastic wrap, fresh leaves last for about two to three weeks in the refrigerator. Don't take them out until just before using, or they will wilt. Curry leaves are an ingredient in most **tarkas:** when toasted in hot oil, they develop a smoky, slightly bitter flavor. They're a digestive tonic.

CURRY POWDER

One ingredient that you *won't* see in this book is curry powder, and I want to explain why. Curry powder is not a single spice but a commercial blend that is a British invention and—since it's often made from inferior (cheap) spices and all sorts of additives—can be harsh and one-dimensional. I never use it.

DAIKON

This mild-flavored, long white radish is known by its Japanese name in the United States, but in India it's called *mooli.* It provides a cool, crisp, satisfying crunch in all sorts of dishes.

DALS

See **Legumes.**

DRIED SHRIMP

See **Shrimp, Dried.**

FENNEL SEEDS

Fennel (*Foeniculum vulgare*) is one of the very oldest cultivated plants; it's indigenous to the Mediterranean but has long been grown else-where. The yellowish brown seeds resemble cumin seeds but have a warm licoricelike flavor. (They contain anethole, a component also found in anise.) Fennel seeds from **Lucknow** are smaller and more refined and sweeter in flavor. Fennel seeds are an appetite stimulant and digestive.

FENUGREEK

Fenugreek seeds are the hard, angular light brown seeds of an herb (*Trigonella foenum-graecum*) in the legume family that's native to southeastern Europe and western Asia (the name means "Greek hay"). Toasting mellows the bitterness of the seeds and gives them a flavor a little reminiscent of maple syrup. Dried **fenugreek leaves** (which are not interchangeable with the seeds) are fragrant and herbaceous. Fenugreek has a long history of use as a medicine.

GINGER

Ginger isn't a root but a rhizome—an underground stem—of a plant (*Zingiber officinale*) that's been cultivated as a culinary and medicinal spice (it's an excellent digestive) for more than three thousand years. Its pungent heat is absolutely indispensable to the cooking of India and Asia. Look for a firm piece of ginger with smooth skin—that's a sign of freshness. Stored in a plastic bag, it keeps in the refrigerator for about two weeks (leave the peel on). When a recipe calls for **sliced ginger,** peel it and cut it crosswise, across the grain. Because the fibers run the length of the rhizome, that will prevent any stringiness. When a recipe calls for the subtlety of **ginger juice,** squeeze the peeled ginger through a garlic press. It turns bitter if not used quickly, so always squeeze it fresh. When I call for **dried ginger,** what I mean is a dried knob (found at Indian markets), which you grate to measure the specified amount. The ground ginger found in the baking aisle of your supermarket will do in a pinch; but don't substitute crystallized or candied ginger. Ginger is a warming spice, and one of the legendary medicinal spices, used the world over for everything from a sore throat to an upset stomach.

GREEN MANGO

In India and Southeast Asia, a ripe mango is treated like a fruit but a green (unripe) mango is treated like a vegetable. When buying a green mango, get one that is truly unripe—it should be as hard as a rock. (Some mangoes are simply green in color and remain that way even when ripe.) If you happen across mangoes from Florida at an ethnic market or a roadside stand down South (they're in season from May until August), snap them up. Unlike imported mangoes, they haven't been treated in a hot water bath to kill insects, so they generally have better texture and flavor.

GREEN MANGO POWDER (*amchoor*)

Green mango is just one of the many souring agents used in India. To make *amchoor*, the flesh of green mangoes is dried in the sun before being ground to a beige powder that is a little fibrous; crumble it well before adding it to a dish.

JAGGERY

This sweetener, made from unrefined sugar cane or palm cane, has almost a caramel flavor. It's sold in pieces that are hacked off from larger cones. Look for pieces that crumble fairly easily. (If it comes in a solid chunk, grate it on a box grater.) Dark brown sugar is a good supermarket substitute; so is the Mexican unrefined sugar called *piloncillo*, found in Latino markets.

KOKUM

This fruit of the evergreen gamboge tree (*Garcinia indica*) is related to the mangosteen, one of the world's most prized tropical fruits. Kokum (pronounced "KOH-come") grows in the rain forests along India's Malabar coast and, like tamarind, is one of several fruity, complex souring agents used in Indian cooking. The darker the kokum, the better the quality; the dried deep purple-brown rinds should be supple, like well-cared-for leather, and slightly sticky inside. Kokum is sold in plastic-wrapped packages at Indian markets and is often labeled "wet kokum." Store it in the freezer.

LEGUMES

Along with rice, legumes are at the heart of Indian food, and I can't imagine life without them. They are nutritional powerhouses and absolutely delicious. When dried beans, peas, lentils, and some seeds are split and skinned, they are called *dals;* the term also refers to the cooked soups, stews, sauces, and dips made from them. Split chickpeas, split pigeon peas, and *urad dal* are also used as flavoring agents, toasted, and used like any other spice. When preparing legumes for cooking, pick them over carefully for stones and other debris, and wash them well.

Chana Dal These are hulled split yellow Indian chickpeas, from the plant *Cicer arietinum*, which are a smaller, nuttier variety than the "garbanzos" more commonly seen in American supermarkets. Indian chickpeas are what are used to make **chickpea flour** (*besan*). In South India, *chana dal* is used as both an ingredient and a spice. *Chana dal* is sometimes labeled "Bengal gram."

Dhana Dal These roasted split coriander seeds have a woodsy, citrusy aroma and flavor. They are used as both an ingredient and a spice.

French Green Lentils These tiny dark green lentils (*lentilles du Puy*) aren't used in India, but they provide a wonderful contrast—in flavor, texture, and appearance—to common Indian lentils.

Kala Chana This close relative of the chickpea is dried until it is a dark reddish brown. It has an earthy flavor.

Masoor Dal (Pink Lentils) The small flat seeds of the plant *Lens culinaris* have been hulled to reveal their coral-pink interior. When cooked, they become yellow, like *toor dal*, but make a thinner, lighter puree. They overcook very easily, so keep an eye on them.

Moong Dal (Mung Beans) The term *moong dal* refers to hulled split yellow seeds of the plant *Phaseolus aureus*. Left whole, the beans are sprouted to make bean sprouts.

Rice Beans The small seeds of this legume (*Vigna umbellata*) are cultivated in Asia and India; they are often eaten with or instead of rice.

Toor Dal (Yellow Lentils) The seeds of the plant *Cajanus cajan* (a member of the pigeon pea family) are hulled and split to reveal a golden interior. They make a thick, creamy puree. They are frequently used in South Indian vegetable stews.

Urad Dal (Black Gram Bean) The term *urad dal* refers to the hulled, split ivory-colored seeds of *Phaseolus mungo*. They are used as both an ingredient and a seasoning.

LONG SQUASH
See **Squash, Long.**

LOTUS ROOT
This native of Asia (*Nelumbo nucifera*) isn't technically a root, but a rhizome, a thick stem from which the roots grow. Pared and sliced, it is mild, slightly sweet, and crunchy like jícama. If fresh when bought, it should last a week or so in the refrigerator.

LUCKNOW FENNEL SEEDS
See **Fennel Seeds.**

MACE
Mace grows on the same tropical tree as nutmeg. When ripe, the tree's apricotlike fruits burst open to reveal black nuts wrapped in a red net called the *aril*. The kernel inside each nutshell is called *nutmeg*; the webby net is called *mace*. The net is removed from the nutmegs, flattened, and dried to form brittle pieces. When I call for a piece of mace in a recipe, that's what I'm referring to. One whole piece is equal to about 1½ teaspoons smaller shards and ½ teaspoon preground mace.

It's a warming spice with a flavor a little deeper than that of nutmeg; combined with green cardamom, it generates lots of heat in the body. It's also considered a carminative (gas reliever) and astringent.

MUSTARD

Tangy **mustard greens,** which come from several different varieties of mustard plants of the *Brassica* genus, are cooked and eaten in India as well as in China and Japan. They are high in vitamins and calcium. In the United States, bottles of thick, golden **mustard oil** are usually marked "not for human consumption" (mustard oil is also used as a topical liniment), but it's a culinary staple in the eastern Indian state of Bengal. Pressed from mustard seeds, it has a characteristic fragrance and heat and should always be brought to its smoking point to tame its aroma before using. **Brown** (sometimes called *red*) **mustard seeds** are indispensable to Indian cooking. After toasting in either a dry skillet or in oil, they take on a nutty flavor. **Yellow mustard seeds** are milder. **Mustard *dal*** are brown mustard seeds (*Brassica juncea*) that have been hulled and split. They are often used as a pickling spice.

NIGELLA SEEDS (*kalonji*)

These shiny, flat triangular black seeds from a plant (*Nigella sativa*) related to the cottage-garden staple love-in-a-mist are used in kitchens from Turkey to India, where they are integral to pickling spices and the Bengali five-spice mixture called *panch phoran.* Nigella seeds are often incorrectly (but commonly) labeled "black onion seeds."

PANKO

These fluffy bread crumbs come from Japan; a spongy square loaf is dried and grated to give the crumbs their unusual texture. After frying, they stay crunchy longer than regular bread crumbs because they absorb less grease.

PAPRIKA

This deep brick-red powder is made from mild chiles. Indian paprika comes from Kashmir, but Hungarian paprika is a good alternative. It is bitter when raw, but becomes mellow and sweet after being cooked. Like other chiles, it is high in vitamin C and stimulates the appetite.

PEPPERCORNS

Intense, biting, fruity, warm, indispensable—the spice trade was built on Indian **black peppercorns,** which are produced by fermenting and drying the green (immature) berries of the *Piper nigrum* vine. Today, black pepper remains the most popular spice on the planet. About twenty varieties are grown in India alone; one of the finest is labeled *Tellicherry,* from the Malabar coast. Freshly ground whole peppercorns are a world apart from the pallid, preground stuff in tins. See also **Szechwan Peppercorns.**

POMEGRANATE SEEDS, DRIED (*anardana*)

The slightly sticky, dark red seeds have a subtle sweet-sour taste and a nice crunch. They're used in northern Indian cooking, which makes sense, as pomegranates are native to nearby Iran. The seeds are often ground to a powder and used as a souring agent, much like *amchoor* (green mango powder).

POPPY SEEDS

The seeds used in northern India (from the flowers of the *Papaver* genus) are white and are often used as a thickener for sauces. They have an almondlike flavor.

RAWA

This is the Hindi name for semolina, coarse ground wheat. The closest approximation in the

United States is Cream of Wheat. Seasoned with a little black pepper, it makes a crisp yet delicate coating for fish and other seafood. Don't substitute American semolina; it takes too long to cook.

RICE
There are as many as twenty thousand different varieties of rice (the seeds of the grass *Oryza sativa*) grown in India, most of them locally. The most famous Indian rice is **basmati,** with its distinctive nutty fragrance and elegant needlelike grains. It's not an everyday rice in India but served on special occasions. Look for aged basmati, which has the best aroma and richest flavor. **Rice flakes** are made of parboiled rice that's been crushed. They make a wonderful crisp coating for seafood.

SALT
As a general rule, I like to use **kosher salt** for meat and **sea salt** for seafood. It just seems to make sense to me. **Black salt,** mined in central India, is actually pinkish gray in color. It has a pungent, smoky tang with an acidic aroma and flavor.

SHRIMP, DRIED BABY
These are not a substitute for fresh shrimp but a flavoring, and don't let their pungent smell intimidate you. They add a deep background flavor to dishes. (Think of what a dab of anchovy paste does for spaghetti sauce.) They're sold in cellophane packages and should be brittle and pink-orange in color. They're widely used in Southeast Asia as well.

SILK SQUASH
See **Squash, Silk.**

SQUASH
Long squash—also known as *bottle gourd, calabash, cucuzza,* and *upo*—is eaten all over the world,

from India to Italy, from the Caribbean to China. It has a mild flavor and firm, smooth texture that's reminiscent of cucumber and zucchini. **Silk squash**—also called *angled loofah* and *Chinese okra*—is eaten all over Asia. It originated in India, though, and it's one of my all-time favorite vegetables. Crisp-tender and mild, it picks up other flavors like a sponge. (Another variety *is*, in fact, a sponge—the loofah that you use in the bath.)

STAR ANISE
This beautiful star-shaped seed pod of a Chinese evergreen (*Illicium verum*) has an aniselike flavor (both star anise and anise seeds contain the essential oil anethole). Primarily thought of as an Asian spice (it's essential to Chinese five-spice powder), it's also used in rich Indian stews and rice dishes.

SZECHWAN PEPPERCORNS
Szechwan peppercorns are botanically unrelated to black peppercorns. Native to south-central China, the spice is made from the dried seed pods of the prickly ash tree. They have a pungent, citrusy flavor and aroma and have a distinctively tingling effect on the palate. Szechwan peppercorns are different from the "Szechwan seasoning" found in the spice aisle of grocery stores, which doesn't actually contain Szechwan peppercorns.

TURMERIC
The bright yellow-orange powder called *turmeric* is the boiled, peeled, dried rhizome (*Curcuma longa*) in the ginger family. Turmeric (which is what gives American ballpark mustard its hue) is bitter when raw; when cooked, it turns earthy and mellow. Considered one of the most important everyday spices in India, it's a natural antiseptic and anti-inflammatory.

sources

Many of the spices and other ingredients such as fresh green and red chiles may be found at grocery stores, fancy foods shops, and Latino, Indian, Middle Eastern, and/or Asian markets. Look for meats such as guinea hens and duck breasts at high-end grocery stores or your local butcher shop. Look for white port at liquor stores and wine shops. Below you will find some of my favorite suppliers for all sorts of things. And if you would like to find out more about my food at Tabla, visit tablany.com.

Bridge Kitchenware
212-838-1901 or 800-274-3435
bridgekitchenware.com
Electric coffee/spice grinders, Silpat nonstick baking sheet liners

The Chile Shop
505-983-6080
thechileshop.com
New Mexico chiles, pasilla de Oaxaca chiles

Chile Today–Hot Tamale
800-468-7377
chiletoday.com
New Mexico chiles, pasilla de Oaxaca chiles

D'Artagnan
800-327-8246
dartagnan.com
Duck breasts, duck confit legs, kid goat, guinea hens, quail, veal demiglace, venison

Dean & DeLuca
800-999-0309
deandeluca.com
Capers packed in salt, French green lentils (*lentilles du Puy*)

Ethnicgrocer.com
Spices, legumes, and other Indian ingredients

Foods of India
212-683-4419
212-644-7057 (fax)
Spices, legumes, and other Indian ingredients

Formaggio Kitchen
888-212-3224
formaggiokitchen.com
Aleppo pepper

Hudson Valley Foie Gras
845-292-2500
hudsonvalleyfoiegras.com
Duck breasts, duck confit legs

Marché aux Delices
888-547-5471
auxdelices.com
Fresh and dried morels

Niman Ranch
510-808-0340
nimanranch.com
Pork chops

Penzeys Spices
800-741-7787
penzeys.com
Spices

Vanns Spices
800-583-1693
vannsspices.com
Spices

index

bass (*continued*)

    wild striped, in fish curry with eggplant and okra, 88–89

bay leaves, 286

beans, summer, fricassee of, 198

beef:

    brisket, barbecued, 155–56

    flank steak, curry leaf–marinated, 151–52

    hamburgers, 153–54

    oxtails, sweet spiced, 159–60

    short ribs, braised, 157–58

    strip loin, coriander-and-mustard-crusted, 149–50

beet(s)

    green mango–marinated fluke with pickled daikon and, 14–15

    roasted, salad, 25–26

Bengal, 88

Berried Treasure, 198

Bombay, xi, xiii, xiv, 59, 96, 99, 134, 208

Brazil, 263

bread crumbs, *see* panko

broth(s):

    coriander, poached halibut in, 64–65

    ginger, poached wild striped bass with, 78–79

    jeera meera, Goan pot-au-feu with, 182–83

    kokum, steamed black sea bass with, 82–83

    spice-infused wild mushroom, 48–49

Brussels sprouts and chanterelles, pan-roasted, 199–200

bulgur, *see* cracked wheat

cabbage:

    braised, 201

    lobster coconut curry with eggplant and, 115–16

calamari, crab-stuffed, with spicy sauce, 121–22

caldo verde with peanuts, 50–51

cardamom, 286

    stewed kid goat with turnips and, 186–87

carrot soup, chilled, 38–39

Cato Corner Farm, 46

cauliflower:

    caldin, 204–5

    puree with chestnuts, 202–3

celery, tomato soup, chilled, with fennel, ginger, and, 34–35

chaat masala spice blend, 286

chaats, 238

chana dal (hulled split yellow Indian chickpeas), 290

cheese toasts, for French onion soup, 46–47

cherry chutney, 231

Cherry Lane Farms, 221

chestnuts, cauliflower puree with, 202–3

chicken:

    cafreal, 128–29

    noodle soup, 52–53

    poached, with salsa verde, 130–31

    roast, with fenugreek, 126–27

    stock, 274

chickpea flour (*besan*), 286

chickpeas, hulled split yellow Indian (*chana dal*), 290

    mushroom, cakes with tomato sauce, 215–16

chickpeas with coconut and tamarind, 206–7

chiffonade, how to make, 8

chile(s), 286–87

    to roast, peel, and seed, 9

    roasted, sauce, pan-roasted red snapper with, 69–70

    sweetbread, fry, 184–85

chive lemon raita, 246

chowder, corn and potato, 44–45

chutneys, 228–40

    apple, 229–30

    cherry, 231

    coconut coriander, 232

    dried-fruit, 233

    lemon, 235–36

    mango, 237

    mint coriander, 234